THE ROLE OF PLACE AND PLAY IN YOUNG CHILDREN'S LANGUAGE AND LITERACY

Edited by Shelley Stagg Peterson and Nicola Friedrich

Dominant assumptions about place tend to be defined in relation to urban communities. To assume a singular construction of urban places misrepresents the experiences, perspectives, and identities of urban children, making their identities become invisible to researchers, educators, and curriculum developers.

Sharing a wide range of perspectives, *The Role of Place and Play in Young Children's Language and Literacy* sheds light on language and literacy learning in play-based early childhood settings where place plays an important role in teaching and learning. Drawing on geographic contexts, including northern rural and Indigenous communities, and giving voice to educational leaders in Indigenous professional learning contexts, as well as speech-language pathologists, this book joins forces with literacy and early childhood education researchers to create an interdisciplinary collage of theory, research, and practice.

Bringing place and play together, a concept Shelley Stagg Peterson and Nicola Friedrich call *playce-based learning*, this book provides new and compelling ways to think about equity and educational opportunity in the language and literacy development of young children, and offers spaces for them to construct their own identities in positive ways.

SHELLEY STAGG PETERSON is a professor in the Department of Curriculum, Teaching and Learning at the Ontario Institute for Studies in Education at University of Toronto.

NICOLA FRIEDRICH is a postdoctoral fellow in the Department of Curriculum, Teaching and Learning at the Ontario Institute for Studies in Education at University of Toronto.

The Role of Place and Play in Young Children's Language and Literacy

EDITED BY SHELLEY STAGG PETERSON
AND NICOLA FRIEDRICH

UNIVERSITY OF TORONTO PRESS
Toronto Buffalo London

© University of Toronto Press 2022
Toronto Buffalo London
utorontopress.com

ISBN 978-1-4875-2921-5 (cloth)   ISBN 978-1-4875-2924-6 (EPUB)
ISBN 978-1-4875-2922-2 (paper)   ISBN 978-1-4875-2923-9 (PDF)

Library and Archives Canada Cataloguing in Publication

Title: The role of place and play in young children's language and
   literacy / edited by Shelley Stagg Peterson and Nicola Friedrich.
Names: Peterson, Shelley, editor. | Friedrich, Nicola, editor.
Description: Includes bibliographical references and index.
Identifiers: Canadiana (print) 20210369434 | Canadiana (ebook) 20210369485 |
   ISBN 9781487529215 (cloth) | ISBN 9781487529222 (paper) |
   ISBN 9781487529246 (EPUB) | ISBN 9781487529239 (PDF)
Subjects: LCSH: Place-based education. | LCSH: Children and the
   environment. | LCSH: Play environments. | LCSH: Language arts
   (Early childhood) | LCSH: Literacy – Study and teaching (Early childhood)
Classification: LCC LC239 .R65 2022 | DDC 370.11/5 – dc23

We wish to acknowledge the land on which the University of Toronto Press operates. This land is the traditional territory of the Wendat, the Anishnaabeg, the Haudenosaunee, the Métis, and the Mississaugas of the Credit First Nation.

This book has been published with the help of a grant from the Federation for the Humanities and Social Sciences, through the Awards to Scholarly Publications Program, using funds provided by the Social Sciences and Humanities Research Council of Canada.

University of Toronto Press acknowledges the financial support of the Government of Canada, the Canada Council for the Arts, and the Ontario Arts Council, an agency of the Government of Ontario, for its publishing activities.

Canada Council   Conseil des Arts
for the Arts   du Canada

ONTARIO ARTS COUNCIL
CONSEIL DES ARTS DE L'ONTARIO
an Ontario government agency
un organisme du gouvernement de l'Ontario

Funded by the   Financé par le
Government   gouvernement
of Canada   du Canada

Contents

List of Figures vii

1 Introduction: Playce-Based Language and Literacy Learning in Early Childhood   3
SHELLEY STAGG PETERSON AND NICOLA FRIEDRICH

2 Valuing Rural and Indigenous Social Practices: Play as Placed Learning in Kindergarten Classrooms   17
KAREN EPPLEY, SHELLEY STAGG PETERSON, AND DENISE HEPPNER

3 Seven Directions Early Learning for Indigenous Land Literacy Wisdom   33
SHARLA *MSKOKII* PELTIER

4 Sámi Children's Language Use, Play, and the Outdoors through Teachers' Lenses   53
KRISTINA BELANCIC

5 Young Children Exploring Identities, Languages, and Cultures in a Multicultural Place   67
MARIA COOPER AND HELEN HEDGES

6 Placing the Child's Hands on Land: Conceptualizing, Creating, and Implementing Land-Based Teachings in a Play Space   81
LORI HUSTON AND STEPHANIE MICHANO-DROVER

7 Negotiating a Place to Belong in an Aotearoa New Zealand Playgroup   95
MARY M. JACOBS

8 The Importance of the Land, Language, Culture, Identity, and Learning in Relation for Indigenous Children   109
    JEFFREY WOOD

 9 If Writing Floats "on a Sea of Talk," How Best to Harness the Waves and Currents of Place and Play?   127
    JUDY M. PARR

10 Scaffolding Community Literacy Practices in Kindergarten Classrooms   143
    NICOLA FRIEDRICH

11 Children's Engagement and Inquiry in Outdoors Contexts as Play- and Place-Based Learning   159
    GISELA WAJSKOP

12 Enriching Learning with the Richness around Us   177
    CHRISTINE PORTIER

13 Exploring Urban Place-Based Play as a Stimulus for "Language in Action" and "Language as Reflection"   195
    JANET SCULL AND KIM O'GRADY

14 The Key Role of the Educator as a Conversational Partner in Play- and Place-Based Learning   211
    JANICE GREENBERG AND SHARON WALKER

15 Language Learning in the Garden: Discoveries from a Collaboration in a North-Central Saskatchewan Indigenous Community   227
    LAUREEN J. MCINTYRE, LAURIE-ANN M. HELLSTEN, AND TYLER BERGEN

16 Conclusion: Questions and Implications Arising from Playce-Based Learning in Communities across Four Continents   243
    SHELLEY STAGG PETERSON

17 Places and Players: An Afterword   253
    MICHAEL CORBETT

Contributors   263

Index   267

Figures

3.1 Holistic *Anishinaabe* Pedagogical Model   38
3.2 Schoolyard Placement of Medicine Circle Cloth, Circular Mat, Blanket   40
3.3 Story Circle Participants "Make Meaning"   43
3.4 Generation of Knowledge in the Story Circle   43
3.5 *Anishinaabe* Ecological Relational Knowledge (AERK) Conceptual Map   45
8.1 Nurturing Guides   111
8.2 The Holistic View of the Child   112
8.3 Native Language Teacher as Cultural Broker   118
8.4 Tipi   119
8.5 Student in One of the Language Programs   123
11.1 Children play at the Escola do Bairro's backyard   165
11.2 Children looking at the pond surrounded by tropical plants from the Brazilian rainforest   166
11.3 Children play with the treehouse pulleys in Escola do Bairro's backyard   168
11.4 Children trying out the pulley to raise a girl in the rope seat   170
11.5 Children measuring how many children are needed to pull up a boy   171
11.6 Writing and drawing about the attempt to raise a child using the pulley   172
11.7 Writing and drawing about the attempt to raise a child using the pulley   173
12.1 Small Worlds   184
12.2 Spring Murals   187
12.3 Little Trees   187
12.4 Wildlife Puppets   188
12.5 Island Maps   190
15.1 The Pre-kindergarten Classroom Garden   233
15.2 Open-Ended Statements and Process Questions Classroom Poster   237

THE ROLE OF PLACE AND PLAY IN YOUNG CHILDREN'S LANGUAGE AND LITERACY

1 Introduction: Playce-Based Language and Literacy Learning in Early Childhood

SHELLEY STAGG PETERSON AND NICOLA FRIEDRICH

In this book, we bring notions of play and place as cultural constructions into conversations about language and literacy. Although the connections between play, language, and literacy have frequently been discussed in the literature on language and literacy teaching and learning in recent decades (see, e.g., Christie & Enz, 1992; Ihmeideh, 2015; Morrow, 1990; Pellegrini & Galda, 1993; Stagnitti et al., 2016), the influence of geography on culturally constructed expectations and assumptions is generally not acknowledged. As Casey (1997) shows, throughout the history of Western thought, place is considered a backdrop to cultural activity, and as such, not influential to understandings of what is deemed to be literacy and constructions of being literate.

The authors of the chapters in this book view play and oral and written language as social practices contextualized within particular places. Some authors emphasize the sociocultural aspects of language and play, while others emphasize the cognitive and developmental aspects. The chapters present examples from around the world of teachers who recognize that "places are pedagogical ... [they] *teach* us about how the world works and how our lives fit into the spaces we occupy. Further, places *make* us: As occupants of particular places with particular attributes, our identity and our possibilities are shaped" (Gruenewald, 2003b, p. 621, italics in original). The teachers whose play-based teaching practices are introduced in this book focus on local practices from geographic margins that range from a school garden and the bush surrounding schools and Aboriginal Head Start sites in Indigenous communities in northern Canada and northern Sweden, to primary classrooms and outdoors play spaces in urban Australia, Brazil, and Canada, to primary classrooms and a community playgroup of new immigrant parents and their children in Aotearoa New Zealand. They find that play pedagogies foregrounding such places offer "a radical perspective from which to see and create, to imagine alternatives, new worlds" (hooks, 1990, p. 150). Children's genuine participation in place-conscious play activities is vital to this radical imagining process.

Across these chapters, the authors variously consider play-based teaching practices that focus on the local in regard to children's language and literacy. Some authors propose ways to foster young children's cultural identity and sense of belonging through a place-conscious approach to learning. Other authors focus on supporting oral and written language by developing curricula based on local resources, activities, interactions, and texts. Many chapters highlight the importance of place within Indigenous communities, contributing to a (re)visioning of place that extends beyond assumptions within settler colonial pedagogical contexts. Indigenous scholars and early childhood educators take up Indigenous ontologies and philosophies in which the nature of being/becoming is embodied in Land. Land is "an Indigenous philosophical construct [that is] both space (abstract) and place/land (concrete); it is also conceptual, experiential, relational, and embodied" (Styres, 2017, p. 49). Their chapters contribute important understandings of the self in relationship to Land and of Land as first teacher.

In this opening chapter, we present an overarching theoretical framework for the research presented in this book. We begin by introducing our theory of language, literacy, identity, power, and culture that we are calling *playce-based learning*. We argue that playce-based learning is especially important in parts of the world where most authors of this book conduct research. We then situate our playce-based learning theory within the body of work that shows how culture has been used in theory and research in early childhood language, literacy, and play. We discuss tenets of educational theories highlighting the importance of place and conclude with a brief overview of the book and a synopsis of the individual chapters.

Role of Play and Place in Language and Literacy: Playce-Based Learning

Play has long been recognized as having "the potential to disrupt, defile and disturb social conventions, rules, manners and routines" (Wood, 2014, p. 146). Wood refers to "dimensions of diversity" (p. 149), a concept which, we suggest, should include diverse local places in which children and their families live. Bringing play and place together, the concept we are calling playce-based learning, creates a "permeable" school space (Dyson, 1993/2016) for children, teachers, and early childhood educators to construct local places as important for their particular worldviews and experiences. Playce-based classroom experiences offer children spaces to construct their communities in positive ways. Through first-hand and imagined experiences with natural and human-created objects from the local environment and guided by teachers, early childhood educators, and other adults in the community, children construct relationships to their community and the natural world within and around it.

Playce-based learning breaks up instructional patterns that isolate children and teachers from their local communities. Teachers' planned and spontaneous interactions with children in play are influenced by the cultural construction of play (e.g., what constitutes play, what is appropriate play within classrooms, the role of play within the school curriculum, expected types of interactions and outcomes of play, roles of objects and types of appropriate objects in classroom play, adult and child roles within play) within the local context, as well as in broader society. The same is true of ways in which oral and written language factor into the play interactions. Social expectations within local and broader communities influence notions of what are considered to be appropriate use of registers, choice of words, non-verbal communication modes, text forms, and so on within any given social interaction.

Place is more than a backdrop to play and young children's language and literacy learning in playce-based classrooms. Direct experiences with real-life events and materials within children's local environment, rather than the vicarious encounters mediated through reading or viewing texts or listening to lectures, are the substance of students' learning. When place is viewed as more than a physical location for learning, teachers and children engage with the local economic, social, and cultural activities of their communities and the natural world in playful ways (Sobel, 2005).

In the next section, we present assumptions and understandings from sociocultural theories of language, literacy, and play that have been influential to our playce-based language and literacy theory.

A Sociocultural View of Oral Language, Literacy, and Play

Play and oral and written language are cultural and historical constructions representing ways in which, over the histories of social groups, choices have been made about expected ways to interact and make sense of the world (van Oers, 2014). Through everyday social activities, children learn possible ways of interacting, as well as possible roles and relationships that may be taken up within those interactions. They construct meanings from those embedded within the social activities

(Boyd & Galda, 2011; Hodgkinson & Mercer, 2011). As children move beyond the familiar and engage in activities in new social contexts, they apply new frames to what they know. They try out hypotheses and refine their ways of interacting and the meanings they have constructed based on responses of others and observations of the effects on natural and human-created objects in their worlds. In this way, cultural practices and meanings of particular social groups are ever-evolving (Boyd & Galda, 2011 Resnick & Snow, 2009). We develop this sociocultural view of oral language, literacy, and play in the following areas.

Oral language. Language is foundational to literacy and all learning, as it represents culturally based ways of organizing understandings of the world and relationships within it (Vygotsky, 1962). Given their emphasis on children's active participation in social activities to support their construction of knowledge, sociocultural theorists advocate for classroom practices that follow principles of what Alexander (2008) calls *dialogic teaching*. Mutually supportive talk among peers and with the teacher creates space for collective, cumulative meaning-making, as children build on their own and others' experiences, ideas, and perspectives to create knowledge. They feel secure that their contributions will be considered and valued, and that the joint meaning-making is moving in a purposeful direction under the teacher's guidance. Interaction within classrooms to support children's language and learning is important, whether children are learning in their mother tongue or in another language (Conteh et al., 2008; Grant & Mistry, 2010). The *exploratory talk* (Barnes, 1976) of children's interactions will be filled with changes of direction and hesitations as children propose ideas that are not fully formed, and will invite others to help fill in gaps in their thinking or point out other ways of thinking about a topic. Discovery of new meanings is made possible when children learn from others in dialogic teaching contexts. As we explain further below, play provides authentic opportunities for exploratory talk, as children collaboratively solve problems and construct meanings in play contexts created from their collective experiences and funds of knowledge.

Literacy. Research underpinned by sociocultural theory foregrounds ways of being and human relationships and interactions in reference to cultural constructions of literacies. Within a sociocultural perspective of literacy, literacy is understood as a set of social practices embedded in cultural and historical contexts (Heath, 1983; Street, 1984). Literacy practices, defined by Barton and Hamilton (2000) as "the general cultural ways of utilizing written language which people draw upon in their lives" (p. 7), are inferred from observing individuals engaging in activities in which literacy plays a role. Individuals use texts to achieve particular purposes, and the ways in which they create and use texts vary across diverse communities (Perry, 2012). Children come to literacy within social situations (Razfar & Gutiérrez, 2003). From their participation in literacy activities within their various communities of practice (Lave & Wenger, 1991), children develop early literacy beliefs, values, and linguistic knowledge (Purcell-Gates, 2007) and generate and test new hypotheses about print (Harste et al., 1982). To assist children in acquiring new literacy skills and behaviours, educators can build on the children's cultural ways of creating and using texts (Purcell-Gates et al., 2011).

Play. Here researchers conceptualize play as a sociocultural construct, recognizing the social and cultural variations of children's play experiences within their families and communities (Campbell, 2005; Taylor, 2013). Wood (2013, p. 8) argues that "everything that children play at, or play with, is influenced by wider social, historical, and cultural factors, so that understanding what play is and learning how to play are culturally and contextually situated processes." Children construct knowledge by attending to ideas, values, perspectives, and material objects that are part of everyday lived experience, building on their funds of knowledge in play (Hedges et al., 2019; Moyles, 2015). In their play, children create understandings based in the physical and social contexts of everyday life, exploring and affirming taken-for-granted relationships and roles; they try out new ways of interacting and being or take on new perspectives of familiar ways.

Children learn through interacting with others and with objects in play and playful activities (Bodrova & Leong, 2009; Vygotsky, 1978). Wood (2013) proposes a pedagogical model (she calls it adult-guided play) that flexibly moves between responsiveness to children's interests and understandings and to curriculum goals. Two assumptions underpin adult-guided play: (a) there is intrinsic value in children's learning and development in play that children choose freely; and (b) adults can support children's learning toward desired learning outcomes through planned scaffolding. Adult guidance is responsive to children's goals and intentions and builds on what children show that they know and can do in their play. Teachers engage in complex decision-making as they interweave children's and pedagogical purposes.

The Need for Place to Be Part of Theories of Language and Literacy

Across decades and international borders, educational theorists have cautioned against distancing children from direct experience with their immediate environment in its physical and cultural manifestations (Bigelow, 1994; Dewey, 1938; Freire, 1972). Relationships with the physical, geographical place, and the cultural constructions of that place, created from interactions of generations of people in particular places, have disappeared from the gaze of language and literacy researchers and theorists.

Children's experience of their community, including its physical spaces, is "mediated by culture, education and personal experience" (Gruenewald, 2003b, p. 626). At the same time, the places themselves are culturally constructed – having been invested with meanings such as "city," "hamlet," "mining town," or "northern community." The language used to talk about places constructs identities in relationship to features of the places, such as geographical location, size of the community, or the primary industry employing many of the children's family members.

Dominant assumptions about place, which tend to be defined in relation to urban communities, are legitimated when place is not considered to be a sociocultural construct. Leaving place out of sociocultural conversations about children's language and literacy marginalizes the experiences and worldviews of children living in places that are considered as "other" to the cultural construction of "urban." This disregard "diverts the attention of citizens, educators, and students from the social, cultural, and political patterns involved in place making" (Gruenewald, 2003b, p. 628). As an example, school curricula, created by provincial, state, or national ministries and departments of education inevitably housed in large urban centres, assume a homogeneous southern urban, middle-class experience, erasing the influence of place as a determining factor in making curriculum relevant to children's experience (Smith, 2002). Because such curricula tend to turn the gaze of teachers and learners away from the land (Nabhan & Trimble, 1995), they do not validate rural and Indigenous children's and families' ways of being and interacting in their worlds.

Also influential to our playce-based theory are place-conscious and place-based educational theorists. We present understandings within these bodies of work, both of which have been influential to the authors of the chapters in this book.

Place-Conscious and Place-Based Educational Theories

Place-conscious educational theory, a concept created by Gruenewald (2003a), is multidisciplinary, and integral to critical pedagogy (e.g., Gruenewald, 2003a, 2003b). Place-conscious theory starts with a view of place as "an expression of culture ... that ... represents the outcome of human choices and decisions" (Gruenewald, 2003b, p. 627). Culture and place are thus viewed as being mutually constructive. Recognition of cultural constructions of place is a starting point for critical pedagogies and curriculum development that challenge dominant practices and perspectives regarding place. By foregrounding local stories, experiences, interactions, and perspectives, teachers resist the "placeless" standardized curriculum; one that "limits, devalues, and distorts local geographical experience" (Gruenewald, 2003a, p. 8). Working from a place-conscious perspective ensures that the curriculum does not obscure children's relationships to the cultural activities, identities, and understandings of the local community.

Particularly influential to the fields of outdoor, environmental, and ecological education (e.g., Cohen & Rønning, 2017; Smith, 2002), place-based theory supports students' understanding of abstract concepts in terms of their connections to students' local communities and natural environments. Place-based education theory is "distinguished from other situated, context-rich teaching and learning modalities (for example: project-based learning) by its unequivocal relationship to place" (Semken et al., 2017, p. 543). Place is foundational to curriculum development, as important goals of place-based pedagogy and curriculum are to deepen students' understanding of and their abilities to live well in their local communities (Sobel, 2004). In place-based classrooms, students and teachers co-construct curricula, using students' questions and interests as a springboard (Smith, 2002). Together, students and teachers participate meaningfully in knowledge and identity construction that is always related to the local phenomena and community (Woodhouse & Knapp, 2000). In the process, they affirm the worth of their community and their identities as community members.

Organization of This Volume

Various contributors to this volume have worked with teachers who foreground the connections to the natural world and to everyday activity in their communities. These teachers use play to co-create their communities as places where interactions with others and the physical environment are defined locally. Their understandings of what constitutes a community are not measured against an "every place" urban template. Although basic tenets from both place-conscious and place-based theory in relation to young children's language and literacy development through play are found in each of the chapters, we have grouped the chapters according to which of the two theories we see as being foregrounded.

Place-Conscious Theory

Karen Eppley, Shelley Stagg Peterson, and Denise Heppner use assumptions of a theory of critical pedagogy of place (Gruenewald, 2003a) to show how northern rural and Indigenous kindergarten teachers' use of local cultural practices is a radical act. These teachers transform dominant assumptions of rurality and Indigeneity, rendering them more relevant to children's lives and experience. They also choose to support children's literacy learning, using text creation practices of mainstream society. Their play-based and place-oriented practices contribute to young children's positive sense of self while engaging in dominant literacy practices that provide access to powerful discourse communities.

In place of Western constructions of teaching and learning, Sharla *Mskokii* Peltier introduces an Anishinaabek ecological relational-knowledge theoretical framework, the *Medicine Wheel*, as well as the *Story Circle* pedagogical process. Reflecting an Indigenous holistic approach to learning, these models support young children in coming to know who they are and where they find themselves in relationship with the seven directions. Knowledge from *Aki* (Land) is lived knowledge, created through ongoing exploration of being in relationship with *Aki*. Education is a lifelong learning process, with schooling being one part.

Kristina Belancic interviewed 11 Sámi teachers in northern Sweden to understand the roles of play and place in children's integration of traditional Sámi knowledge and the minority Sámi language in informal spaces outside the classroom. The participating teachers provided many examples of ways in which place is influential to the kinds of play in which Sámi children engage and whether they use Sámi or Swedish in their talk during play activities.

Maria Cooper and Helen Hedges' analysis of play interactions of two 4-year-old boys of blended Pasifika heritage and their teacher provides insights into ways in which language and cultural knowledge specific to each boy's heritage, together with that of their experiences in Aotearoa New Zealand, contributed to their identity construction. The boys wove cultural knowledge of home and their shared community into collaborative meaning-making in play activities. Play provided a foundation for exploring and creating meanings and identities.

Lori Huston and Stephanie Michano-Drover foreground the cultural and physical constructions of place as they describe how an Indigenous early learning program in a northern Canadian Indigenous community successfully navigated mainstream expectations and regulations to create a playground that embodied Indigenous land-based ways of teaching and learning. The authors further discuss implications arising from the early childhood educators' experiences in developing culturally appropriate play spaces in Indigenous communities.

To highlight how parent expertise can inform children's sense-making as they negotiate meanings in their first language in a multilingual playgroup, Mary Jacobs describes the activities of a group of young children in an intercultural playgroup in Aotearoa New Zealand. Rather than focusing on the geographical space in which the playgroup is located, she makes the case for conceptualizing the playgroup itself as a negotiated place, one in which children assign and convey meaning through interactions with other children and with adults.

Jeffrey Wood shares his experience incorporating the principles of land, culture, identity, and relationships into teaching and pedagogy in three northern First Nations communities and schools in Ontario, Canada. Underpinning the language programs is the understanding that "language comes from the land, culture comes from language, identity comes from culture, and all learning is done in relation." Teachers brought their communities' Indigenous languages to life through games and other supportive, holistic experiences.

Place-Based Theory

Bridging the two perspectives of place, Judy Parr considers how notions of place and play, influenced by the physical landscape and by culture within New Zealand contexts, can be channelled to the development of children's writing as they progress through primary school. She demonstrates how, through the use of a popular New Zealand text, *The School Journal*, teachers were able to draw on the children's lived experience and their language and culture, enabling them to see themselves as writers and to see their world as germane to writing.

Bringing place-based education theory to conversations about play and literacy, Nicola Friedrich discusses three kindergarten teacher teams' intentional use of social practices within their rural communities to support young children's literacy learning. In the process, she suggests thinking about guided play (Weisberg et al., 2016) as more than teacher scaffolding to support language and skill development. The intentional guidance is meant to support children's take-up of community practices as literate members of a rural community where particular written texts are created to solve problems and carry out social interactions important to the community.

In Gisela Wajskop's chapter, place-based learning informs the outdoors-based curriculum of a private lab school in the city of São Paulo, Brazil. Teachers in the school support children's learning through inquiry projects that highlight the intrinsic relationship between nature and culture. Children observe, ask questions, and explore ideas, as they create and modify their provisional and spontaneous theories about scientific concepts, with teachers respectfully listening to their play-based talk and challenging them to deepen their understandings.

Christine Portier shares examples from multiple classroom initiatives in three northern Alberta classrooms to illustrate how natural and human-created environments allow for the contextualization of curriculum. Throughout the chapter, drawing on concepts of place from multiple disciplines (e.g., Comber, 2016; Jack, 2010; Sobel, 2004) and from tenets within guided play (Weisberg et al., 2016), she demonstrates how the teachers started from place to foster collaborative and playful student interactions, shape the design of multiple interactive activities, and encourage imaginative extensions.

Janet Scull and Kim O'Grady examine the intersection between children's imaginative place-based play supplemented by teacher-facilitated discussions and their language development (i.e., content, vocabulary, syntax, and register). By conceptualizing the children's use of language in play as "language in action" and their language during discussion as "language as reflection" (Martin, 1985), the authors suggest teachers can negotiate the challenges of context-reduced language for children in early years classrooms.

Janice Greenberg and Sharon Walker bring their experience and perspectives as speech-language pathologists to conversations about play, place, and language. They show how teachers can be intentional in creating outdoors contexts for children to talk and learn. At the same time as teachers prepare potential topics for sustained conversations with children, they pay heed to opportunities to support children's language, literacy, and vocabulary by spontaneously responding to what children say and do. Place is a consideration, as conversations in the outdoors reflect the natural and agricultural environment. The conversations are playful in terms of children's use of their imagination to consider not only what the physical environment shows them but also to think creatively about what might be.

Drawing from action research within a North-Central Saskatchewan Indigenous community, Laureen McIntyre, Laurie-ann Hellsten, and Tyler Bergen highlight the place-based language and literacy learning in play in a pre-kindergarten class. They share the story of one teacher who implemented a garden-based learning program, Little Green Thumbs, in her classroom. Using data drawn from video clips showing interactions between the children and their teacher, the authors demonstrate how the garden provided the children with a natural experiential background in which the children could develop their language in terms of form (i.e., phonology, morphology, syntax), content (i.e., semantics), and use (i.e., pragmatics) through play.

REFERENCES

Alexander, R. (2008). Culture, dialogue and learning: Notes on an emerging pedagogy. In N. Mercer & S. Hodgkinson (Eds.), *Exploring talk in school* (pp. 91–114). Sage.

Barnes, D. (1976). *From communication to curriculum.* Penguin.

Barton, D., & Hamilton, M. (2000). Literacy practices. In D. Barton, M. Hamilton, & R. Ivanic (Eds.), *Situated literacies: Reading and writing in context* (pp. 7–15). Routledge.

Bigelow, B. (1994). *Rethinking our classrooms: Teaching for equity and justice.* Rethinking Schools.

Boyd, M.P., & Galda, L. (2011). *Real talk in elementary classrooms: Effective oral language practice.* Guilford.

Campbell, S. (2005). Secret children's business: Resisting and redefining access to learning in the early childhood classroom. In N. Yelland (Ed.), *Critical issues in early childhood education* (pp. 146–162). Open University Press.

Casey, E. (1997). *The fate of place: A philosophical history.* University of California Press.

Christie, J., & Enz, B. (1992). The effects of literacy play interventions on preschoolers' play patterns and literacy development. *Early Education & Development, 3*(3), 205–220. https://doi.org/10.1207/s15566935eed0303_1

Cohen, B. J. & Rønning, W. (2017). Place-based learning: Making use of nature in young children's learning in rural areas in Norway and Scotland. *Cad. Cedes, Campinas, 37*(103), 393–418. https://doi.org/10.1590/CC0101-32622017176129

Comber, B. (2016). *Literacy, place, and pedagogies of possibility.* Routledge.

Conteh, J., Kumar, R., & Beddow, D. (2008). Investigating pupil talk in multilingual contexts: Socio-cultural learning, teaching and researching. *Education 3–13, 36*(3), 223–235. https://doi.org/10.1080/03004270802217660

Dewey, J. (1938). *Experience and education.* Macmillan.

Dyson, A.H. (1993/2016). *Negotiating a permeable curriculum: On literacy, diversity, and the interplay of children's and teachers' worlds.* Garn Press.

Elkonin, D.B. (1998). *Psicologia do Jogo.* Martins Fontes.

Freire, P. (1972). *Pedagogy of the oppressed.* Herder and Herder.

Goncü, A. (1999). *Children's engagement in the world: Sociocultural perspectives.* Cambridge University Press.

Grant, K., & Mistry, M. (2010). How does the use of role-play affect the learning of year 4 children in a predominately EAL class? *Education 3–13, 38*(2), 155–164. https://doi.org/10.1080/03004270903130796

Gruenewald, D.A. (2003a). The best of both worlds: A critical pedagogy of place. *Educational Researcher, 32*(4), 3–12. https://doi.org/10.3102%2F0013189X032004003

Gruenewald, D.A. (2003b). Foundations of place: A multidisciplinary framework for place-conscious education. *American Educational Research Journal, 40*(3), 619–654. https://doi.org/10.3102%2F00028312040003619

Harste, J.C., Burke, C.L., & Woodward, V.A. (1982). Children's language and world: Initial encounters with print. In J.A. Langer & M.T. Smith-Burke (Eds.), *Reader meets author/Bridging the gap: A psycholinguistic and sociolinguistic Perspective* (pp. 105–131). International Reading Association.

Heath, S.B. (1983). *Ways with words*. Cambridge University Press.

Hedges, H., Cooper, M., & Weisz-Koves, T. (2019). Recognising and responding to family funds of knowledge. In S. Alcock & N. Stobbs (Eds.), *Rethinking play as pedagogy* (pp. 107–120). Routledge.

Hodgkinson, S., & Mercer, N. (2011). Introduction. In N. Mercer & S. Hodgkinson (Eds.). *Exploring talk in school*, (pp. xi–xviii). Sage.

hooks, b. (1990). *Yearning: race, gender, and cultural politics*. South End Press.

Ihmeideh, F. (2015). The impact of dramatic play centre on promoting the development of children's early writing skills. *European Early Childhood Education Research Journal, 23*(2), 250–263. https://doi.org/10.1080/1350293X.2014.970848

Jack, G. (2010). Place matters: The significance of place attachments for children's well-being. *British Journal of Social Work, 40*, 755–771. https://doi.org/10.1093/bjsw/bcn142

Morrow, L.M. (1990). Preparing the classroom environment to promote literacy during play. *Early Childhood Research Quarterly, 5*, 537–554. https://doi.org/10.1016/0885-2006(90)90018-V

Moyles, J. (2015). *The excellence of play* (4th ed.). Open University Press.

Nabhan, G., & Trimble, S. (1995). *The geography of childhood: Why we need wild places*. Beacon Press.

Pellegrini, A.D., & Galda, L. (1993). Ten years after: A re-examination of symbolic play and literacy research. *Reading Research Quarterly, 28*(2), 162–175. https://doi.org/10.2307/747887

Perry, K. (2012). What is literacy? A critical overview of sociocultural perspectives. *Journal of Language and Literacy Education, 8*, 50–71. Retrieved from http://jolle.coe.uga.edu/wp-content/uploads/2012/06/What-is-Literacy_KPerry.pdf.

Purcell-Gates, V. (2007). Complicating the complex. In V. Purcell-Gates (Ed.), *Cultural practices of literacy: Case studies of language, literacy, social practices, and power* (pp. 1–22). Routledge.

Purcell-Gates, V., Melzi, G., Najafi, B., & Orellan, M.F. (2011). Building literacy instruction from children's sociocultural worlds. *Child Development Perspectives, 5*, 22–27. https://doi.org/10.1111/j.1750-8606.2010.00144.x

Razfar, A., & Gutiérrez, K.D. (2003). Reconceptualizing early childhood literacy: The sociocultural influence. In N. Hall, J. Larson, & J. Marsh (Eds.), *Handbook of early childhood literacy* (pp. 34–47). Sage.

Resnick, L.B., & Snow, C.E. (2009). *Speaking and listening for preschool through third grade*. International Reading Association.

Saracho, O.N., & Spodek, B. (2006). Young children's literacy-related play. *Early Child Development & Care, 176*(7), 707–721. https://doi.org/10.1080/03004430500207021

Semken, S., Ward, E.G., Moosavi, S., & Chinn, P.W.U. (2017). Place-based education in geoscience: Theory, research, practice, and assessment. *Journal of Geoscience Education, 65*, 542–562. https://doi.org/10.5408/17-276.1

Smith, G.A. (2002). Place-based education: Learning to be where we are. *Phi Delta Kappan, 83*(8), 584–594. https://doi.org/10.1177%2F003172170208300806

Sobel, D. (2004). *Place-based education: Connecting classrooms & communities*. The Orion Society.

Stagnitti, K., Bailey, A., Hudspeth Stevenson, E., Reynolds, E., & Kidd, E. (2016). An investigation into the effect of play-based instruction on the development of play skills and oral language. *Journal of Early Childhood Research, 14*(4), 389–406. https://doi.org/10.1177%2F1476718X15579741

Street, B. (1984). *Literacy in theory and practice*. Cambridge University Press.

Styres, S.D. (2017). *Pathways for remembering and recognizing Indigenous thought in education: Philosophies of Iethi'nihsténha Ohwentsia'kékha (Land)*. University of Toronto Press.

Taylor, A. (2013). *Reconfiguring the natures of childhood*. Routledge.

van Oers, B. (2014). Cultural-historical perspectives on play: Central ideas. In L. Brooker, M. Blaise, & S. Edwards (Eds.), *The SAGE handbook of play and learning in early childhood* (pp. 56–66). Sage.

Vygotsky, L.S. (1962). *Thought and language*. MIT.

Vygotsky, L.S. (1978). *Mind in society: The development of higher psychological processes*. Harvard University Press.

Vygotsky, L.S. (1979). *Pensamento e Linguagem*. Edições Antídoto.

Weisberg, D.S., Hirsh-Pasek, K., Golinkoff, R.M., Kittredge, A.K., & Klahr, D. (2016). Guided play: Principles and practices. *Current Directions in Psychological Science, 25*(3), 177–182. https://doi.org/10.1177/0963721416645512

Wood, E. (2014). The play-pedagogy interface in contemporary debates. In L. Brooker, M. Blaise, & S. Edwards (Eds.), *The SAGE handbook of play and learning in early childhood* (pp. 145–156). Sage.

Woodhouse, J., & Knapp, C. (2000). *Place-based curriculum and instruction.* ERIC Document Reproduction Service No. EDO-RC-00-6.

2 Valuing Rural and Indigenous Social Practices: Play as Placed Learning in Kindergarten Classrooms

KAREN EPPLEY, SHELLEY STAGG PETERSON, AND DENISE HEPPNER

In this chapter, we make a case for play in kindergarten classrooms as a tool for placed learning, drawing on assumptions of critical pedagogy of place (Gruenewald, 2003a). Snapshots of children's play in a northern rural Canadian community and two northern Indigenous communities provide a forum for examining and questioning the dominant social constructions of rurality and Indigeneity as inferior to constructions of urbanity and non-Indigeneity. The play narratives are presented as "everyday micro-political acts" (McDonnell, 2018, p. 12), where children and teachers highlight and reflect on the practices of their communities through dramatic play and sand centre play. We draw on the narratives to discuss the affordances of play for learning about place.

Our work is based on a view of play as an authentic forum supporting children's learning across the curriculum. When engaged in play interactions, children draw on funds of knowledge and experiences (Hedges et al., 2011; Moll & Gonzalez, 2004) to learn possible roles, relationships, perspectives, and meanings for understanding and interacting with others in their social worlds (Vygotsky, 1978). Play is an integral part of classroom learning activities when the children's funds of knowledge (Moll & Gonzalez, 2004) enable meaning-making across the curriculum. Play is also a forum for teachers to learn about each child in their classroom as someone "whose social sense and knowledge resources come from a diversity of involvements as a friend, a family member, and a participant in community and popular cultures" (Genishi & Dyson, 2009, p. 19). These observations and understandings are important to creating play opportunities that support place-conscious learning.

The teachers in the study made intentional decisions to replace homogenized play opportunities in their early childhood classrooms with opportunities that intentionally link to the children's lives in Canadian First Nations rural communities. In so doing, the teachers actively positioned children as place makers and participants in the socio-political processes (Gruenewald, 2003a) that constitute the rural social space in which they live. While the play opportunities described in the vignettes are "local" in the sense that the children engaged in locally relevant activities through their play, the children's connections to tradition, stories, and culture transcend space and time (Blair, 2001). Their play, situated in the bounded space of the classroom and based on the places of their daily lives, bridged space and time. Likewise, the placed nature of their play blurred distinctions between education, work, play, childhood, and adulthood (Corbett & Horner, 2019). The teachers engaged the children at school as people in a place. This, we argue, is a radical act.

Play, Place, and Critical Pedagogy

The teachers' decisions to use play as a tool to position children's outside-of-school lives, identities, and histories at the centre of their classroom lives can be understood through the lens of critical pedagogy of place. A critical pedagogy of place:

> means challenging each other to read the text of our own lives and ask constantly what needs to be transformed and what needs to be conserved. In short, it means making a place for the cultural, political, economic, and ecological dynamics of places whenever we talk about the purpose and practice of learning. (Gruenewald, 2003b, p. 11)

Critical pedagogy of place brings critical pedagogy to bear on place-based education. Place-based education is often enacted as local ecological and experiential learning, especially in rural places (Haas & Nachtigal, 1998; Theobald, 1997). A key difference between place-based education and critical pedagogy of place is the way in which critical theory, with its centralized concern about power relations, is brought to bear on place. A criticism of place-based education is that it is blind to urbanization and globalization, race, ethnicity, and colonization (Gruenewald, 2003b). Explicit attention to these constructs is central to critical pedagogy of place.

Reinhabitation and decolonization are twin goals of critical pedagogy of place and are connected to the intentional maintenance or transformation of places (Gruenewald, 2003b). Gruenewald defines *reinhabitation* as learning "to live well socially and ecologically in places that have been disrupted and injured" and *decolonization* as "learning to recognize disruption and injury and to address their causes" (p. 9). As applied to education, he describes critical pedagogy of place as a means through which to unlearn norms associated with dominant culture in favour of "more socially just and ecologically sustainable ways of being in the world" (p. 9). Doing so requires thinking around what needs to be transformed (critical) and what needs to be conserved (place-based). Places in this view are understood not as neutral, local geographies, but rather as socially produced and politically connected to local, regional, national, and global contexts (Eppley, 2019).

Given the northern Indigenous communities in which our research is conducted, Bowers' (2008) perspective, centring on the invisibility of culture, particularly Indigenous cultures, must be considered. From Bowers' point of view, critical pedagogy of place activates a tension between traditional cultural practices and the expectation of progress (*transformation*) inherent in modernity generally and in critical pedagogy specifically. And, further, that critical analysis of a community's position within economic globalization requires acceptance of modernity's key tenets as replacements for traditional ways of knowing and environmental stewardship (see Smith, 2008).

The following vignettes are descriptions of video excerpts showing how three teachers offered invitations for play that engaged children in new opportunities for placed learning.

Northern Canadian Contexts

The first vignette comes from Denise's (author three's) ethnographic doctoral research study in Tipiyimisiw, a northern Indigenous community in Saskatchewan.

The other two vignettes come from Shelley's six-year collaborative action research guided by the four R's of Indigenous research: respect, relevance, reciprocity, and responsibility (Kirkness & Barnhardt, 1991). Research centred on participating teachers' concerns and questions. There was a high degree of collaboration and dialogue between teachers and researcher. Importantly, both teachers and researchers benefit from the project (Messiou, 2019). This is research "*in* and *for* rural communities" (Corbett & White, 2014, p. 1). Given our focus on place, we believe it is important for readers to get a clear sense of the communities involved in our research. Accordingly, we describe the communities in greater detail.

Tipiyimisiw, A Northern Rural Indigenous Community

Tipiyimisiw First Nation, a northern Saskatchewan community, has approximately 700 registered members living on reserve. Accessible by road, Tipiyimisiw is approximately 40 kilometres north of an urban centre. The school, community administration, and health centre provide the majority of employment in the area. The health centre's mission is to provide holistic, culturally appropriate services. They provide not only medical care, mental health services, and dental assistance, but also house a daycare and Aboriginal Head Start Program. Tipiyimisiw School, where Graham teaches, is a pre-kindergarten to Grade 8 school situated in the core area of the Tipiyimisiw First Nation. The school staff members are either from the community or a neighbouring First Nation community. Most of the staff and many of the students are related to each other and the school has a familial atmosphere. The mandate of Tipiyimisiw School is to maintain high academic standards and develop with pride the cultural uniqueness of each student via traditional teachings.

Aspen, A Northern Rural Community

Aspen, a northern rural Alberta community, has a population of approximately 2700, including farm families within the town catchment. It is located more than 200 kilometres from an urban centre. Aspen has an agricultural and resource-based economy that attracts families from elsewhere, although the school population primarily comprises children whose parents and possibly grandparents of European backgrounds have attended the school. A few parents of school-aged children in nearby First Nations communities have chosen to register their children in Aspen school, rather than in the federally funded and locally administered schools in their community. Aspen has elementary and high schools in both the public and Catholic school divisions. The public elementary school has both half-day and full-day kindergarten for children who turn 5 years old in the year they begin kindergarten. Kindergarten is not compulsory, but most Aspen parents of 5-year-old children enrol their children in kindergarten. Many teachers have lived and worked in Aspen for most of their teaching careers. Polly, the teacher of the sole kindergarten class in the public school, has been teaching her centre-based kindergarten class for more than 30 years.

Poplar Lake, a Northern Rural Indigenous Community

Poplar Lake, an Indigenous Ontario community, has a population of close to 400 people living on reserve. Accessible by road, Poplar Lake is approximately 500 kilometres from an urban centre. There is some mining in the area, though not in Poplar Lake itself. The larger employers in the community are the school and the community administration.

The health centre in Poplar Lake offers health services by nurses year-round and is staffed by a doctor for one week out of every five. Poplar Lake students can attend their community's school from kindergarten through Grade 8. Parents can enrol their children in junior kindergarten during the year that the children turn 4 years of age and in senior kindergarten in the year that children turn 5 years old. Kindergarten is not compulsory and many parents choose to enrol their children only in senior kindergarten. Students must leave Poplar Lake and board with families in communities hundreds of kilometres from their own families, or complete online courses through distance education programs, in order to attend high school. The three kindergarten classes in Poplar Lake School are taught by Indigenous early childhood educators, some of whom are from Poplar Lake and some of whom are from other First Nations communities, as well as Trisha, who has a BEd from an Ontario institution offering an online Indigenous bachelor of education program. Trisha has been a kindergarten teacher for the duration of the collaborative action research project, but the other two kindergarten classes have seen almost yearly turnover during this time.

In the following section, we describe and discuss vignettes from each teacher's classroom, drawing on critical pedagogy of place assumptions. Teachers and communities have been assigned pseudonyms.

Vignette One: Storytelling in the Tipiyimisiw School

Graham, an elementary school teacher in the Tipiyimisiw School, uses play within the classroom to intentionally develop his students' knowledge and understanding of the local community and culture. For example, one day he brought his daughter's pet rabbit to class to show his students. Graham introduced the rabbit by its whimsical Cree name: Muchoo (bug) Wapuss (rabbit). He explained, "Muchoo Wapuss. Bugs Bunny. Middle name is 'S'. Bug S. Bunny!" Holding the students in rapt attention, he then shared his Indigenous community's legend of how the rabbit lost its tail in the process of hanging it down to help a friend get out of a pit. In sharing this traditional story Graham legitimized his community's Indigenous discourses within which spiritual and communal teaching (helping a friend) is privileged over scientific explanations of phenomena (a short, flashy white tail confuses predators during a chase).

Children later role-played the characters of the story, reinforcing and extending their cultural learning. Through play, Graham's students created meaning and developed their cultural identity at school. Working against the homogenizing potential of formal schooling, Graham developed children's sense of Tipiyimisiw as a rural social space in which geography interacts with culture (Cresswell, 2015; Reid et al., 2010). Meaning about and of a place such as Tipiyimisiw is produced and reproduced through social interactions and "active engagement with our landscape"; narratives are constructed and maintained in "connection to the significant cultural histories and moralities ... stored within our storied landscapes" (Johnson, 2012, p. 831). In a dialogic production of knowledge, Graham's students gathered meaning *from* this landscape while identity was incorporated and maintained based *upon* the landscape. Each story arising from the active engagement of being-in-place "is a text within the metanarrative of a particular culture, aiding through its remembrance, the continual re/creation of that society" (Johnson, 2012, p. 833). Muchoo Wapuss is part of a storied landscape of placed knowledge that works to create and recreate the Indigenous culture of Graham and his students.

Engaging and culturally sustaining (Paris & Alim, 2017), Graham's instruction through storytelling and role play was authentically connected to the students' lives and place. His teaching also had a critical element in that the storytelling resided in a third space between official and unofficial knowledge (Soja, 1996) where placed identities meet sanctioned knowledge (Mills & Comber, 2013) within a history of colonization.

In exploring Indigenous understandings of the rabbit's tail, a critical pedagogy of place challenged and subverted the deficit status of Indigenous knowledge within dominant discourses. Local cultural knowledge and the epistemologies of the community were viewed as legitimate, valuable, and appropriately integrated into the official space of school (Brayboy & Castagno, 2009). This enabled the Indigenous students to see themselves reflected authentically within the classroom and in the curriculum (Bell & Brant, 2015). The cultural capital of Indigenous understandings was valued and held power within the classroom, and more powerful Indigenous identities were constructed. Graham's classroom practice aligns with Parr's findings that effective teachers "use talk, place and play to build bridges between the linguistic and cultural worlds"(p. 139, this volume) that their students inhabit.

A critical pedagogy of place values and honours the global, national, and personal resources of Indigenous communities. Creating space for children to follow up on Indigenous storytelling in play activities places Indigenous knowledge and practices at the forefront of curriculum. We argue that this is a radical act, as it resists the historical and ongoing assimilative forces of mainstream schooling that have marginalized and attempted to erase Indigenous languages, culture, and perspectives that continue to "colonize the minds of [Indigenous] children" (Moore, 2017, p. 46). In adopting a critical pedagogy of place grounded within Indigeneity we acknowledge the multiplicity of ways in which people relate to, interpret, and make meaning from/of the world (Johnson, 2012). In doing so, we uncover and affirm place-based cultural knowledge as significant to our ontology. With acknowledgment of the importance of place for many epistemologies, *place* might offer "a 'common ground' between Western and Indigenous thought" (Johnson & Murton, 2007, p. 127).

Vignette Two: Rural and Blue-Collar Work in the Sand Play Centre

In her Aspen kindergarten classroom serving a mix of Indigenous and European Canadian children, Polly uses contexts and texts from her students' lives in her play-based classroom. Her teaching practices enhance students' literacy learning, while simultaneously developing positive identities by affirming the social practices that are part of everyday experience in the lives of Aspen community members. These practices are closely tied to place, as they reflect community members' approaches to addressing challenges and capitalizing on the affordances of their northerly geography and climate.

The importance of place to children's meaning-making is evident in Polly's classroom. The weather and distinct seasons, and also the great distances between the children's farm homes and the town of Aspen and the closest major urban centre, place limitations on and open up possibilities for social interaction in and around the community of Aspen (Sampson & Goodrich, 2009). Driving on gravel roads is an everyday part of many children's lives as they travel to their small-town school by bus. Polly used play to provide opportunities for students to give meaning to these experiences (Giroux & Simon, 1989) through the material resources she brought to the classroom and the ways in which she and the children used the resources in play centres. The 5- and 6-year-old children's play at the sand centre in her classroom, for example, included building roads in the sand with toy bulldozers and excavators and then creating signs to show that road bans were in effect. (Road ban signs indicate that heavy trucks and other equipment cannot be filled to full capacity when driving on the soft country roads in the spring as the frost comes out of the ground.) With the goal of introducing meaningful text creation as part of children's play, Polly modelled the creation of the signs (a drawing of a big truck with a diagonal line through it) and then left popsicle sticks and stiff paper at the sand centre so students could create signs to enhance their sand play.

Polly's play-based curriculum was a "permeable" curriculum (Dyson, 2016) that provides opportunities for integrating local literacies and concepts into the official curriculum as represented in provincial expectations. Knowledge creation is a dynamic and fluid process, as children and their teachers explore the rules and ways of getting things done in their community, while responding to the challenges and affordances of their particular environments. In reflective conversations that take up a critical pedagogy of place stance, Polly and the researcher proposed that she and the children might talk about the ways in which legislators have addressed the problem posed by the spring thaw on local roads (e.g., giving opinions on whether the road bans are an effective way to solve the problem of rutted, impassable roads when heavy vehicles are allowed to drive over the soft, wet spring roads). These kinds of conversations serve to highlight practices that benefit community members and generate ways to transform community practices to serve greater numbers of community members. Local in the sense that they are about the immediate environment, yet in developmentally appropriate ways, these conversations enable the children to consider broader questions of how systems of government impact their daily lives.

Children's play is "an important arena for children's cultural participation, encompassing its role in exploring, questioning, producing and reproducing social norms and subjectivities" (McDonnell, 2018, p. 11). In Polly's classroom, for example, children imagined themselves in adult roles as road construction workers, farmers hauling grain in large trucks to elevators for shipment to markets, and heavy equipment operators working in the local resource extraction industries. Polly created spaces in her classroom for children to take up roles of important adults in their lives doing blue-collar jobs, jobs that are positioned in the mainstream urban- and white-collar oriented discourses as undesirable and of low status. In their sand centre play, children constructed understandings that challenged dominant discourses positioning blue-collar work. Taking up a critical pedagogy of place provides a forum for transforming assumptions about roles and relationships among those who work across the primary/secondary/tertiary industry spectrum (Berg & Frost, 2005; Lucas, 2011).

Vignette Three: Dramatic Play of Indigenous Cultural Practices Tied to the Land

At the centre of the curriculum co-created by Trisha and the Elders of Poplar Lake community is the key assumption of Indigenous epistemology – that experience is a legitimate way of knowing (Kovach, 2009). By placing land-based practices of their community at the centre of the curriculum, Trisha, the Elders, and the children disrupted dominant notions of curriculum as coming from ministries and departments of education in southern urban centres. They resisted the sense of "everywhereness" and cultural/historical neutrality that comes with a curriculum that is assumed to be appropriate for all children in the province, regardless of their place-influenced cultural identities.

Trisha and her kindergarten students travelled with the Elders by bus to go sucker fishing, using snares and their hands to catch the fish. The Elders showed children how to scale, fillet, and smoke the fish with a smoker constructed of corrugated metal and small logs. Throughout the following weeks, the children created fishing snares and went pretend sucker fishing in the dramatic play centre. They filled up buckets with objects that were assigned roles as suckers, used pretend knives to scale and fillet the "fish," and built a pretend smoker in the classroom to smoke them. They also drew pictures and wrote about their experiences, sharing their writing and drawings with peers and their teachers.

Trisha's and the Elders' teaching is culturally sustaining pedagogy (Paris & Alim, 2017), in that they drew on the linguistic cultural knowledge of their Indigenous community. Their land-based teaching, however, transcends the fostering of linguistic and cultural pluralism. Trisha and the Elders did not set out to add or reinforce cultural practices and knowledge to the children's funds of knowledge. Nor did they limit themselves to the important work of ecological learning about stream health or food systems. Instead, they worked from place-specific and critical pedagogies at the intersection of the environment, culture, and formal schooling (Gruenewald, 2003b). The collaborative teaching and learning among the children, the teacher, and the Elders was both critical and place-based.

Decolonization and reinhabitation are foundational to a critical pedagogy of place (Gruenewald, 2003b). The teaching and learning interactions at the stream site and in Trisha's classroom were decolonizing practices in the sense that the activities were a means through which to "unlearn" dominant culture via the contestation of mainstream assimilationist and genocidal discourses that have been institutionalized in policy and practice over generations. Such discourses and the associated policies have led to "the gradual loss of [Indigenous] world-views, languages, and cultures and the creation of widespread social and psychological upheaval in Aboriginal communities" (Battiste, 2008, p. viii). The losses have led to generations of Indigenous children being deprived of a fundamental part of their cultural and racialized identities. Trisha and the community Elders resisted homogenizing forces by engaging the children in activities that were culturally and historically located within their Indigenous community. While their work was decolonizing, it also supported reinhabitation. The stream was more than a moving body of water that supported the ecologically sensitive practices of fishing to feed community members. It was the site of the children's construction of Indigenous identities and a tool for passing Indigenous knowledge via traditional ways of teaching and learning that had been constructed and reconstructed over many generations. The children and adults practised reinhabitation in their learning of cultural knowledge that supports and sustains people and ecosystems (Bowers, 2001).

Concluding Thoughts

The First Nations Elders' and classroom teachers' decisions cannot be fully understood as the exclusive domain of theories about funds of knowledge (Moll & Gonzalez, 2004). Furthermore, culturally sustaining pedagogy (Paris & Alim, 2017) does not adequately frame the teachers' decisions. Critical pedagogy of place is a more robust theoretical tool with which to make sense of the teachers' invitations to play because it enables thinking about the children's lived experiences, cultural identities, and geographic locations. It is also a useful theoretical lens through which to understand how community Elders and teachers considered and acted on their thinking about how dominant cultural practices intersect with traditional cultural practices.

The teachers' resistance to homogenized curriculum, including pop culture play and other standardized schooling practices associated with dominant cultural practices, is the enactment of a placed, critical stance in the classroom. The vignettes in this study appear to contradict Bowers' (2001, 2008) assertion that the transformative component of a critical pedagogy of place might be incompatible with the goals of northern rural and Indigenous teachers within a dominant paradigm of economic globalization. For example, the children's free-choice dramatic play often included elements of popular culture such as zombies, Minecraft, or superheroes. The Indigenous Elders regarded these pop culture discourses as an assimilative force and thus tried to redirect the children's play. The Elders and teachers expressly resisted what they understood as the potential of popular culture as a pedagogy of erasure (Eppley, 2011). The teachers replaced these and other place-less play experiences with locally and culturally meaningful ones, and in so doing, honoured the shared cultural histories and lived experiences of the children. In contrast, pop culture play in Black urban classrooms is often seen as a means of resistance to the hegemony of school literacy (Dyson, 2003; Evans, 2004; Shegar & Weninger, 2010).

Northern rural and Indigenous teachers' identities, their pedagogies, and the context in which teachers live and teach are mutually constitutive (Walker-Gibbs et al., 2018) Teachers may find that their responsibility towards honouring the cultural ways of rural and Indigenous communities, and their responsibility towards teaching the curriculum, are often in conflict (Moore, 2017). The curriculum often contains dominant perspectives of "rural" and "Indigenous" that undervalue and/or dismiss the lives, knowledge, and perspectives of rural and Indigenous community members. Teachers who live in the same rural and/or Indigenous community in which they teach may find that their positioning as employees within a mainstream institution signifies their adoption of dominant urban, non-Indigenous perspectives. Yet, they and their students live, learn, and play in communities understood within socially constructed discourses as lacking in personal, social, or economic potential. There is a disconnect between their positioning as a teacher and as a community member. These understandings manifest in a form of institutionalized obstacles to social justice for students and identity conflicts for teachers (Eppley & Shannon, 2015).

Teachers like Trisha, Polly, and Graham challenge the dominant perspectives of "rural" and "Indigenous" as homogeneous constructs, positioning the knowledge, perspectives, and experiences of children and adults in their communities as significant and powerful. Their play-based, permeable curriculum places the symbols, activities, values, and events that community members value as defining their community's identity, and which are often connected to the physical environment, at the centre of the curriculum. These stories, events, and social gatherings "provide the social interaction through which meanings are mediated and in doing so also provide the context in which individuals articulate who they are" (Sampson & Goodrich, 2009, p. 904). Teachers communicate strong messages about the cultural richness of their local communities when they invite community members to the classroom and integrate community events and ways of being, including ways to earn a living, into classroom learning experiences. Play in kindergarten classrooms is a tool for placed learning that resists what Corbett (2007) has described as dominant messages about northern rural Indigenous and non-Indigenous communities being places to leave because they do not offer as much for young people as southern urban communities. Bringing northern Indigenous and rural practices into classrooms, we argue, is a radical act in its assertion of the rightful place of these practices and perspectives in the school curriculum.

ACKNOWLEDGMENTS

We acknowledge that our research has been conducted on lands of First Nations peoples whose ancestors were signatories to Treaty 6, 8, and 9. We honour the culture of the First Nations and strive to uphold our treaty obligations as we share the knowledge created through our research. We are grateful to the children, teachers, parents, and community members who participated in our research and acknowledge the funding support of the Social Sciences and Humanities Research Council of Canada.

REFERENCES

Battiste, M. (2008). The struggle and renaissance of Indigenous knowledge in Eurocentric education. In M. Villegas, S.R. Neugebauer, & K.R. Venegas (Eds.), *Indigenous knowledge and education: Site of struggle, strength, and survivance* (pp. 85–91). Harvard Educational Publishing Group.

Bell, N., & Brant, T. (2015). *Culturally relevant Aboriginal education.* Pearson Canada.

Berg, P., & Frost, A.C. (2005). Dignity at work for low wage, low skill service workers. *Industrial Relations, 60,* 657–682. https://doi.org/10.7202/012339ar

Blair, S. (2001). Travel routes, dreaming tracks and cultural heritage. In M. Cotter, B. Boyd & J. Gardiner (Eds.), *Heritage Landscapes: Understanding Place and Communities* (pp. 41–51). University of Southern Cross Press.

Bowers, C.A. (2001). *Educating for eco-justice and community.* University of Georgia Press.

Bowers, C.A. (2008). Why a critical pedagogy of place is an oxymoron. *Environmental Education Research, 14*(3), 325–335. https://doi.org/10.1080/13504620802156470

Brayboy, B.M.J., & Castagno, A.E. (2009). Self-determination through self-education: Culturally responsive schooling for Indigenous students in the USA. *Teaching Education, 20*(1), 31–53. https://doi.org/10.1080/10476210802681709

Corbett, M. (2007). *Learning to leave: The irony of schooling in a coastal community.* Fernwood.

Corbett, M. & Horner, F. (2019). "I never had a childhood": Narratives of work, play, and loss in postwar rural Atlantic Canada. In C. Mitchell & A. Mandrona (Eds.), *Our rural selves: Memory and the visual in Canadian Childhoods* (pp. 80–97). McGill-Queen's University Press.

Corbett, M. & White, S. (2014). Introduction: Why put the "rural" in research? In M. Corbett & S. White (Eds.), *Doing educational research in rural settings: Methodological issues, international perspectives, and practical solutions* (pp. 1–4). Routledge.

Cresswell, T. (2015). *Place: An introduction.* Wiley-Blackwell.

Dyson, A. (2003). *The brothers and sisters learn to write.* Teachers College Press.

Dyson, A. (2016). *Negotiating a permeable curriculum: On literacy, diversity, and the interplay of children's and teachers' worlds.* Garn Press.

Eppley, K. (2011). Reading mastery as pedagogy of erasure. *Journal of Research in Rural Education, 26*(13). https://doi.org/info:doi/

Eppley, K. (2019). Close reading: What is reading for? *Curriculum Inquiry, 49*(3), 1–18. https://doi.org/10.1080/03626784.2019.1631701

Eppley, K. & Shannon, P. (2015). Literacy education for the lumps and divots of smart cities and rural places. In S. Williams & A. Grooms (Eds.), *Educational opportunity in rural contexts: The politics of place* (pp. 59–73). Information Age Press.

Evans, J. (Ed.). (2004). *Literacy moves on.* David Fulton Publishers.

Genishi, C., & Dyson, A.H. (2009). *Children, language and literacy: Diverse learners in diverse times.* Teachers College Press and National Association for the Education of Young Children.

Giroux, H., & Simon, R. (1989). Popular culture and critical pedagogy: Everyday life as a basis for curriculum knowledge. In H. Giroux & P. McLaren (Eds.), *Critical pedagogy, the state, and cultural struggle* (pp. 236–292). State University of New York Press.

Gruenewald, D. (2003a). Foundations of place: A multi-disciplinary framework for place-conscious education. *American Educational Research Journal, 40*(3), 619–654. https://doi.org/10.3102%2F00028312040003619

Gruenewald, D. (2003b). The best of both worlds: A critical pedagogy of place. *Educational Researcher, 32*(4), 3–12. https://doi.org/10.3102%2F0013189X032004003

Haas, T. & Nachtigal, P. (1998). *Place value.* ERIC Press.

Hedges, H., Cullen, J., & Jordan, B. (2011). Early years curriculum: Funds of knowledge as a conceptual framework for children's interest. *Journal of Curriculum Studies, 43*(2), 185–205. https://doi.org/10.1080/00220272.2010.511275

Johnson, J.T. (2012). Place-based learning and knowing: Critical pedagogies grounded in Indigeneity. *GeoJournal, 77*(6), 829–836. https://doi.org/10.1007/s10708-010-9379-1

Johnson, J.T., & Murton, B. (2007). Re/placing Native science: Indigenous voices in contemporary constructions of nature. *Geographical Research, 45*(2), 121–129. https://doi.org/10.1111/j.1745-5871.2007.00442.x

Kirkness, V.J., & Barnhardt, R. (1991). First Nations and higher education: The four R's – respect, relevance, reciprocity, responsibility. *Journal of American Indian Education, 30*(3), 1–15.

Kovach, M. (2009). *Indigenous methodologies: Characteristics, conversations, and contexts.* University of Toronto Press.

Lucas, K. (2011). Blue-collar discourses of workplace dignity: Using outgroup comparisons to construct positive identities. *Management Communication Quarterly, 25*(2), 353–373. https://doi.org/10.1177%2F0893318910386445

McDonnell, S. (2018). Nonsense and possibility: Ambiguity, rupture and reproduction in children's play/ful narratives. *Children's Geographies.* https://doi.org/10.1080/14733285.2018.1492701

Messiou, K. (2019). Collaborative action research: Facilitating inclusion in schools. *Educational Action Research, 27*(2), 197–209. https://doi.org/10.1080/09650792.2018.1436081

Mills, K. & Comber, B. (2013). Space, place, and power: The spatial turn in literacy research. In K. Hall, T. Cremin, B. Comber, & L. Moll (Eds.), *International handbook of research in children's literacy, learning, and culture.* Wiley-Blackwell.

Moll, L.C., & Gonzalez, N. (2004). Engaging life: A funds-of-knowledge approach to multicultural education. In J. Banks & C.A. McGee Banks (Eds.), *Handbook of research on multicultural education* (pp. 699–715). Jossey-Bass.

Moore, S. (2017). *Trickster chases the tale of education.* McGill-Queen's University Press.

Paris, D. & Alim, S. (Eds.) (2017). *Culturally sustaining pedagogies: Teaching and learning for justice in a changing world.* Teachers College Press.

Parr, J. (2022). If writing floats "on a sea of talk," how best to harness the waves and currents of place and play. In S.S. Peterson & N. Friedrich (Eds.), *The role of place and play in young children's language and literacy* (pp. 127–141). University of Toronto Press.

Reid, J., Green, B., Cooper, M., Hastings, W., Lock, G., & White, S. (2010). Regenerating rural social space? Teacher education for rural-regional sustainability. *Australian Journal of Education, 54*(3), 262–276. https://doi.org/10.1177%2F000494411005400304

Sampson, K.A., & Goodrich, C.G. (2009). Making place: Identity construction and community formation through "sense of place" in Westland, New Zealand. *Society and National Resources, 22,* 901–915. https://doi.org/10.1080/08941920802178172

Shegar, C. & Weninger, C. (2010). Intertextuality in preschoolers' engagement with popular culture: Implications for literacy development. *Language and Education, 24*(5), 431–437. https://doi.org/10.1080/09500782.2010.486861

Smith, G. (2008). Oxymoron or misplaced rectification. *Environmental Education Research, 14*(3), 349–352. https://doi.org/10.1080/13504620802194273

Soja, E. (1996). *Thirdspace: Journeys to Los Angeles and other real-and-imagined places*. Blackwell.

Theobald, P. (1997). *Teaching the commons: Place, pride, and the renewal of community*. Westview Press.

Vygotsky, L.S. (1978). *Mind in society: The development of higher psychological processes*. Harvard University Press.

Walker-Gibbs, B., Ludecke, M., & Kline, J. (2018). Pedagogy of the rural as a lens for understanding beginning teachers' identity and positionings in rural schools. *Pedagogy, Culture & Society, 26*(2), 301–314. https://doi.org/10.1080/14681366.2017.1394906

3 Seven Directions Early Learning for Indigenous Land Literacy Wisdom

SHARLA *MSKOKII* PELTIER

"Hello Sharla. I think you'd better get outta the house NOW. The grass fire is two feet from the back corner of my trailer. I called for the firetruck!"

My next-door neighbour's phone call was alarming to say the least. I quickly woke my two young boys and we were outside in minutes. I put a blanket over their heads so that they would not see the fire next door and held their hands tightly. After guiding them away from the fire and into the maple bush, I removed the blanket. Our eyes were as wide as saucers as we looked up and saw an orange glow above the trees.

I explained to my boys, "It's a fire in the meadow, this side of Auntie Stella's. She is ok and the firetruck is coming. Someone started a grass fire today and it got out of control in the field."

"Where's daddy?" my youngest son asked.

"He's in town visiting uncle," I assured him.

The smell of smoke was strong and the sound of grass and bushes going up in flames was distinct. "What should we do? Is the fire gonna burn up our place, mama?" asked my oldest boy.

"Well," I answered, "the firetruck is coming to put water on the fire. We will stay here where we are safe. Let's think about our animal and plant friends in the meadow. I hope they can be safe too. We can say their names and send words to them." Each of us took turns naming every plant and animal we could think of.

We said things like, "Hop fast, peeper frogs. Jump away, bunnies. Fly high fireflies. Strawberry plants and raspberry bushes, be safe. Stay alive, sweetgrass." Before we had named all of the creation we knew, the firetruck arrived. We heard all the commotion and soon they had taken care of the fire.

This story is presented as a segue into a consideration of *Anishinaabe* family early learning cultural practices geared towards ensuring the child is grounded in Place and relationship to *Aki*[1] for a healthy sense of identity and belonging. Place-based learning is compatible with relational ways of being and Indigenous land-literacy is conducive to early language and literacy learning.

My two sons and I experienced the grass fire 20 years ago when they were 4 and 6 years of age. Sharing this story brings to mind our love for nature and sense of *Odenang*/where the heart is. My husband and I are *Anishinaabek*[2] and we raised our boys on Manitoulin Island on Wikwemikong Unceded First Nation, Ontario. *Anishinaabek* believe that children are gifts. Each child is unique and brings wonderful contributions to our community and nation. Our role as parents and community members is to protect and nurture the child. Immersed in a relational way of being, our young children are situated at the centre of relationships.

The grass fire story is grounded in relationship to Place and *Aki*. As the mother of preschool boys in the midst of a dangerous and potentially traumatic incident, I ensured their safety and directed our attention to the safe and familiar, grounding place of the maple bush. Family life experiences (play, exploration, culture-based activities such as gathering and using local medicinal plants) developed our meaningful relationships with the waters, trees, plants, animals, and insects. Speaking our good wishes sent gratitude and acknowledgment for our relationships in all directions. We engaged together in our cultural ways of living in a relational and good way. Although my boys were young, they were acquiring land literacy knowledge – without rain, the soil, grasses, plants, trees, and ponds dry out and fire comes through.

I chose to begin this chapter with a parent-child lived experience story in honour of the oral storytelling tradition and passing on of cultural knowledge to centre the contributions of Indigenous Knowledges and relational ways of being within the broader socio-political reconciliatory context. Respect and understanding for different ways of knowing, seeing, doing, and being towards educational transformation are reflected in *Anishinaabe* early learning educational processes grounded in Place and *Aki*. In this respect, I share insights stemming from my doctoral research (Peltier, 2016), and my worldview perspectives as an *Anishinaabe* grandmother and researcher-participant who introduced *Anishinaabe* ecological relational knowledge (AERK) into a northeastern Ontario classroom by utilizing a holistic teaching/learning process.

---

1 *Aki* is the term that refers to "Land" in this chapter.
2 *Anishinaabek* is used here to refer to the *Anishinaabe* peoples: the Algonquin, Chippewa, Delaware, Mississauga, Odawa, and Ojibway and Pottawatomi people of the Great Lakes Region.

This chapter focuses on an Indigenous philosophy of education and pedagogical approach. The term Indigenous refers to the First Peoples that occupied the continents of the world and is used in this research context to refer to all First Peoples[3] – unique in our own cultures but common in our experiences of colonialism and our understanding of the world (Wilson, 2008, p. 15). Scholars from diverse academic and cultural perspectives have provided information about Indigenous Knowledge as a process situated within a context of relationships. Indigenous Knowledge is a way of knowing, seeing, doing, and being that involves observing, listening, engaging in life activities, and developing skills modelled by family and community members. Cree philosopher Ermine (1995) discusses Indigenous Knowledge as an interaction of life experience, relational collectivity, and inner knowing; in his view "experience *is* knowledge" (p. 104). The philosophy that knowledge comes from the *Aki* is exemplified by "a broad sense of knowledge with a specific place and the pedagogy contained within the stories that were conceived within that place" (Kulnieks et al., 2010, 19). Indigenous Knowledge requires a reflective process of deep meaning-making so that our stories and oral tradition stimulate remembering; and when we retell stories, we contribute to knowledge transmission and new knowledge generation.

Global concern for the environment and increasing awareness of Indigenous cultural values and respect for *Aki* command an authentic role for Indigenous people and validation of Indigenous ecological perspectives. Ecological relational knowledge – ways of knowing interrelationships and interconnections with *Aki* and each other – is foundational to *Anishinaabe* ways of knowing, seeing, doing, and being. As new understandings facilitate resolution of historical trauma and strengthening of healthy relationships, we can collectively promote biophilia[4] and Indigenous Knowledges. Incorporating AERK in early learning and schooling contexts is especially important in this promotion.

Indigenous ways of knowing are grounded with Land. Knowledge comes from the Land and Indigenous Place-based learning is tied to the local context. This chapter presents a culturally relevant learning and land literacy approach for early child care and development contexts by (1) providing an *Anishinaabek* ecological relational knowledge theoretical framework, pedagogical process model, and conceptual map based

---

3 *Aki* is Anishinaabemowin (the Aboriginal language and language dialects of the Anishinaabek, referred to as Ojibway). In this chapter, terms in *Anishinaabemowin* are italicized. Words that are typically not capitalized appear in this document with a capital to denote an Indigenous voice and Indigenous perspective in this paper.
4 Biophilia refers to the love for nature and non-human beings (Cajete, 1999).

on research with children (Peltier, 2016); and (2) illustrating *Anishinaabe* worldview perspectives and parents' role in early child development.

Anishinaabek Ecological Relational Knowledge Theoretical Framework, Pedagogical Model, and Conceptual Map

Theoretical Framework

Indigenous Knowledge comes from *Aki*. Each of us is situated in a specific Place. My identity and self-development are grounded in *Odenong* – my home and community of origin. The Place that I come from is called *Mnjikaning*. It is a place where two fresh water lakes meet and people have gathered to fish and trade for 5500 years. I grew up on Lake Couchiching, which is in the Great Lakes area of Ontario. My father taught me how to live with the lake in a respectful way so that we could harvest fish, eat, and make a living selling bait and guiding. The lake is our life. It is the foundation for who I am and where I come from. I *am* the Water. I *am* the Land. What I do to the Water I do to myself. What I do to the Land I do to myself.

The Medicine Circle is a framework for examining and understanding Indigenous constructs such as the cosmic order and unity of all things (Dumont, 2006). Bopp et al. (1989) explored the teachings of the Medicine Circle, an ancient symbol of Indigenous people of Turtle Island (North America), and described it as "a symbolic tool that helps us to see interconnectedness of our being with the rest of creation" (p. 41). Utilizing the Medicine Circle, relationships are expressed in sets of four (e.g., physical senses – sight, hearing, touch, taste; four dimensions of wholistic learning – spiritual, emotional, physical, mental; life on *Shkagamik-kwe*/Mother Earth – mineral, plant, animal, human; four cardinal directions – east, south, west, north). "The Medicine Wheel shows the universe reflected in our being – visualizing oneself in the center, connected equally to all points by the power of will towards idealism [which] ... makes all great causes possible ... a response of the heart ... essentially an emotional attraction to what is good" (Bopp et al, 1989, p. 50).

The Medicine Circle frames an Indigenous pedagogical approach within relational interconnections and learner self-awareness towards an ideal, wholistic balance. Lifelong learning involves developing self-awareness and balance among the aspects of oneself – the mind, spirit, body, and feeling/heart – an awareness that in turn "embraces the mental, spiritual, emotional and physical aspects of the individual, the family, the community, and Shkagamikwe as a whole" (Graveline, 1998, p. 54).

Pedagogical Process Model

The Medicine Wheel is foundational and frames the Wholistic *Anishinaabe* Pedagogical Model in Figure 3.1 (below). This Indigenous Pedagogy is wholistic in that all aspects of the learner are engaged by thinking, writing (white), intuitive reflecting, visioning, listening (yellow), experiencing, doing, drawing (red), relating, feeling, and storying (black).

An Indigenous cosmovision ideology is shown by the two colours forming the background of the schematic. Our way of knowing within an Indigenous Knowledge paradigm and pedagogical process negotiates the physical world (green) as well as the unseen (blue).

The *Anishinaabe* pedagogical model is grounded within an inclusive community of respect and mutual understanding and in an Indigenous pedagogical process that is wholistic and relational. An Indigenous pedagogy in a school classroom environment, as well as in the larger educational context of life-long learning through lived experience and story, engages all aspects of the learner for embodied knowledge, and the teacher-learner relationship is reciprocal. The child is teacher and learner. The teacher is also learner. Central to an Indigenous pedagogy is the process of coming to know in a community of engagement. Land informs the knowledge of how we are to live in a good way within a particular Place. How we relate with each other and the creation and our engagement in learning is informed by our understanding of being *with* Place. Experiences and stories illuminate biophilia and balanced reciprocity in relationships.

Anishinaabe Storywork Circle Pedagogy

The three components in the *Anishinaabe* storywork Circle pedagogy are Teaching stories, reflective experiences in Place, and story Circles. The following describes each component with an example:

Grandmother Teaching Story: Embedding AERK Concepts and Principles in Story. A grandmother exudes many aspects of living Indigenous Knowledge. I shared AERK in the Grandmother Teaching Stories that I have gained from my experience as a parent, grandmother, and educator as well as stories passed down to me from Elders and Keepers-of-*Anishinaabemowin*. In the Indigenous educational process, Elder stories about experiences and observations of the natural environment represent knowledge through stories passed from generation to generation. The storyteller imparts their own life and experience into the telling of stories and the listeners filter the story through their own experience and reflective thinking. They make it relevant to their own life. I paid

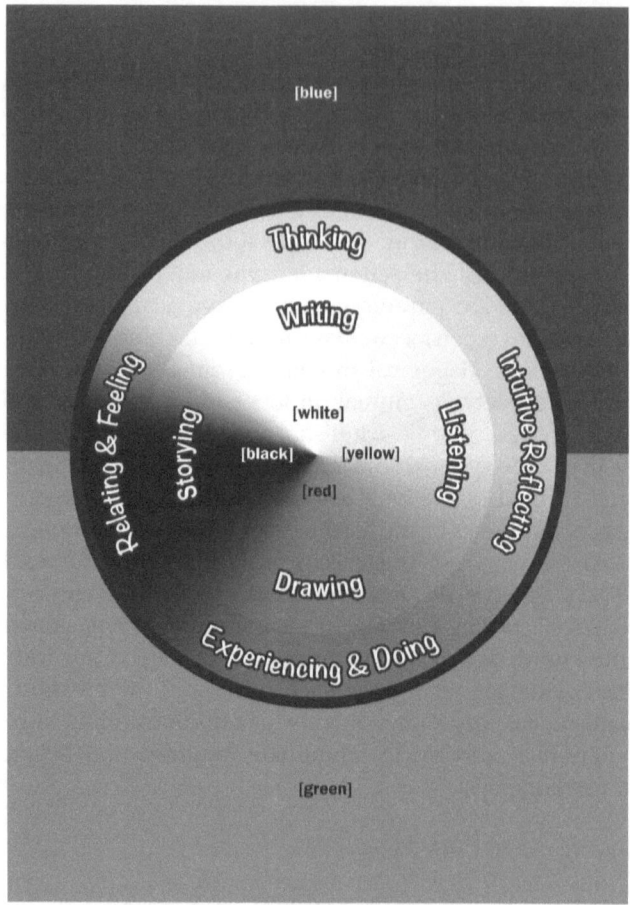

Figure 3.1 Wholistic *Anishinaabe* Pedagogical Model

Source: Redrawn figure based on "An Anishinaabe Perspective on Children's Language Learning to Inform," in "Seeing the Aboriginal Child," by S. Peltier, 2017, *Language and Literacy, 19*(2), Special Issue.

particular attention to aspects of Place/context, philosophical principles, and *Anishinaabemowin* concepts in the Grandmother Teaching Stories that I shared with the students. The incorporation of *Anishinaabemowin* conveys worldview perspectives and exemplifies an Indigenous paradigm and ways of knowing. In this pedagogical approach, I introduced and repeated several concepts and labels in *Anishinaabemowin* in context to the students in order to provide an explanation of Indigenous worldview with particular emphasis on conceptions of AERK (i.e., *Mishomis*/Grandfather Rock, *Odehwegan*/drum, *Nibi*/water, *Asemaa*/tobacco, *Aki*/Land).

I drew on my Grandmother Teaching Bundle in the Teaching Stories and referred to the items to facilitate comprehension of abstract concepts. Bundle components included *Mishomis*; *Odehwegan* (hand drum and drum stick); *Nibi*/water (drinking water and copper water vessel); pouch of *Asemaa*; electronic candle (symbol of community Fire Circle); Medicine Circle cloth; circular mat; large blanket for us to sit in a Circle.

Figure 3.2 (below) illustrates how the Medicine Circle cloth, circular mat, and blanket were configured in the schoolyard as visual referents to support Grandmother Teaching Stories and Relational Wheel Teachings that illustrate a philosophy of interconnections and interdependence with our Self, family, community, nation, world, and universe. As I shared a Grandmother Teaching Story about quietness within and attention to balance of the four aspects of personal being for wellness, I pointed out the four quadrants of the Medicine Circle cloth (white, yellow, red, black) to illustrate the four aspects of a person. I shared a story about pride in the man my son has become and how I thanked him for choosing me to be his parent and I pointed to the centre of the Circle, the place of the child. When I shared Relational Wheel teachings, the family was acknowledged and represented by the centrally placed Medicine Circle with the child as central. The mat (purple) that the Medicine Circle cloth was situated on formed a circular border around the Medicine Circle and this was explained to represent relationship with the community. Additionally, it was pointed out that the circular mat represented an Indigenous concept of time as being circular and cyclical, non-linear. For example, our care-horizon is longer than our life (past, present, and future are interconnected and we consider the choices we make and our actions as impacting the next seven generations). We imagine that "the ancestors are living their future through us." The area of the large rectangle blanket (pink – where the story Circle participants sat during Circles outside in the schoolyard) was described as representing our relationship with our nation (First Nation, Canada), and the grass of the schoolyard around the periphery (green) delineated the world. What lay beyond the grass signified our relationship with the universe.

The Relational Wheel Teaching Stories illustrate the philosophy that our way of Being extends outward in all directions to the cosmos. We can conceptualize the interconnected and interdependent features of a Relational Way of Being when we imagine dropping a Pebble into a pond – a change in one of these interconnected layers sets into motion change in all. *Nibwaakaawin*/a state of Being is rooted in the understanding of

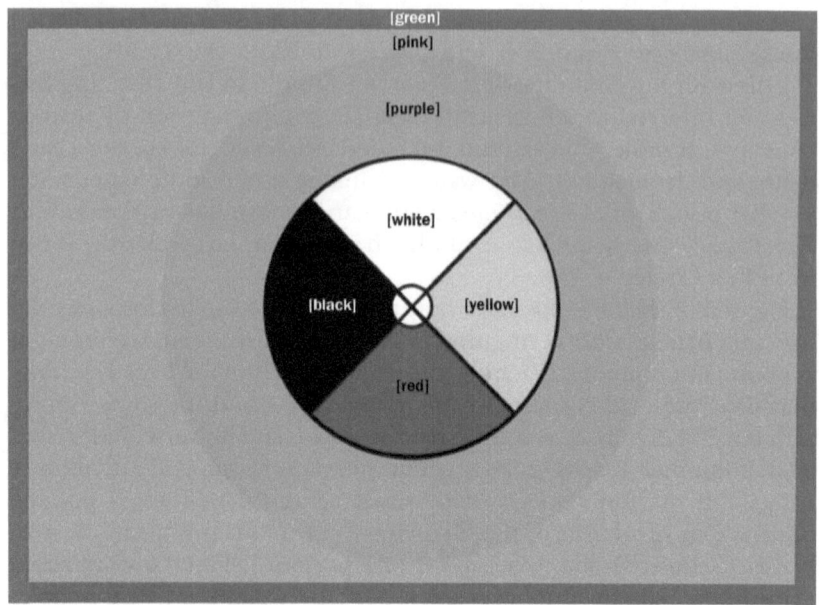

Figure 3.2 Schoolyard Placement of Medicine Circle Cloth, Circular Mat, Blanket

and respect for the interconnectedness of all life where all things are interdependent. *Nibwaakaawin* acknowledges "all my relations," which includes *Negwaadodem*/the whole clan of family/blood relatives as well as feelings of *Weh*/connection to community, society, and all of creation. *Nibwaakaawin* is tied to the concept of volition or choice to act in a way that supports rebalancing and harmony. To exemplify *Nibwaakaawin*, we gathered on the blanket on a particularly windy day and directed our attention to the movement of the trees, grass, and clouds, and envisioned sharing our breath with the trees.

The Grandmother Teaching Story component of this storywork Circle pedagogy epitomizes the oral tradition and the listener's process of meaning-making. The AERK demonstrated in the Grandmother Teaching Stories in this research were relational to *seven directions*, reflecting an Indigenous wholistic approach to learning: *Aki*/the Land; *four* directions of the Medicine Wheel; *above* the Earth/Sky world; and *underneath*/ancestors. These Anishinaabe ecological relational Teaching Story concepts were included:

- Medicine Wheel philosophy (inner space reflection and volitional balance of spiritual, physical, emotional, and mental aspects of the

person), four colours and cardinal directions (yellow-east, south-red, black-west, white-north).
- Relationship and interconnections of self to family, community, nation, and universe, sky world (movement of sun, clouds, moon – June/*Waabnonii Giizis*/Blooming Moon), *Shkagamik-kwe*/Mother Earth (plants, strawberries/*Odemininan*, animals, *Nibi*/water, air and fire), *Gaaniniigaaniijek*/Ancestors, harmony, and reciprocity.
- Individual and collective presence in the Circle (learning/teaching, listening, respect, and belonging).

The following is an example of a Grandmother Teaching Story I shared with the students and their teacher. It brings forward appreciation of Indigenous peoples' contributions to the world (aquaculture), illustrates the economy of trade among nations and sophistication of Indigenous relational, land-based Knowledge prior to colonization, and speaks of identity and belonging. The story tells about the gathering place at the narrows between Lake Couchiching and Lake Simcoe. The people of *Mnjikaning* built and took care of a large fish fence or corral, containing many species of fish. The area was sandy, with shallow water that ebbed and flowed between the two lakes, a perfect environment for aquaculture. People of different nations, from close by and afar, travelled to trade items made from copper, turquoise, and clay. The people of *Mnjikaning* always had a ready supply of fresh fish as well as preserved, smoked fish. As recently as 20 years ago, the remains of the fish fence were still intact beneath the sand. These remnants of the cedar and balsam saplings were studied by scientists with permission of our First Nation community and were confirmed by carbon dating testing to be over 5500 years old. My ancestors are an ancient people. We refer to ourselves as "The People of the Fish Fence."

Reflective Experience in Place: Reconnecting to *Aki*/Land. This exercise offered an opportunity for personal reflection on the Grandmother Teaching Story, and to enhance awareness of Self and interconnectivity with surroundings, and "being of a place." I modelled for the students how to ground the Self by walking barefoot to find their Place in the schoolyard. Standing or sitting, while quieting the body and mind during alone-time, brings focus to the moment, and engaging all of the senses heightens perception of relationship to Place. After each Grandmother Teaching Story, students were given a clipboard, pencil, and paper, and were given 15 minutes for their reflective experience in Place. I sounded my hand drum to call them back for a Story Circle.

Story Circle. After each reflective experience in Place, we sat together in a Story Circle on the blanket. Each Story Circle was a response to the invitation: "What did you notice about the Teaching story and time with *Aki*?" The classroom teacher and students participated by telling a story, sharing their writing or drawing, or exercising the option of passing if they did not wish to speak.

The Story Circle provided a safe and respectful place in the classroom for listening, thinking, and reflecting on what is shared, with the option of speaking. During our first Story Circle, I introduced *Mishomis*/Grandfather Rock to the participants, explaining that the rock is the oldest part of *Shkagamik-kwe*/ Mother Earth and knows everything that was ever said or done here on *Aki*. I described my relationship with Grandfather Rock as a balanced, healthy one that is based on reciprocity – he helps me remember things and in return I bring him to visit with students and hear their stories. I treat him with kindness and care, just like I would treat my real grandfather. Grandfather Rock was referred to as *Mishomis* (Grandfather) and was central to our story Circle process to elicit respect and an orderly flow within the Circle. *Mishomis* represented for us a tangible reminder to listen respectfully, remember, and share openly from the heart, in response to the students' sharings and personal life connections. Huston and Michano-Drover (this volume) also describe how Indigenous early childhood educators used the teachings around the Grandfather Rock to introduce children to their community's teachings.

The process honoured coming to know in inner ways as well as through oral expression. Stories shared were accepted as representing the storyteller's "truth." Each participant was instructed to take what they could from each sharing and to leave the rest with the central fire/candle. The Story Circle participants were instructed to listen respectfully without judging others, to remember what is shared, and to share openly from the heart. The participants took turns holding *Mishomis*/Grandfather Rock and passing him, hand to hand, in a clockwise direction around the Circle. The person holding the stone was the speaker, invited to speak if they wished. When finished, he or she passed the stone to the person on the left. Thus, the Circle flowed in a clockwise direction, following the route of the sun as perceived by *Anishinaabek* people, and extending from the heart on their left side. Story Circle participants had the option of passing the stone to the next person without sharing. Usually the stone was passed around the Circle twice to allow participants time to reflect and respond to what others shared. The passing of the stone to the next person signalled that the person had finished their turn at sharing.

The Circle Process of Anishinaabe Ecological Relational Knowledge Creation

The schematic below (Figure 3.3) illustrates the clockwise movement of *Mishomis* within the story Circle. The Circle participant's cultural

Seven Directions Early Learning 43

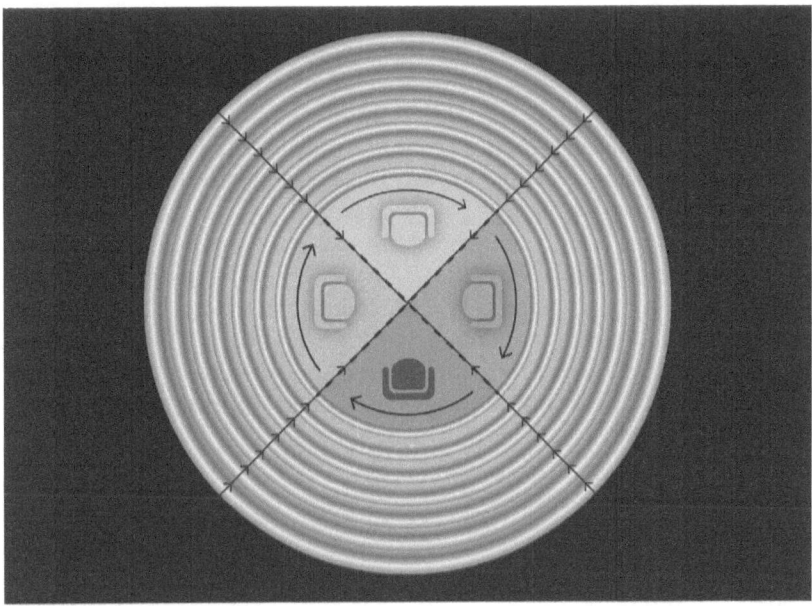

Figure 3.3 Story Circle Participants "Make Meaning"

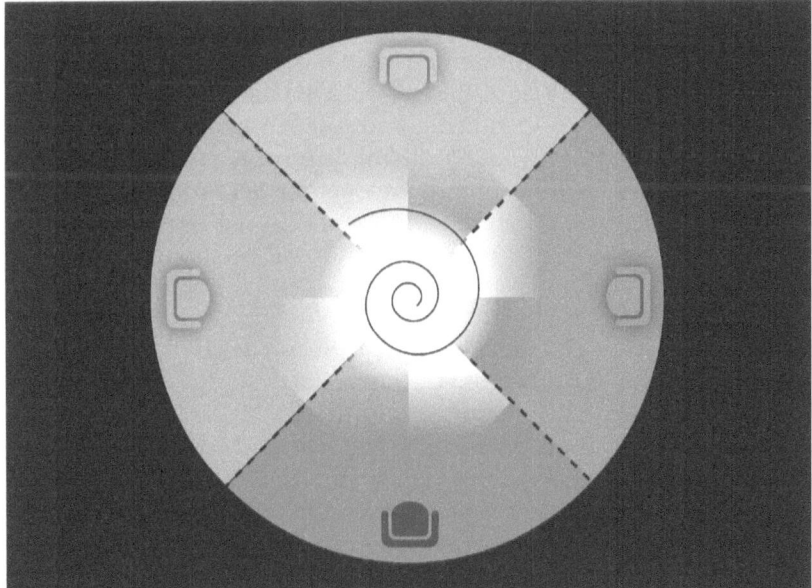

Figure 3.4 Generation of Knowledge in the Story Circle

knowledge, prior experiences, frames of reference, and knowledge from *Gaaniniigaaniijek* (the ancestors) are represented by the concentric circles (rainbow colours). The storytelling process within the Circle honours the individual and *Debwewin* (personal and wholistic truth rooted in their heart). A sense of community is created as each person listens and/or shares (inclusiveness), and everyone is valued and seen as equally important (equity).

Figure 3.4 represents the generative aspect where new knowledge is created within the Story Circle experience. Each participant shares knowledge with the other Circle participants, and cumulatively this process creates new understandings. The new knowledge from the Story Circles in this research project is referred to as *Kinoomaadiziwin*, revealing participants' understanding of aspects of *Anishinaabe* ecological relational knowledge.

Anishinaabe Ecological Relational Knowledge Conceptual Map

Figure 3.5 (below) illustrates the conceptual knowledge generated by Story Circle participants. This knowledge was situated within understanding interrelationships and interconnections with *Aki* and each other within the specific knowledge system context of localized (northeastern Ontario *Anishinaabe*) content, meaning, and protocols.

The AERK themes represented in the Story Circles are embodied knowledge. Colour groupings are associated in the schematic to represent aspects of wholistic knowing: thinking (white), intuitive reflecting (yellow), experiencing and doing (red), and feeling and relating (black). Indigenous people acknowledge that not everything is known and understood, and this is represented in the schematic by situating *Anishinaabe* ecological relational knowledge on a dark background.

Living with Place: *Anishinaabe* Worldview Perspectives and Parents' Role in Early Child Development

A young Indigenous child's parents, grandparents, and language- and Indigenous Knowledge-keepers support the child to know who they are and where they find themselves in relationship with the seven directions. The teachings and experiences are valued and honoured within the context of family and community life.

Figure 3.5 *Anishinaabe* Ecological Relational Knowledge (AERK) Conceptual Map

Indigenous land-literacy is a lifelong learning process that begins from birth and where the child is central within a relational way of being. Over the course of the life-path journey, an individual acquires *Nibwaakaawin*. Indigenous Knowledge-keepers, language-keepers, grandmothers, and grandfathers provide guidance and support towards the acquisition of this land-literacy wisdom. The term *Weh* refers to our feelings of connection that gradually develop from the process of heart-knowledge interacting with mind-knowledge so that a person feels connection with not only family and community but outward to society, *Aki*, and the universe.

Cultural ways of honouring the child and supporting their early development are significant to grounding them to Place during their early years. These culturally based early child development practices were almost extinguished due to colonial policies and racist interference, but are being revitalized in our families and communities today. An Indigenous child's early learning is primarily guided by the parents, grandparents, and family members. The kinship structure of the *Anishinaabe* family is extensive beyond blood relatives. *Negwaadodem* refers to the whole clan of family and community kinship inclusive of ancestors. Kinship terms of endearment are modelled and the child shows respect for those who teach and care for them by calling them, "auntie," "uncle," "*Nookmis*/grandmother," and "*Mishoomis*/grandfather."

The child's transition from the Spirit World to their Earthly Walk is honoured in birthing and early development ceremonies and parenting practices. In infancy, the swing/hammock and moss bag/cradleboard honour the child's transition to the family, and the young child's sacred naming ceremony includes an announcement of their unique name and personal colours to the creation and family/community.

As the young child approaches their next stage of life at the age of 7 or 8 years, a rite of passage celebration honours their life-stage transition from "small child" to "big-child," with family and community acknowledgment and with new responsibilities and expectations. At this time, the circle of loving and nurturing relationships extends beyond the child's home as they visit and engage with friends and participate in community activities.

During our time parenting young children, my husband and I utilized an Anishinaabe pedagogical approach that allowed our two boys to participate in all family activities and to experience and appreciate connection to the seven directions. The young child is exposed to the language and activity in its entirety, and they participate at a level in line with their language and acquired skills. For example, when cleaning freshly harvested fish, our older boy (age 8) had a sharp knife to remove the head and cut the fish alongside his father, while our younger son (age 6) had a tiny jackknife to safely participate as he could.

Table 3.1 (below) illustrates aspects of the seven-direction learning that my young children (before the age of 7 years) were immersed in to develop identity, a sense of belonging, and a relational way of being. Understanding where they are and the importance of Place grounds them to *Odenang*/where the heart is.

Table 3.1 Aspects of Seven-Direction Relational Early Learning

	Aspects of Relationship	Lived Knowledge
1. *Aki*/Land	Respect and reciprocity in relationships with animals and plants, food, medicines.	Ask for what is needed by offering *asemaa*/tobacco and addressing: berries, spring water, fish, trees for firewood. Take only what we will use. Share with family and Elders in the community. Appreciate microcosms and observe rocks, flowers, insects, frogs, snakes in their natural environment (observe and explore with care, there is no need to always bring these home – they are at their home with their relatives).
	Nibi/Water	Acknowledge and sing to *Nibi*/water at the pond, lake, stream, and in ceremony.
	Fire	Respectfully build and care for a fire that has a specific purpose, always with guidance from father, uncle, or grandfather. Never play with fire.
2. Medicine Circle Cardinal Directions and Aspects of Self	EAST Visioning and intuitive, spiritual	The door of our Tipi/Lodge faces east, that place where the sun comes up. Gratitude expressed by greeting a new day or the rain, showing happiness for life by singing/drumming and dancing at the powwow.
3. Medicine Circle	SOUTH Experiencing and doing, physical	Hearing talk about where we are going on trips, seeing maps used and visiting "Pinelli's," down south at Niagara, going to the powwow down south at Buffalo/New York. Physical skills such as holding an infant and being attentive to a younger child by sharing drinks and snacks, playing with them, and keeping them safe. Participating in the harvest by helping untangle the fish net, picking berries, wrapping moose meat for the freezer.
4. Medicine Circle	WEST Feeling, relating, emotional	That place where the sun sets is in the west. Emotional such as using voice to release physical pain by yelling or screaming when hurt. Expressing feelings with words, "I love _____." "I like _____." "I don't like _____."

(*Continued*)

Table 3.1. (Continued)

	Aspects of Relationship	Lived Knowledge
5. Medicine Circle	NORTH Knowing, thinking	Hearing talk about where we are going on trips, seeing maps used and going north to "Bill and Emily's farm" by Timmins, driving way up north to Chisassibi/James Bay. Respectful consciousness to anticipate others' needs and respond as a helper – extending an arm to offer an Elder support when walking. Fetching/carrying things for an Elder. Engaging in an activity quietly and listening when adults are together and when in ceremony.
6. Sky World and Above	Clouds, thunder, lightning, Northern Lights, andstars	When on the lake or road, hearing talk about rain or snow clouds and observing this. Anticipating a storm and moving indoors when hearing thunder, seeing lightning, noting when the leaves turn in response to the wind. Laying down on *Aki* to observe the clouds, stars, and shapes in the night sky. Enjoying the energy from the sounds and colours of the Northern Lights.
7. Ancestry and *Gaa-niniigaaniik*/ Ancestors	Family/kin and community members who have gone on to the Spirit World. Awareness that the ancestors walked here before us.	Stories and artifacts from veterans, Chiefs/community leaders. Stories connecting the child to Places where ancestors lived. Annual memorial ceremonies for family members who have passed on to the Spirit World.

Anishinaabek Ecological Relational Knowledge and Reconciliation

A ripple effect is occurring in the collective consciousness of Indigenous peoples and Canadian society following the Truth and Reconciliation Commission of Canada's (TRC's) Report and Calls to Action (Truth and Reconciliation Commission of Canada, 2015a and 2015b). This new wave of interest and attention includes immersion in a process of coming to terms with historical and ongoing colonial harm to Indigenous family and community systems, and Indigenous languages and knowledges.

Haskell and Randall's (2009) idea of "disrupted attachments" resonates with Indigenous peoples in Canada today. Disrupted attachments result from severed attachment to land, customs, culture, governance, languages, and ways of life, and from the reverberations of "complex trauma" involving harms in relationships with the self and relationships with others (p. 48). Haskell and Randell show that "the effects of and responses to traumatic events are "transmitted" across generations" (p. 51), and conclude, "[our] social justice vision of healing, recovery, equality, and transformation ... includes attention to the conditions of wellness and resilience, and attention to directions for healing from trauma" (p. 52).

Indigenous intergenerational trauma as a result of colonization is becoming obvious in these times of truth and reconciliation. This reality demands the creation of space to critically examine our role as educators and early learning practitioners. Forging new relationships must include healing the negative and hurtful relationship between Indigenous people and schooling based in "Western" approaches. Conceptualizations of child development and play remain largely "Western"; with constructions of knowledge about play and young children's learning and well-being within a sociocultural paradigm being informed by ideological discourses and play-based pedagogies (Peterson & Riehl, 2016). It is important to apply critical theoretical perspectives to taken-for-granted beliefs, discourses, and practices in relation to early learning and play in the context of Indigenous children (Gerlach et al., 2014). Play in early child development is a normalizing construction situated within systemic relations of power and historical, political, and socio-economic structures. Indigenous children's play experiences within their homes may be shaped by intergenerational occupational injustices, as parents' own lack of participation in childhood play experiences are transferred forward to the next generation.

An educator who works towards inclusivity and reconciliation values the child's life experience, relationships, and cultural knowledge systems such as the earth, family, and community, and creates space for Indigenous learners and knowledge keepers in the classroom. Indigenous people have heard about Truth and Reconciliation; many are still waiting to be recognized and invited more fully into shaping the processes that affect them in relation to others, including their communities, families, and children. Commitment to a learning journey to understand local protocols and known Indigenous resource people is demonstrated by reaching out to Indigenous people in their rural, urban, or First Nation community and establishing trust. In order to bring Indigenous

Knowledge into the classroom, the teacher approaches Indigenous people to create a relationship and ask for their support. Indigenous Knowledge is about relationships and the process of coming to know. It is about lived relationships and is grounded in community. An educator who is considering integrating Indigenous Knowledge into their classroom walks alongside Indigenous people who are knowledge-keepers. This may include language keepers, Elders, students' family and community members, and skilled resource people who model ways of being, knowing, and doing in the context of the school and school community. Even an Indigenous teacher does not bring Indigenous Knowledge into their classroom on their own. As Wood (this volume) states, "language teachers in the three schools ensure that learning is always supported and contextualized on the land, combined with cultural learning in relationship" (p. 119).

In place of Western constructions, I offer Story Circle process, *Anishinaabe* relational ways of seeing, doing, being, and knowing, and seven directions cultural perspectives of Place-based learning for the young child. Early child care and development contexts can be informed by an Indigenous early learning paradigm where knowledge that comes from *Aki* is lived and a child's experiences are reflected upon over their lifespan, creating deeper knowledge and meaningful connections. Education is a lifelong learning process and schooling is one aspect of education. Indigenous Knowledge extends beyond environmental science, land-based learning, stories from books, and cultural performances. Place-based learning in an early learning context supports ongoing exploration of being in relationship with Place to develop biophilia/love for nature and the necessary receptivity to sense Place wholistically.

Hop fast, peeper frogs. Jump away, bunnies. Fly high fireflies. Strawberry plants and raspberry bushes, be safe. Stay alive, sweetgrass.

Education and play are intertwined with *Anishinaabe* daily life and events, even dangerous events such as the one recounted at the beginning of the chapter. In interacting with my children when we were threatened by wildfire, I travelled into their world to create a playful situation that at the same time helped them understand the event in relation to deeper life learning. In this process, my children also became teachers, as children are the playful masters of their own experience.

REFERENCES

Bopp, J., Bopp, M., Brown, L., and Lane, P., Jr. (1989). *The sacred tree.* Four World Development Press.

Cajete, G. (1999). Reclaiming biophilia. In G. Smith, & D. Williams (Eds.), *Ecological education in action: On weaving education, culture, and the environment*, 189–207. State University of New York Press.

Dumont, J. (2006). *Indigenous intelligence*. University of Sudbury.

Ermine, W. (1995). Aboriginal epistemology. In M. Battiste & J. Barman (Eds.), *First Nations education in Canada: The circle unfolds*, 101–112. UBC Press.

Gerlach, A., Browne, A. & Suto, M. (2014). A critical reframing of play in relation to indigenous children in Canada. *Journal of Occupational Science*, 21(3), 243–258. https://doi.org/10.1080/14427591.2014.908818

Graveline, J. F. (1998). *Circle works: Transforming eurocentric consciousness*. Fernwood Publishing.

Haskell, L., & Randall, M. (2009). Disrupted attachments: A social context complex trauma framework and the lives of Aboriginal peoples in Canada. *Journal of Aboriginal Health*, 5(3), 48–99. https://doi.org/10.3138/ijih.v5i3.28988

Huston, L., & Michano-Drover, S. (2022). Placing the child's hands on the land. In S.S. Peterson & N. Friedrich (Eds.), *The role of place and play in young children's language and literacy* (pp. 81–94). University of Toronto Press.

Kulnieks, A., Longboat, D., & Young, K. (2010). Re-indigenizing curriculum: An eco-hermeneutic approach to learning. *AlterNative: An International Journal of Indigenous Scholarship*, 6(1), 15–24. https://doi.org/10.1177%2F117718011000600102

Peltier, S. (2016). *Demonstrating Indigenous storywork Circle pedagogy: Creating conceptual space for ecological relational knowledge in the classroom*. [Unpublished PhD dissertation]. Laurentian University.

Peterson, S.S., & Riehl, D. (2016). Rhetorics of play in kindergarten programs. *Brock Education Journal*, 25(2), 22–34. https://doi.org/10.26522/brocked.v25i2.498

Truth and Reconciliation Commission. (2015a). *Honouring the truth reconciling for the future: Summary of the final report of the Truth and Reconciliation Commission of Canada*. http://www.trc.ca/assets/pdf/Honouring_the_Truth_Reconciling_for_the_Future_July_23_2015.pdf

Truth and Reconciliation Commission. (2015b). *Truth and Reconciliation Commission of Canada: Calls to action*. http://trc.ca/assets/pdf/Calls_to_Action_English2.pdf

Wilson, S. (2008). *Research is ceremony: Indigenous research methods*. Fernwood Publishing Company Limited.

Wood, J. (2022). The importance of the land, language, culture, identity and Learning in relation for Indigenous children. In S.S. Peterson & N. Friedrich (Eds.), *The role of place and play in young children's language and literacy* (pp. 109–126). University of Toronto Press.

4 Sámi Children's Language Use, Play, and the Outdoors through Teachers' Lenses

KRISTINA BELANCIC

Introduction: History of Sámi Education in Sweden

This chapter draws on interviews with 12 Sámi teachers to explore their perceptions of the role of play and place in learning Sámi language and culture for Sámi children (ages 9 and 11) in two Sámi schools in the Swedish part of Sápmi. In this context, I refer to place as outdoors where Sámi children play during recess. The outdoors is important as it gives voice and choices to children in determining what, how, when, and where they learn.

I begin by introducing the Sámi context and Sámi education, including the roles of place and play in the Sámi National Curriculum. The land of the Sámi Indigenous people, Sápmi, stretches across Finland, Norway, Russia, and Sweden. There is no precise information about the Sámi population in Sápmi, as no institution is responsible for collecting demographic data related to the Sámi people, but approximations of the total Sámi population in Sápmi are in the range of 50,000–100,000 (Pettersen, 2011). In Sweden, the number of Sámi people is between 15,000 and 30,000; however, not all of them speak Sámi (Outakoski, 2015). In the Swedish part of Sápmi, five Sámi languages are spoken: North Sámi, Lule Sámi, South Sámi, Pite Sámi, and Ume Sámi. All five Sámi languages are listed as endangered languages, according to UNESCO (2019).

Due to Sweden's assimilation policy between the 1920s and 1950s, the language of instruction in Sámi schools was Swedish, although Sámi children's mother tongue was Sámi (Sjögren, 2010). As a result, the status of the Sámi languages declined, and many Sámi people chose not to speak Sámi with their own children. In 1977, the Swedish state reaffirmed the status of the Sámi people as Indigenous people and pledged to support Sámi traditions, culture, language, and education through legislation (Mörkenstam & Lawrence, 2012). Not only for Sámi Indigenous people in Sweden but for Indigenous people all over the world, the school context is an important pillar and support for language development. Today, Sámi children can attend one of the five Sámi schools in Sweden. The languages of instruction in these schools, which offer Grades 1 to 6 (ages 6 to 12), are both Sámi and Swedish. However, after Grade 6, Sámi children have to attend a Swedish school to complete their compulsory education.

In 2011, a new Sámi National Curriculum (SNC) was established for Sámi schools. One of the main goals of the SNC is for students to be functionally bilingual, in terms of speaking, reading, and writing in the Sámi and Swedish languages. The SNC differs from the Swedish National Curriculum in its focus on Sámi traditions, culture, values, and language. Sámi children studying the Sámi language can choose between Sámi as a first language (L1) or Sámi as a second language (L2). Sámi children living in an environment where the language has a strong presence often choose to study Sámi as an L1. Others choose to study it as an L2 because they have had little exposure to the language (Sullivan et al., 2019). Thus, not all of the children have the same language proficiency in Sámi. In her study, Outakoski (2015) points out that many Sámi children are bilingual and multilingual, but for some Sámi children in Sweden, Sámi schools are often the only context in which they can use Sámi.

Sámi Curriculum, Play, and Place

Although there is no mention of the outdoors as a learning space for Grades 4 and 5 (ages 9 to 11) (Skolverket, 2019), the SNC recognizes play as important for helping children to acquire knowledge, particularly in the early years (Grade K–3 of schooling) (Skolverket, 2019). Play is an activity that involves exploring, experimenting, jumping, running, climbing, and learning; as part of or in combination with outdoor activity it triggers both physical and cognitive development (Fisher et al., 2010). Whether activities are adult-led or child-led (Eberle, 2014), play supports children's writing, language acquisition, mathematics, and conceptual learning (Saracho & Spodek, 2006; Wajskop & Peterson, 2015).

In particular, sociodramatic play has been found to enhance children's emotional and social development. According to Smilansky and Shefatya (1990), sociodramatic play is "a form of voluntary social play activity" (p. 3) where children create imaginary worlds, characters, and scenarios which relate to the real world. During sociodramatic play, children create stories and roles that reflect their everyday experiences. Through such play, children learn to socialize, communicate, negotiate, think creatively, and solve problems. Crucial to sociodramatic play is the interaction with peers "to enable social engagement and the practice of social and language skills" (Morrissey et al., 2017, p. 178). Sociodramatic play is a practice for meaning-making, as it relies on understanding cultural expectations and rules and understanding others' perspectives (Fromberg Pronin, 2015; Saracho & Spodek, 2006). Please note that throughout this chapter, I use the term *play* to refer to *sociodramatic play*.

In addition to sociodramatic play, the notion of place consciousness is important in my research, as both culture and place are constructive to human understanding and to students' academic achievement (Gruenewald, 2003). Previous research (Lloyd et al., 2018; Shamah & MacTavish, 2009; Smith, 2002; Sobel, 2004) focusing on place-based learning has shown that outdoor play and learning are significant contributors to children's overall development and learning. Place consciousness, as taken up in my study, is about the relationship between Sámi culture and the history and geography of places where Sámi children live and learn. Interactions with wildlife, such as reindeer herding, fishing, and hunting, are important parts of Sámi schooling, as are oral history and storytelling (Jannok Nutti, 2007). Sámi teachers are aware of the importance of the reindeer corral for language teaching and learning. Hornberger and Outakoski (2015) explain that the reindeer corral "is a site of overlapping, polycentric social and societal spaces such as family needs, community practices, regional Sápmi identities, and national educational policies, but also of school spaces such as classroom lessons, school policies, and curricular demands" (p. 44). Indigenous language, culture, tradition, and livelihoods "exist in a deep and holistic engagement with [their] places" (Mustonen, 2018, p. 66), particularly outdoor places. Sámi children (ages 6 to 9 years) whose schooling included being outdoors in the forest increased their use of the Sámi language, and the children were able to transform and connect acquired knowledge to other subjects (Jannok Nutti, 2008).

While a number of studies focus on the child's perspective on outdoor play and show that the combination of outdoor activity and play encourages children's communication, and develops language and collaboration skills, few studies focus on the teacher's perspective (Fjørtoft & Sageie, 2000; Jarman, 2008; Norling & Sandberg, 2015). In one study (Norling & Sandberg, 2015), participating teachers were aware of the outdoors as a language-learning facilitator; however, they had few opportunities to enhance children's development through outdoor learning.

In the following section, I describe my methods for gathering and analysing interview data to explore the roles of play and place in Sámi children's learning in Swedish Sámi schools.

Methods

Prior to data collection, I met with the head of the Sámi Education Board and the principals of two of the Sámi schools. We discussed the schools, the learning environment, and the challenges that teachers faced. One of the principals showed interest in the project. Later, upon learning about my project, another principal expressed interest in taking part. Since this project used an Indigenous methodology approach, considerable time was needed to develop relationships and establish communication with the schoolteachers and children. Additionally, I had one online meeting with parents of children in the participating schools to inform them about the project.

Data Collection and Analysis

Over 8 weeks, I gathered data through classroom observations and interviews with Grade 1–6 Sámi teachers and Sámi children, who were 9 to 11 years old, in the two participating schools. Eleven Sámi primary schoolteachers, with teaching experience ranging from 6 months to 38 years, participated in the study. I conducted semi-structured interviews, each between 20 and 60 minutes in length. I used probing and follow-up questions (e.g., "Can you expand, please?," "What do you mean?," "Tell me more."). All interviews were audio-recorded and transcribed. The interviews were conducted in Swedish. The quotations from the transcribed data that are presented in the findings are translated from Swedish into English by the author.

In the interviews, the teachers were asked about their language use in the school context, their language use in the family environment, what they thought about the future of the Sámi languages, and the schoolchildren's knowledge and attitudes towards Sámi. During the interviews, teachers talked about Sámi children's language use during play and how they perceived the role of play in school.

All interviews were analysed to explore the teachers' perceptions of play, place, and language use in Sámi schools. I used key terms (e.g., play, free play, sociodramatic/pretend play, game, outdoor, cards, language, place, space, outside) to code the transcripts.

Teachers' Perspectives on Language Use in Play and the Role of Place

In the analysis process, I identified three overarching themes: (1) playce matters for language learning, (2) playce matters for cultural awareness, and (3) peers' language preference and fluency matter in outdoor play. The first theme, *playce matters for language learning*, relates to learning Sámi as a first and second language in outdoor contexts, and learning languages together with others through outdoor play. The second theme, *playce matters for cultural awareness*, refers to the cultural background of Sámi children and shows how pretending to be reindeer herders impacts on their language choice and language use. This theme highlights the importance of the outdoors, as real-life reindeer herding happens only outside. The third theme, *peers' language preference and fluency matter in outdoor play*, shows that children learn through playing outdoors while interacting with more competent peers.

In the following sections, I elaborate on these themes, drawing from interview data.

Playce Matters for Language Learning

In the following excerpt from a participating Grade K–6 teacher's interview, the link between play and place for language learning is highlighted. In this case, the teacher describes children who have Sámi as their first language as needing to develop their Swedish knowledge and vice versa:

> When children are outdoors during recess, they speak Swedish when they play ... When learning a new language, the children play in that new language, so you do not have to be afraid that children speak Swedish a lot when they play when the home language is Sámi. It could be that children are on their way to learning a new language and therefore use it while playing.

In this statement, the teacher attributes children's language use and play to a particular outdoor place. She explains that Sámi children enjoy learning a new language in the schoolyard, as they incorporate the "new language" (Swedish) in their play. Her perspective, that regardless of the language (e.g., first or second language) students' use of language(s) during outdoor play supports their overall language development, is supported by previous research (Lloyd et al., 2018). The outdoors as a place also provides children with a sense of belonging and contributes to the foundation of children's identities (Norling & Sandberg, 2015). Similarly, Fjørtoft and Sageie (2000) found that children's engagement in play in outdoor environments is crucial for developing language and collaboration skills in a variety of domains at the same time.

The teacher's assurance to Sámi parents that they "do not have to be afraid that children speak Swedish a lot when the home language is Sámi" reflects her awareness that many Sámi parents are afraid their children's use of Swedish at school will diminish their use of the Sámi language. It seems that this view of language use has an impact on how the teacher sees the tension between Sámi as a minority language and Swedish as a majority language. She is confident that as long as both Sámi and Swedish are spoken in the school and in the children's home environment, there is no reason to believe that Sámi will die out.

Also making connections between place, play, and language learning, a Grade 2–6 teacher believes that pupils learn language while playing outdoors at the schoolyard:

> Children's language use depends on their needs. You can use language(s) in different contexts. Sometimes I used to think like that when the children play outdoors, then they use Swedish and that is a way of learning a language. So, you do not have to worry about the increased Swedish language use … Here at this school we have several languages and children must also learn to speak and use Swedish … and then it is easier for children to use Swedish through a role … to play and be someone else when speaking Swedish.

Here, the teacher comments on the role and position of the Swedish language in the Sámi society and the Sámi school. This teacher notices that children have the potential to become strong Swedish-language speakers, too, as play and place play important roles in the development of children's language skills. Another teacher adds that Sámi children "use Swedish when they play outdoors, but they otherwise use Sámi in school." These teachers point out the importance of the schoolyard as a safe and negotiated place for the children to play and to learn a language through interactions with others (Smith, 2002). For the Sámi pupils, speaking Swedish while pretending to be someone else is a way of learning Swedish. Similarly, a Grade K–6 teacher explains, "The children are Sámi-speaking so they use Sámi a lot. However, they can use some Swedish words also … and when they play … well, it depends on the kind of play but for the most part they use Sámi." All three teachers refer to how the children's language use depends on the play context and that play provides an opportunity for children to learn a second language as well as develop their first language (Mistry & Sood, 2015).

Playce and Cultural Awareness

The interconnectedness of language and culture is reflected in a participating Grade K–6 teacher's observation that "children play in Sámi;

however, their language choice depends on the game ... They use Swedish when playing with cars and Sámi when playing as reindeer herders." Reindeer herding takes place outdoors in nature and is vital to Sámi people and their culture. For some Sámi children, reindeer herding is part of their real-life experience and culture. In this statement, the teacher sees play as a cultural activity where children have an opportunity to replay stories from a particular event and give new meaning to the context.

Since reindeer herding is based on pupils' real-life experiences, it connects the children to place and provides them with opportunities to share and further discover new meanings in these experiences (Smith, 2002). In their play, children share the same culture and reality, "acting like they are other people in another place and time" (Lillard et al., 2013, p. 2).

It is not enough for teachers to understand that children use different languages when they play. Instead, it is important to listen to what children do when they play outdoors "to get a sense of the conceptual and social understanding of children's play" (Wajskop & Peterson, 2015, p. 19). As Gisela Wajskop (this volume) adds it is important for teachers to listen to children's talk when playing to understand "children's knowledge of everyday life" (p. 163).

Also, the schoolyard as a place helps teachers understand that place stimulates children's development through playing, exploration, and stimulation by others in an outdoor setting (Morgan, 2010). But also, as Gisela Wajskop (this volume) indicates that listening to and challenging children's experience through place-based play mediates their learning.

Playce Influences Peers' Language Preference

Language use during outdoor play depends on pupils' language fluency and preferences of their peers, as pointed out by a Grade K–6 teacher: "If a child does not speak good Sámi, then they [the group] switch to another language [Swedish]." If Sámi-speaking children play together outdoors on the schoolyard, they use Sámi; however, if a less fluent Sámi-speaking child joins the game, the fluent Sámi speakers switch and adapt their language to that of the less fluent Sámi-speaking child. By changing the language to Swedish, the Sámi children welcome the less fluent-speaking child to be part of the outdoor play.

Similarly, I observed two Sámi-speaking children playing a game together on the school's playground outdoors. Two Sámi children played a game in Sámi when a less fluent Sámi-speaking child joined the game; the two Sámi children switched to Swedish. This example shows how during outdoor play, the two Sámi children switch to Swedish to enable the other child to join the game. Perhaps it also indicates that the two Sámi children are aware of the peer's lack of proficiency in Sámi and therefore switched to Swedish. The two children were not "just" playing. They were also socializing through play by allowing the other child to join the game that in turn influenced the children's language choice. Both examples identify the schoolyard as a cultural and geographical place that provides children with the opportunity to draw on their cultural knowledge; the children realize that those who are more competent have to support the less competent, they value the friendship of peers, and they create a space where it is acceptable and safe to use any language.

Even though the above examples show that Sámi children adapt their language to Swedish, a Grade 3–6 teacher indicates that non-speaking or less fluent Sámi children may benefit from more competent peers in outdoor playing activities as well. She explains, "If more Sámi children talk Sámi during play in the outdoor school place, then other children will join the game and switch to Sámi." Similarly, a Grade K–6 teacher believes that play is a way for non-Sámi-speaking children to use Sámi together with others: for "children [who] are Sámi-speaking and for some children who do not have Sámi, it [play] is a way to engage in Sámi and undergo language immersion together with others." However, equally important is the teacher's role in creating learning opportunities by understanding what children do with their language, and by acting as a scaffolder during play (see Gisela Wajskop, this volume).

These examples, in contrast to the first and second example, illustrate how Sámi children learn together with more competent peers in the schoolyard and show that stronger Sámi-speaking children support less fluent children (cf. Ervin-Tripp, 1991). Interaction with peers is beneficial for language learning, but communication with peers at a higher level of language proficiency possibly supports scaffolding and results in a positive social experience (Mistry & Sood, 2015). In addition to its role in play, the schoolyard as a place enables children's engagement in communication (Jarman, 2008) and provides them with language choice and more freedom to play and explore without adult control (Tovey, 2007).

Another example highlighting peers' language preference in outdoor play was observed in one of the Sámi schools. Every day during recess, all the Sámi children from Grades 1 to 6 gathered together to play "Under the Wings of the Hawk" on the schoolyard. Before the game started, the children negotiated to choose one pupil to stand on one side of the field and be "the hawk." The other players stood on the opposite side of the field. Then, the hawk cried, "Under the wings of the hawk!," to which the others responded, "What colour?" The hawk picked and shouted out the name of a colour. All the children who were dressed in the colour that the hawk called out had immunity and could not be taken. All the other children had to run to the opposite side without being caught by the hawk. Those who were caught became new hawks. The game continued with the new hawks choosing another colour. The game ended when only one participant was remaining. The last participant then served as the hawk in the next round of the game. This game was, for all the Sámi children, an opportunity to participate in a play activity and to use the Sámi language in a particular place. Norling and Sandberg (2015) highlight the importance of play activity for children to perform meaning-making together with other peers in their immediate environment. The game and the place provided all pupils the possibility to construct their knowledge by participating and interacting outdoors together with peers.

During this game, the children developed a relationship with the outdoor place that was their schoolyard. Given that the connection to the outdoors and nature is valued in the Sámi context (Jannok Nutti, 2008), the children's meaning-making through language and action was a product of their own choices within their cultural context.

Änggård (2012) pointed out that outdoors sociodramatic play is a rich context for children's meaning-making, as the outdoors is loaded with symbolic meanings that children use in constructing their Sámi identities. By playing the "hawk" game every day at the same spot, the place became an identity marker for the Sámi pupils. The place became important for them as the children chose and decided what, when, where, and how they would learn. This game is an example of how to integrate play and place, and to develop meaning (Stolz, 2015) in children's interaction. Even though less-fluent or non-Sámi-speaking children recited the Sámi phrases of the game from memory, they were still learning Sámi words in an authentic context. They were able to speak and hear Sámi. In line with this observation, a participating Grade 4–6 teacher pointed out that, because of children's lack of knowledge of Sámi games, the children play Swedish games. They use Swedish to play these games. This teacher proposed that if more games in Sámi such as "Under the Wings of the Hawk" are provided to Sámi children, there will be greater language development in Sámi, as language will be connected to place and children's real-life experience.

Teachers' Reflections about Place and Play for Sámi Language Learning and Culture Awareness

In this chapter, I have provided a snapshot of teachers' perceptions of the roles of play and place on children's use of Swedish and Sámi in

Sámi schools. As teachers reported, their pupils were capable of making their own language choices in the schoolyard during play. Sámi children's decisions influenced their own and other's actions. They switched from speaking Sámi to speaking Swedish so that less-fluent Sámi speakers could understand them, for example. Peers respected their language choices and understood the need to adapt in order for the play to continue (Lindahl, 2005). Additionally, the examples show that children were learning together and developing different skills (e.g., cultural awareness or socialization) through playing in the schoolyard. The schoolyard as a place not only offered opportunities for language learning but also enabled the children to acquire and value the knowledge and skills involved in local cultural activities. For example, pretend play of Sámi cultural practices, such as in reindeer herding, offers a great opportunity for language development and language learning (Saracho & Spodek, 2006). Children learn together and from each other during play as each of them brings together their own experience from home and school. Also, playing with each other possibly contributes to the maintenance of the Sámi languages and culture in the Sámi schools (cf. Kyratzis, 2014).

Vygotsky's (1967) sociocultural perspective on language describes language as a cultural necessity for developing and sharing knowledge among members of a community. This view of language is evident in Sámi pupils' reindeer-herding play activity as it relates to the cultural background of Sámi children. The Sámi languages are rich in terminology for reindeer and reindeer husbandry. Both are important parts of Sámi traditional knowledge. As such, the Sámi pupils experience Sámi language use during reindeer herding and it is not surprising that they use Sámi during the outdoor play activity in the school. The example shows that the children's play, for instance where they take up roles as reindeer herders, has an impact on their language choice and language use. Further, it indicates the importance of place, as the reindeer herding takes place in particular places in the world. Reindeer-herding play enables children to connect to the places where they live and provides them with opportunities to share and deepen their understandings of Sámi social values and family practices. The culture of children's Sámi communities is reflected in their play. Culture and language are closely intertwined; as children learn and use language in their play, they are learning culture (Gaskins, 2014).

In this study, some Sámi pupils had Sámi as their first language and Swedish as their second language, while others had Swedish as their first language and Sámi as their second language. Yet, others used Swedish and Sámi in their homes equally. Regardless of pupils' first and second language, outdoor play provided a context for children's use of their first and second languages. Grøver et al. (2016) explain that playing together with peers in a second language may contribute to language learning as the learners encounter a range of possibilities to make use of those languages. At the same time, using the first language during outdoor play possibly helps to understand the second language (e.g., memorizing words). The game "Under the Wings of the Hawk!" demonstrated how pupils, together with peers, used and learned the Sámi language in outdoor play.

The teachers in the Sámi schools who participated in the study have provided numerous examples and observations that highlight the importance of providing pupils with various play activities that reflect their experiences, interests, and culture to stimulate and support language use and development. They thus open our eyes to the potential of the schoolyard as a rich place for language and cultural learning.

REFERENCES

Änggård, E. (2012). Att skapa platser i naturmiljöer: Om hur vardagliga praktiker i en I Ur och Skur-förskola bidrar till att ge platser identitet. Creating places in the natural environment: How everyday preschool practices in all kinds of weather give places identity. *Tidsskrift for Nordisk barnehageforskning*, 5(1), 1–16. https://doi.org/10.7577/nbf.414

Eberle, S.G. (2014). The elements of play: Toward a philosophy and a definition of play. *American Journal of Play*, 6(2), 214–233.

Ervin-Tripp, S. (1991). Play in language development In B. Scales, M. Almy, A. Nicolopoulou, & S. Ervin-Tripp (Eds.), *Play and the social context of development in early care and education* (pp. 84–98). Teachers College Press.

Fjørtoft, I., & Sageie, J. (2000). The Natural environment as a playground for children: Landscape description and analyses of a natural playscape. *Landscape and Urban Planning*, 48(1–2), 83–97. https://doi.org/10.1016/S0169-2046(00)00045-1

Fromberg Pronin, D. (2015). How nonlinear systems inform meaning and early education. In D. Formberg Pronin & D. Bergen (Eds.), *Play from birth to twelve: Contexts, perspectives, and meanings* (3rd edition, pp. 419–434). Taylor and Francis. https://doi.org/10.4324/9781315753201

Fisher, K., Hirsh-Pasek, K., Golinkoff, R.M., Singer, D.G., & Berk, L. (2010). Playing around in school: Implications for learning and educational policy. In A.D. Pellegrini (Ed.), *The Oxford handbook of play* (pp. 341–363). Oxford University Press. https://doi.org/10.1093/oxfordhb/9780195393002.013.0025

Gaskins, S. (2014). Children's play as cultural activity. In L. Brooker, M. Blaise, & S. Edwards (Eds.), *The Sage handbook of play and learning in early childhood* (pp. 31–42). Sage.

Grøver, V., Lawrence, J., & Rydland, V. (2016). Bilingual preschool children's second-language vocabulary development: The role of first-language vocabulary skills and second-language talk input. *International Journal of Bilingualism, 22*(2), 234–250. https://doi.org/10.1177/1367006916666389

Gruenewald, D.A. (2003). Foundations of place: A multidisciplinary framework for place-conscious education. *American Educational Research Journal, 40*(3), 619–654. https://doi.org/10.3102/00028312040003619

Hornberger, N., H., & Outakoski, H. (2015). Sámi time, space, and place: Exploring teachers' metapragmatic statements on Sámi language use, teaching, and revitalization in Sápmi. *Confero: Essays on Education, Philosophy and Politics, 3*(1), 9–54. https://doi.org/10.3384/confero.2001-4562.150618

Jannok Nutti, Y. (2007). *Matematiskt tankesätt inom den samiska kulturen: Utifrån samiska slöjdares och renskötares berättelser. Mathematical thinking within the Sámi culture: On the basis of the stories of Sámi Handicrafters and reindeer herders* (Licentiate thesis). Luleå University of Technology.

Jannok Nutti, Y. (2008). Outdoor days as a pedagogical tool. In A. Ahonen, E. Alerby, O.M. Johansen, R. Rajala, I. Ryzhkova, & E. Sohlman (Eds.), *Crystals of schoolchildren's wellbeing – Cross-border training material for promoting psychosocial well-being through school education* (pp. 199–207). University of Lapland.

Jarman, E. (2008). Creating spaces that are "communication friendly." *Mathematics Teaching Incorporating Micromath*, (209), 31–33.

Kyratzis, A. (2014). Peer interaction, framing, and literacy in preschool bilingual pretend play. In A. Cekaite, E. Teubal, S. Blum-Kulka, & V. Grøver (Eds.), *Children's peer talk: Learning from each other* (pp. 129–148). Cambridge University Press. https://doi.org/10.1017/CBO9781139084536.011

Lillard, A.S., Lerner, M.D., Hopkins, E.J., Dore, R.A., Smith, E.D., & Palmquist, C.M. (2013). The impact of pretend play on children's development: A review of the evidence. *Psychological Bulletin, 139*(1), 1–34. https://doi.org/10.1037/a0029321

Lindahl, M. (2005). Children's right to democratic upbringings. *International Journal of Early Childhood, 37*(3), 33–47. https://doi.org/10.1007/BF03168344

Lloyd, A., Truong, S., & Gray, T. (2018). Place-based outdoor learning: More than a drag and drop approach. *Journal of Outdoor and Environmental Education, 21*(1), 45–60. https://doi.org/10.1007/s42322-017-0002-5

Mistry, M., & Sood, K. (2015). *English as an additional language in the early years: Linking theory to practice*. Routledge.

Morgan, P. (2010). Towards a developmental theory of place attachment. *Journal of Environmental Psychology, 30*(1), 11–22. https://doi.org/10.1016/j.jenvp.2009.07.001

Mörkenstam, U., & Lawrence, R. (2012). Självbestämmande genom myndighetsutövning? Sametingets dubbla roller. Self-determination through government exercise? Sami parliament's dual roles. *Statsvetenskaplig Tidskrift, 114*(2), 207–239.

Morrissey, A.-M., Scott, C., & Rahimi, M. (2017). A comparison of sociodramatic play processes of preschoolers in a naturalized and a traditional outdoor space. *International Journal of Play, 6*(2), 177–197. https://doi.org/10.1080/21594937.2017.1348321

Mustonen, T. (2018). "He might come back": Views on Sámi cultural and linguistic revitalisation from Finland. In G. Roche, H. Maruyama, & Å. Virdi Kroik (Eds.), *Indigenous efflorescence: Beyond revitalisation in Sápmi and Ainu Mosir*. ANU Press.

Norling, M., & Sandberg, A. (2015). Language learning in outdoor environments: Perspectives of preschool staff. *Nordisk Barnehageforskning: Nordic Early Childhood Education Research, 9*(1), 1–16. https://doi.org/10.7577/nbf.749

Outakoski, H. (2015). *Multilingual literacy among young learners of North Sámi: Contexts, complexity and writing in Sápmi* (Doctoral dissertation). Umeå University.

Pettersen, T. (2011). Out of the backwater? Prospects for contemporary Sami demography in Norway In P. Axelsson & P. Sköld (Eds.), *Indigenous peoples and demography: The complex relation between identity and statistics* (pp. 185–196). Berghahn.

Saracho, O.N., & Spodek, B. (2006). Young children's literacy-related play. *Early Child Development and Care, 176*(7), 707–721. https://doi.org/10.1080/03004430500207021

Shamah, D., & MacTavish, K.A. (2009). Making room for place-based knowledge in rural classrooms. *Rural Educator, 30*(2), 1–10. https://doi.org/10.35608/ruraled.v30i2.448

Sjögren, D. (2010). *Den säkra zonen: Motiv, åtgärdsförslag och verksamhet i den särskiljande utbildningspolitiken för inhemska minoriteter 1913–1962. The safety zone: Motives, suggested measures and activities in the separative education policy targeted at national minorities 1913–1962* (Doctoral dissertation). Umeå University.

Skolverket. (2019). *Läroplan för sameskolan, förskoleklassen och fritidshemmet 2011: Reviderad 2019. Curriculum for the Sámi school, the pre-school class and the leisure-time centre 2011: Revised 2019*. Fritze distributör.

Smilansky, S., & Shefatya, L. (1990). *Facilitating play: A medium for promoting cognitive, socio-emotional and academic development in young children* Psychological & Educational Publications.

Smith, G.A. (2002). Place-based education: Learning to be where we are. *Phi Delta Kappan Magazine, 83*(8), 584–594. https://doi.org/10.1177/003172170208300806

Sobel, D. (2004). *Place-based education: Connecting classrooms and communities*. Orion Society.

Stolz, S.A. (2015). Embodied learning. *Educational Philosophy and Theory, 47*(5), 474–487. https://doi.org/10.1080/00131857.2013.879694

Sullivan, K.P.H., Belancic, K., Lindgren, E., Hanna, O., & Vinka, M. (2019). The global in the local: Young multilingual language learners write in North Sámi (Finland, Norway, Sweden). In A. Sherris & J.K. Peyton (Eds.), *Teaching writing to children in indigenous languages: Instructional practices from global contexts* (pp. 235–253). Taylor & Francis.

Tovey, H. (2007). *Playing outdoors: Spaces and places, risk and challenge.* Open University Press.

UNESCO. (2019). *Unesco atlas of the world's languages in danger.* http://www.unesco.org/languages-atlas/index.php

Vygotsky, L.S. (1967). Play and its role in the mental development of the child. *Soviet Psychology, 5*(3), 6–18. https://doi.org/10.2753/RPO1061-040505036

Wajskop, G. (2022). Children's engagement and inquiry in outdoors contexts as play and place-based learning. In S.S. Peterson & N. Friedrich (Eds.), *Role of place and play in young children's language and literacy* (pp. 159–176). University of Toronto Press.

Wajskop, G., & Peterson S.S. (2015). Dramatic play as a meaning-making and story-making activity. *Early Childhood Education Journal 43*(1), 17–20.

5 Young Children Exploring Identities, Languages, and Cultures in a Multicultural Place

MARIA COOPER AND HELEN HEDGES

In our increasingly globalized world many countries have experienced multiple waves of migration. Despite its small size and somewhat isolated geographical position in the world, Aotearoa New Zealand is no exception. While recognizing the multiple languages that migrants bring to the island nation, Aotearoa New Zealand maintains a political commitment to the Māori as its Indigenous people and to the Māori language. However, this commitment has come about following a colonial history of assimilationist policies. Knowledge of the Indigenous Māori language, culture, and history – and positive attitudes towards them – are not yet universally shared within the nation. Migration adds a layer of complexity to this commitment. In policy and practice, the country is still discerning what an increasingly diverse population might mean for social cohesion, economic prosperity, and responsive and contemporary relationships.

Within educational policy, the early childhood curriculum document *Te Whāriki* (Ministry of Education [MOE], 1996, 2017), which concerns children aged from birth to 6 years of age, prioritizes a commitment to Te Tiriti o Waitangi (the Treaty of Waitangi), a partnership agreement signed in 1840 between Māori chiefs and British colonial representatives. The recently revised curriculum highlights this responsibility towards the Indigenous Māori language and culture while also acknowledging and adapting to a multicultural present and future: "Unique in its bicultural framing, *Te Whāriki* expresses our vision that all children grow up ... strong in their identity, language and culture. It emphasises our bicultural foundation, our multicultural present and the shared future we are creating" (MOE, 2017, p. 2). The document also states that the country has a particular responsibility for migrants from neighbouring Pacific Islands countries: "*Te Whāriki* specifically acknowledges the educational aspirations of Pasifika peoples, who derive their identities from Pacific Island nations with which New Zealand has strong historic and present-day connections" (MOE, 2017, p. 7). There are several Pacific Island countries with strong historical, political, and economic associations. These include Samoa, the Cook Islands, Fiji, Tonga, Niue, Tokelau, and Tuvalu.

In this chapter, we discuss place, play, language, and culture in a globalized world as manifested in an early childhood education setting in Aotearoa New Zealand. We highlight ways that place, play, and language might contribute to children building a sense of belonging and cultural identity. While English remains the most widely used language in Aotearoa New Zealand, and a political commitment exists in relation to Māori, migrant families add much language and cultural richness to the country. Children participating in early childhood education create opportunities to explore and learn from each other – and their teachers – as they share the languages, features of culture, and knowledges specific to their family lives and experiences. As children do so, they are developing learner and cultural identities. They are also working to develop a sense of belonging in relation to both heritage countries and the place in which they live.

It is vital that teachers, families, and children value these cultural knowledges and experiences as Aotearoa New Zealand shifts from historical policies around assimilation to policies that prioritize Indigeneity and highlight diversity, belonging, and acceptance. For these and other reasons, our chapter is firmly grounded in sociocultural theory, a theory that recognizes the place of history in shaping culture as a phenomenon that children participate in and contribute actively to (Vågan, 2011). Roth (2006) offers the following socioculturally informed definition of identity: "who we are for ourselves and who we are in relation to others" (p. 3).

The term *place-based education* is derived from studies of human geography. When underpinned by sociocultural theory, place-based education is more than a geographical backdrop to learning activities. Teachers and learners are engaged in pedagogical relationships that explicitly and implicitly demonstrate knowledge, attitudes, and values towards places, languages, and cultures. Place-based education offers a focus on context, history, and relationships that is useful when building curriculum, culture, and community (Penetito, 2008) to foster participation, belonging, and identity development. For all those who have lived in Aotearoa New Zealand for one or more generations, there may be a mixture of confusion and resistance as well as welcome and acceptance for new immigrant families. For more recent immigrants, there are many political, historical, and cultural considerations and decisions to grapple with as they discern who they are and who they want to be in their communities and the country that now forms "home" in terms of the place they reside. Immigrants in Aotearoa New Zealand engage in identity construction as well as develop a sense of belonging when they draw on knowledge of Māori language and practices to honour the Indigenous peoples.

Early childhood education centres are a microcosm of such ongoing complexity and change in the world. They are settings where diverse families are welcomed and children share their ideas and experiences as they play, learn, and talk together. As the early childhood curriculum document states, "Today New Zealand children are growing up in a diverse society that comprises people from a wide variety of cultures and ethnicities. *Te Whāriki* supports children from all backgrounds to grow up strong in identity, language and culture" (MOE, 2017, p. 7). In our chapter *place* is understood as the spaces where Indigenous and heritage languages and cultural practices are fostered by children, families, and teachers in pedagogical relationships. People may or may not be fluent in these heritage languages, and may not even have personally lived in the countries where they are spoken. These languages influence levels of participation, senses of belonging, and developing cultural identities, along with wider knowledges, attitudes, and values towards places, languages, and cultures.

The goals of place-based education are to situate teaching and learning in local activities, values, experiences, and phenomena (Smith, 2002). With a few notable exceptions (e.g., see Podmore et al., 2016), both Māori and Pasifika communities have struggled to develop, support, and maintain community centres in Aotearoa New Zealand that undertake pedagogical interactions in languages other than English. Most children of all cultural backgrounds attend settings where English is the primary language of interactions. For early childhood education teachers in Aotearoa New Zealand, implementing place-based education is a complex task. First, teachers need to have in-depth knowledge and understanding of *te reo* and *tikanga Māori* (Māori language and cultural practices) to meet the primary commitment stated in *Te Whāriki*. Teachers require not only these competencies but knowledge and respect for all the children and families that participate at the centre, and for the diverse ethnicities and backgrounds they represent. This increasingly demands diverse ways to create curricula that recognize and value these children and families (Podmore et al., 2016).

What might such community complexity mean for children's developing sense of belonging and identity building in a multicultural place? Our chapter provides insights into the play activities, and cultural experiences and values, of two 4-year-old boys of blended Pasifika heritages. The interaction between the boys shows how they shared and enacted some of their language-related knowledge, experience, and behaviours. In doing so, they appeared to be locating what it means to live in Aotearoa New Zealand while also exploring elements of belonging and identity related to the nations and cultures of their heritages.

Background and Context

Te Whāriki, as a literal translation from Māori, means a mat for all to stand on. The aspiration statement in the document views children as "competent and confident learners and communicators, healthy in body, mind, and spirit, secure in their sense of belonging and in the knowledge that they make a valued contribution to society" (MOE, 2017, p. 5). *Te Whāriki* is framed by four principles: partnerships with families and communities–*whānau tangata*, empowerment–*whakamana*, relationships–*ngā hononga*, and holistic development–*kotahitanga*. The curriculum values play and exploration: "A curriculum *whāriki* for young children provides a rich array of primarily play-based experiences. By engaging in these, children learn to make sense of their immediate and wider worlds through exploration, communication and representation" (MOE, 2017, p. 15). Early childhood education centres therefore offer significant opportunities to assist children to explore and develop their languages, cultures, and identities through play, exploration, communication, and representation.

In this chapter we analyse an interaction that took place during a project we developed to explore young children's interests, inquiries, and working theories in relation to their everyday lives in their families, communities, and cultures. The project was a partnership between us, as university-based researchers, and centre-based teacher-researchers, who used a number of qualitative data-generation methods (see Hedges & Cooper, 2014 for details). The two 4-year-old boys in this interaction attended Small Kauri Early Childhood Education Centre, a privately owned but community-focused mixed age group setting for children aged 6 months to 5 years old. Small Kauri's teachers provided a well-resourced environment that enabled children to select freely from the play experiences, interact together throughout the day, and be supported to learn from peer interactions and from teacher knowledge and responses. As will be illustrated, this access included musical instruments – and spaces and encouragement to play these and to sing – and a computer to seek information. This interaction was transcribed from video data that a teacher-researcher gathered. Ethical guidelines based on principles of respectful relationships, voluntary participation, informed consent, and children's ongoing assent were enacted throughout the study. Credit – naming the centres, teachers, and children – was offered to recognize the participants' involvement in the research (Cullen et al., 2009) and was largely accepted.

Simeon and Hunter both represented a growing mixed-ethnicity demographic. Hunter is a New Zealand–born child with a Cook Island Māori mother and Samoan father, both of whom had been born in Aotearoa New Zealand themselves, following their parents' migration. Hunter is the second child in his family to attend the centre; his older sister had also attended prior to going to school. The teacher-researchers visited Hunter and his family; they were one of many families and children who were visited at home. Family visits were used to gain deeper insights about him and his family in relation to their life experiences, use of languages, and aspirations for their son (Cooper & Hedges, 2014). Simeon had migrated recently with his family to Aotearoa New Zealand from Fiji, where he was born. His father is Fijian-Indian and his mother Chilean. Like Hunter, he is the younger of two children and has an older sister at primary school. As Simeon was not visited at home, we are not aware of his or his family's languages capacities or the language and culture-related aspirations of Simeon's parents. In this interaction, we explore ways that the boys shared their languages and cultures and melded these with what they saw as significant about language and culture in Aotearoa New Zealand. While this chapter is focused on spoken language as a cultural tool, we also see the way that music, gesture, movement, and dance are part of a broader communicative and representational toolkit (Wells, 1999) that children draw on to express their motivations and messages. As Mary Jacobs highlights, "Children draw on the linguistic and cultural resources of their homes to represent and communicate multimodally and they attempt to expand these resources to understand other people, themselves, and the communities they participate in" (this volume, p. 106).

Simeon and Hunter's Interaction

In the following interaction the participants were Simeon and Hunter, and their teachers, Trish and Rosie.

> TRISH: Toru whā … *[3, 4 in Māori – a widely understood way to begin singing a song]*
> SIMEON: *Starts singing God of Nations [the New Zealand national anthem in English] while banging a drum; Hunter strums a guitar alongside. Simeon sings the opening verse then stops.*

TRISH: What about Māori – can you do the Māori one? *[meaning the national anthem in Māori that uses the same tune]*

SIMEON: Yep. Maybe, maybe a haka one. [*Simeon suggests a haka, a Māori challenge he would have seen performed before sports events as he has an interest in sports.*]

TRISH: What about the Māori national anthem?

SIMEON: No I can't sing that. What about, I want to sing the Māori haka one. *Hunter, who has been listening intently nearby, starts singing ka mate, ka mate [the first line of a famous haka] while holding a guitar. Simeon stands up and asks Hunter to join him. Hunter chooses to continue playing the guitar while Simeon performs.*

SIMEON: Ka mate, ka mate, ka mate, he! [*slaps his knees and arms as he says the first few and the last word of the commonly performed haka*]

HUNTER: No, it's like this: ka mate ka mate, ka ora ka ora. [*continuing the start of the haka while still sitting with guitar.*]

SIMEON: [*Instead of responding to Hunter*] I want the soccer team one.

HUNTER: What's the soccer team one? [*Was he wondering if there was a soccer haka?*]

SIMEON: They've got a, this was a Chile one ... Maybe a Chile one. Maybe a Fiji one! [*Starts to hum the tune accurately and bang the drums. Hunter joins in on the guitar.*] Finished! Can I see a Chile one? Chile music!

Trish suggests Simeon ask Rosie about Chilean music as Rosie's cultural background is Chilean. Simeon does so and they agree to look for Chilean music on the computer using YouTube. Hunter has followed and watches and listens intently again.

ROSIE: You want to see Chilean music or Chilean anthem?

Simeon chooses the anthem. Rosie searches it on the computer. They all listen together. On the screen is the Chilean flag and Rosie explains that it's "her flag." Rosie sings along to the anthem. Simeon listens. Hunter strums the guitar. Rosie continues singing the anthem until it finishes. Simeon asks her if they can search for some other anthems.

SIMEON: I like the Fiji one.

ROSIE: Do you know the words? [*Rosie searches for the Fijian anthem on the computer and finds rugby players from the last World Cup.*]

SIMEON: Fiji. Maybe I want to see the team one.

ROSIE: The rugby players are singing?

SIMEON: Yeah. Ok.

Rosie finds a video with Fijian rugby players lined up before a game to sing the national anthem. They continue watching.

SIMEON: Samoan Fiji?

ROSIE: This is Fiji. Samoa has another anthem. Every country has one. So the Chilean one, the Fijian one ... We need to ask Binita [a teacher with Fijian heritage] how to sing this one, I don't know the words ... Shall we put on the All Blacks one, the New Zealand one? [*Rosie plays a clip showing the players and the crowd singing the anthem.*] Look at those boys, they're wearing the New Zealand All Blacks t-shirts.

SIMEON: Maybe a haka! [*They watch the clip of the haka that follows the national anthem.*] I want to go to New Zealand versus Chile! [*Rosie explains Chile doesn't have a national rugby team, that they play soccer.*] [*video footage ends*]

Hunter and Simeon – Play, Place, Language, Belonging, and Identity Exploration

This interaction occurred in an early childhood education setting that enabled children's interests to be fostered (Hedges & Cooper, 2016). In this case, the interest was a deep inquiry exploring the ways languages, cultures, and identities can be learned through playing, watching, and supporting sporting activities. The inquiry was evident in the musical activity that Simeon and Hunter began together, exploring national anthems and the haka that the All Blacks perform before rugby games. It evolved into Simeon leading an investigation into Fijian and Chilean anthems. Hunter followed, albeit as a less overtly active participant than he was at the beginning of the interaction, when his sharing of expertise was evident.

Simeon initiated and engaged actively with their shared interest in multiple national anthems and sports. Team sports – playing, supporting, and spectating – are popular in many countries around the world, and Aotearoa New Zealand is no exception. National teams often succeed on the international stage at a level beyond expectations relative to the country's small population. In rugby, the New Zealand All Blacks are likely the most recognizable team at international events. After the national anthem is sung at the beginning of important games, the team also performs a haka.

Teacher Trish responded organically to the boys' interest in music and national anthems. As the resulting cultural weaving evolved, Trish encouraged them to sing the national anthem in Māori to honour and foster the commitment to *te reo* and *tikanga Māori* that is present in *Te Whāriki*. Simeon appeared to be less familiar with a haka and so perhaps conflated anthems and a haka as synonymous due to their co-presence at sporting events. Hunter showed more knowledge of a haka in his accurate rendition, but perhaps out of excitement, unfamiliarity, or confusion, Simeon cut Hunter off. When Simeon indicated he was not familiar with the Māori version of the national anthem and asked about Chilean anthems, Trish suggested he go to Rosie, who was of Chilean heritage.

In doing so, Trish was both recognizing cultural expertise that she did not have and supporting Simeon to identify with a teacher who shared an aspect of his mixed ethnicity. Simeon then eagerly pursued his own interest in national anthems that related to his shared cultural heritage with Rosie.

Hunter was an active contributor in the first part of the interaction. In particular, he showed his interest and competence in music through playing the drums and guitar, due to family expertise and values (see Cooper & Hedges, 2014). As the interaction progressed, what has not been captured in the text of the transcript but can be viewed in the video footage is the intent, albeit non-verbal, way that Hunter followed Simeon. He watched the YouTube clips, listened carefully to Rosie, and gently and quietly strummed his guitar throughout. Rosie had not seen the first part of the interaction so perhaps responded to Simeon's more overt approach and Trish's request by exploring Simeon's inquiry into a heritage she shared with him.

In summary, this episode is richly illustrative of an amalgam of political, cultural, and historical features related to place: place of birth, place associated with languages and/or heritage, and place of current living. In early childhood education centres where children can pursue interests with teachers, joint and reciprocal participation leads to opportunities for children to explore their identities, languages, and cultures together.

Discussion: Identities, Cultural Competences, and Relational Pedagogy

Identities development is an ongoing and fluid phenomenon. In this interaction, Simeon and Hunter illustrated ways young children communicate current understandings about languages, cultures, identities, and belonging actively, and weave their own cultural knowledge organically into playful exchanges with each other. They use play as a foundation to explore, share, and develop useful further understandings with each other and their teachers. This example demonstrates that it is likely that multiple identities merge, develop, and change regularly as people interact together. Pasifika early childhood education scholarship is a still-developing arena of study (Mara, 2013). In this section, we draw on the work of two Samoan scholars (Anae, 2016; Tuafuti, 2010) and one Cook Islands scholar (Mara, 2013), all of whom were based in Aotearoa New Zealand, to deepen our understandings of cultural considerations of identities and place-based education. We propose some considerations for relational pedagogies that take account of place and identities. We then raise concerns about language use and retention issues pertinent to achieving the aim of emphasizing "our bicultural foundation, our multicultural present and the shared future we are creating" (MOE, 2017, p. 2).

We begin by offering some ways to understand Hunter's participation in this interaction that acknowledge and validate his cultural competence, confidence, and understandings of appropriate communication. The metaphor of *teu le va* (Anae, 2016; Mara, 2013) describes a form of Samoan relational ethics. *Va* is a space that has physical, relational, and spiritual dimensions. As a concept, it places respectful, nurturing relationships at the centre of all activities and interactions, valuing commitment to and compassion for others in an effort to ensure that interactions are reciprocal and mutually empowering. *Teu le va* is also a verb; it denotes action which suggests that each partner in a relationship actively looks after, values, and cherishes the relational space. In early childhood education, *teu le va*, or nurturing relationships with others, might be evident in Pasifika children's respect for their peer friendships as well as with teachers. Hunter illustrates competence in knowing when to contribute to the relationship and also when to stay quiet and be a good friend who supports and listens. Pasifika children learn to prioritize serving others and thinking of others before themselves (Mara, 2013).

Teu le va may connect with another Pasifika value, that of knowing when to speak and when not to, a quality that may be misunderstood as lack of participation or interest. Listening, observing, and speaking are all valued undertakings. This cultural norm is typically introduced to children in their home and community contexts (e.g., at church), but is often challenged by teachers who may make assumptions about what this manner of not speaking means. Tuafuti (2010) describes a Pasifika *culture of silence* in educational contexts and explains that one should not assume that this silence is a passive process. Instead, silence is a culturally appropriate behaviour that involves deliberate choices about speaking and listening. Knowing when, where, and how to speak, and when to stay silent are aspects of nuanced cultural and communicative competencies valued in relationships in the context of Pasifika culture. Hunter was embedded in Pasifika values through his home and community experiences and was likely mindful of both of these concepts.

As this interaction illustrates, there are many possible opportunities in early childhood education centres for children to share their own languages and cultural values and interests that differ from the centre's dominant or instructional language/s, in this case English. Teachers can foster opportunities for children to share and engender knowledge of, and pride in, their identities. Mary Jacobs reminds us that "when young children are responded to as confident communicators as they play across modes and languages, they can see that their ways of communicating and representing are meaningful in the early childhood settings where they belong" (this volume, p. 106). Further, a sense of belonging and building identities is not restricted to either a place of birth or a place of living, but reflects the richness of experiences in a modern world. We therefore turn now to some considerations for relational pedagogies.

In early childhood education centres teachers can promote children's cultures and identities development first through careful and culturally appropriate provision of choices of resources and activities. In this way, children are encouraged to express values and follow interests, knowing that their cultural tools, resources, and activities are recognized and valued. Trish's willingness to undertake and learn from visits to family homes as part of her teacher-researcher role led to new understandings about Hunter's languages background and his musical expertise; the insights she gained changed curricular provision and relational pedagogical interactions at his early childhood education centre (see Cooper & Hedges, 2014). The relational interactions between teachers and children – and teachers' understanding of the cultural values and behaviours underpinning children's participation in these interactions –encourage children's shared experiences to flourish and foster inclusion, equity, and diversity. Relational interactions are also pivotal to empowering children's ongoing building of multiple identities in relation to places of birth, heritage, and living.

In our selected episode, both teachers provided appropriate resources and responded sensitively and encouragingly to guide and support the boys' inquiry. Relational pedagogy is a term that describes the teachers' approach; it requires teachers to know children and their families exceptionally well and to use this knowledge in meaningful responses (Hedges & Cooper, 2018). We add two Pasifika concepts relevant to relational pedagogy in this chapter. We encourage teachers to understand and engage with these concepts, but also to take appropriate opportunities to invite children into conversations. In these ways, shared understandings are enriched and perspective taking is fostered. Our analysis also brings attention to the importance of peers as relational learners who collaboratively share, explore, and challenge each other's knowledge and are therefore relational pedagogues themselves.

To sum up, teachers help to create the conditions for children's multiple languages, cultures, and identities to be fostered and thrive in a multicultural world. Nevertheless, as Baker (2011) points out, bilingualism – in his book the term refers to two or more languages – is an individual, societal, and political construct. Our chapter illustrates that it is not an easy task for children to grow stronger in multiple languages, cultures, and identities, and develop a sense of belonging in relation to place. As noted earlier, *Te Whāriki* prioritizes attention to the Indigenous language and culture, Māori, with the aim that all children will become familiar with the language and cultural protocols. Prioritizing *te reo* and *tikanga Māori* assumes good language models. Yet as Ritchie (2013) has argued, the commitment and competence required to honour the commitments embedded in *Te Whāriki* bring about significant challenges for teachers and communities that still need addressing.

Layered on the commitment to *te reo* and *tikanga Māori* is the commitment to Pasifika peoples, and beyond that to all learners: "our multicultural present and the shared future we are creating" (MOE, 2017, p. 2). With respect to the significant differences in cultures and identities among Pasifika peoples that such a generic term masks, Mara (2013) pointed out that there is as yet insufficient research and scholarship to inform early childhood teacher education or teacher practices supportive of Pasifika children. Baker (2011) notes that much international research has identified the multiple social, cultural, and cognitive benefits of multilingualism. Yet, the assumption here is that these groups of people are fluent in their languages, cultures, and identities. It is likely that many Pasifika children in Aotearoa New Zealand are not strong in this way owing to the challenges of navigating mixed cultures and insufficient exposure to heritage languages in their homes and communities.

Issues of languages expertise are important when considering ways children develop knowledge, belonging, and identity. Political and societal structures and preferences have meant that Pasifika migrants of earlier generations in Aotearoa New Zealand were discouraged from retaining their languages or, perhaps under pressure, chose to prioritize learning English to access broader opportunities such as education and employment outside the home. As a result, there are a decreasing number of fluent speakers in each generation. The situation of Hunter's family exemplifies that children's language and cultural backgrounds in Aotearoa New Zealand are increasingly complex. This matter then requires attention to children's, teachers', and families' views, knowledge, and agency in developing understandings and practices in a multicultural place in a global world (Schwartz & Palviainen, 2016).

Conclusion

Our chapter raises considerations of the multiple meanings of place-based education, meanings that extend beyond geographical boundaries, history, and culture to embrace connotations of belonging and identity. Our analysis and interpretation perhaps typify Schafft and Youngblood Jackson's (2010) point that place-based education involves a complex mix of social relationships with cultural and political histories and practices. Place-based education in early childhood education centres in Aotearoa New Zealand is a complex endeavour; it takes into account the commitments to Māori and Pasifika peoples stated in the curriculum document, *Te Whāriki*, and the effects of migration on the country in the past 50 years. Language usage is an expression of place, belonging, culture, and identity. Knowledge and a sense of pride and ownership of heritages is vital in Aotearoa New Zealand if, as a first priority, the language and culture of the Indigenous people, Māori, is to continue its revival and to flourish. The problem of language retention has arisen similarly in relation to Pasifika peoples as the effects of migration and early assimilation policies endure in second- and third-generation children. In a globalized world, *place* as a concept is increasingly complex as languages reflect histories, heritages, and countries that children – and sometimes their parents – may not have personally experienced.

As a microcosm of these societal changes in Aotearoa New Zealand, early childhood education centres serve a critical role for all children and families. In this chapter we analysed a play-based and playful interaction between Simeon and Hunter and their teachers, Trish and Rosie. We illustrated the complexities of young children exploring identities, languages, and cultures in a multicultural place that prioritizes a commitment to an Indigenous language and culture. We offered Pasifika culturally based concepts as possible explanations for Hunter's overall participation. We raised points that illustrate the meaning of Roth's (2006) definition of identity as "who we are for ourselves and who we are in relation to others" (p. 3) to showcase children's active interest in the languages and cultures of others they interact with in educational settings. This exploration of identities, languages, and cultures in the multicultural place that is Aotearoa New Zealand is a multifaceted undertaking. It requires teachers to have a dedicated commitment to languages retention and relational pedagogy.

ACKNOWLEDGMENTS

We thank all the children, families, and teachers who chose to participate in the project. In particular, in relation to this chapter, we thank the teachers at Small Kauri Early Childhood Education Centre and the families of Simeon and Hunter for their participation. We acknowledge the

Ministry of Education funding via the Teaching and Learning Research Initiative and the ethical approval of the project by the University of Auckland Participants Ethics Committee. We also thank our research assistant extraordinaire, Monica Bland, for her work editing and transcribing video footage from the project.

REFERENCES

Anae, M. (2016). Teu le va: Samoan relational ethics. *Knowledge Cultures*, 4(3), 117–130. https://addletonacademicpublishers.com/contents-kc/859-volume-4-3-2016/2835-teu-le-va-samoan-relational-ethics

Baker, C. (2011). *Foundations of bilingual education and bilingualism* (5th ed.). Multilingual Matters.

Cooper, M., & Hedges, H. (2014). Beyond participation: What we learned from Hunter about collaboration with Pasifika children and families. *Contemporary Issues in Early Childhood*, 15(2), 165–175. https://doi.org/10.2304/ciec.2014.15.2.165

Cullen, J., Hedges, H., & Bone, J. (2009). Planning, undertaking and disseminating research in early childhood settings: An ethical framework. *New Zealand Research in Early Childhood Education*, 12, 109–118. https://search.informit.org/doi/10.3316/INFORMIT.055340906250874

Hedges, H., & Cooper, M. (2014). *Inquiring minds, meaningful responses: Children's interests, inquiries and working theories*. Final report to Teaching and Learning Research Initiative. NZCER. http://www.tlri.org.nz/sites/default/files/projects/TLRI_Hedges%20Summary%28final%20for%20website%291.pdf

Hedges, H., & Cooper, M. (2016). Inquiring minds: Theorizing children's interests. *Journal of Curriculum Studies*, 48(3), 303–322. https://doi.org/10.1080/00220272.2015.1109711

Hedges, H., & Cooper, M. (2018). Relational play-based pedagogy: Theorising a core practice in early childhood education. *Teachers and Teaching: Theory and Practice*, 24(4), 369–383. https://doi.org/10.1080/13540602.2018.1430564

Jacobs, M. (2022). Negotiating multiple ways of knowing in an Aotearoa New Zealand playgroup. In S.S. Peterson & N. Friedrich (Eds.), *The role of place and play in young children's language and literacy* (pp. 95–108). University of Toronto Press.

Mara, D. (2013). *Teu le va:* A cultural knowledge paradigm for Pasifika early childhood education in Aotearoa New Zealand. In J. Nuttall (Ed.), *Weaving Te Whāriki: Aotearoa New Zealand's early childhood curriculum document in theory and practice* (2nd ed., pp. 55–70). New Zealand Council for Educational Research.

Ministry of Education (MOE). (1996). *Te Whāriki/He whāriki matauranga mō ngā mokopuna o Aotearoa: Early childhood curriculum*. Learning Media.

Ministry of Education (MOE). (2017). *Te Whāriki/He whāriki matauranga mō ngā mokopuna o Aotearoa: Early childhood curriculum*. Ministry of Education.

Penetito, W. (2008). Place-based education: Catering for curriculum, culture and community. *New Zealand Annual Review of Education, 18*, 5–28. https://doi.org/10.26686/nzaroe.v0i18.1544

Podmore, V., Hedges, H., Keegan, P., & Harvey, N. (Eds.). (2016). *Teachers voyaging in plurilingual seas: Children learning in more than one language*. New Zealand Council for Educational Research.

Ritchie, J. (2013). Te Whāriki and the promise of early childhood education and care grounded in a commitment to Te Tiriti o Waitangi. In J. Nuttall (Ed.), *Weaving Te Whāriki: Aotearoa New Zealand's early childhood curriculum document in theory and practice* (2nd ed., pp. 141–156). New Zealand Council for Educational Research.

Roth, W.-M. (2006). Identity as dialectic: Making and re/making self in urban schooling. In J.L. Kincheloe, K. Hayes, K. Rose, & P.M. Anderson (Eds.), *The Praeger handbook of urban education* (pp. 143–153). Greenwood.

Schafft, K.A., & Youngblood Jackson, A. (2010). Introduction: Rural education and community in the twenty-first century. In K.A. Schafft, & A. Youngblood Jackson (Eds.), *Rural education for the twenty-first century: Identity, place and community in a globalizing world*. Pennsylvania State University.

Schwartz, M., & Palviainen, Å. (2016). Twenty-first-century bilingual education: Facing advantages and challenges in cross-cultural contexts. *International Journal of Bilingual Education and Bilingualism, 19*(6), 603–613. https://doi.org/10.1080/13670050.2016.1184616

Smith, G.A. (2002). Place-based education: Learning to be where we are. *Phi Delta Kappan, 83*(8), 584–594. https://doi.org/10.1177%2F003172170208300806

Tuafuti, P. (2010). Additive bilingual education: Unlocking the culture of silence. *MAI Review, 1*, 1–14. http://www.review.mai.ac.nz/mrindex/MR/article/view/305/397.html

Vågan, A. (2011). Towards a sociocultural perspective on identity formation in education. *Mind, Culture, and Activity, 18*(1), 43–57. https://doi.org/10.1080/10749031003605839

Wells, C.G. (1999). *Dialogic inquiry: Towards a sociocultural practice and theory of education*. Cambridge University Press.

6 Placing the Child's Hands on Land: Conceptualizing, Creating, and Implementing Land-Based Teachings in a Play Space

LORI HUSTON AND STEPHANIE MICHANO-DROVER

The beautiful environment of northwestern Ontario, Canada, supports learning. It is a vast area consisting of dense bush and countless freshwater lakes and rivers, including the third-largest freshwater lake on Mother Earth, referred to as Lake Superior. In this chapter, we describe the design and building of the outdoor play space at the Biigtigong Nishnaabeg Children & Family Learning Centre, a licensed child care centre situated within this northern environment. The overarching goal of the play space is to reflect Indigenous ways of being and knowing, recognizing relationships between the self and the natural world, through the implementation of land teachings. The maintenance of balance and harmony within all relationships to nature is fundamental in land-based education. The "reality is based on mutual reciprocity, the rule of paying back what has been received from nature" (Cajete, 2000, p. 73).

In our chapter, we tell the story of Indigenous Early Childhood Educators (IECEs) and their community members designing and building an outdoor play space that incorporates culture connected to land-based teachings. Throughout the process, the IECEs and community members consulted with the community's Elders and Knowledge Keepers, individuals who are "highly respected because of a lifetime of acquiring wisdom and knowledge through continuous experiences and apprenticing with their forebears" (Snively & Williams, 2016, p. 37). Elders play an important role in passing down traditional teachings through the generations, often through "stories, symbols, models, and metaphors" (Snively & Williams, 2016, p. 33). Canada's system of compulsory residential schools for Indigenous children barred generations of children from living with Elders. Consequently, many teachings were not passed on. Today, the role of Elders is essential for closing "generation gaps created by legacies of residential schools while strengthening Aboriginal pride and kinship" (Sutherland & Swayze, 2012, p. 90).

Stephanie, one of the authors, and her colleagues faced challenges in creating the culturally appropriate outdoor play space for their child care centre, challenges that went beyond simply a lack of resources. Typically, play space designs in early learning centres do not reflect the Indigenous community's traditional culture in an obvious way. These spaces tend to resemble those of mainstream urban play spaces, with swing sets and other mainstream standing structures and smaller toys. Provincial licensing requirements do not align with the goals and needs of the children and families in the community. For example, provincial regulations often require child care centres to fence play spaces or obtain signed permission slips for children to step outside the fences. Stephanie and her colleagues set out to ensure the realities of their outdoor play space would remove barriers that might prevent the children's access to community bush lines, events, and local gatherings. In accordance with Indigenous traditions, we begin our chapter by situating ourselves in terms of our cultural, historical, and geographical relationships to the people and the natural world of northern Ontario.

Tánishi, Hello, I am Lori Huston, I am of mixed descent, a combination of Métis, Scottish, and British. My lineage is connected to the Red River Métis people; my great-great-grandmother was born in Tobacco Creek, Manitoba. I currently live in Thunder Bay, Ontario, but was raised in Red Lake, a small town in northwestern Ontario. Red Lake, a town of about 4,000 people on the shores of a large lake, was the site of a Hudson's Bay Company fur-trading post in the late 1800s. Today, gold mining is an important industry that contributes to the town's culture and is a source of employment for its residents. Red Lake has a significant Indigenous population and serves as a hub to surrounding remote fly-in First Nation (FN) communities. Growing up in Red Lake, I witnessed the contributions of white settlers to inequalities between Indigenous and non-Indigenous peoples. Indigenous peoples' ways of knowing occupy many aspects of my life. My background includes 12 years of coordinating an Indigenous ECE post-secondary diploma program with Oshki-Wenjack in Thunder Bay, Ontario. I have observed and supported the IECEs in the realities of inequalities – barriers they face due to their limited access to resources and support for early childhood education.

Boozhoo, my name is Stephanie Michano-Drover. I am an Ojibway from Biigtigong Nishnaabeg, a First Nation community situated on the north shore of Lake Superior, northeast of Thunder Bay, Ontario. My First Nation community has approximately 1,200 members, with 500 physically living in the community. My community is on the west bank of the mouth of the Pic River, where there are giant rolling sand dunes within a triangular area bounded by Lake

Superior to the west, the Pic River to the South, and by a sharp rock face to the northwest. The area north of the rock face terrain consists of low rock outcrops, spruce forests, and muskeg. The sand was deposited by meltwater running off of the continental glaciers about 10,000 years ago, when the Pic River was much larger than it is today. I am the Early Childhood Supervisor at the Biigtigong Nishnaabeg Children & Family Learning Centre in my community. I have many years of experience working in the field of child care, from front line staff to my current position. I'm married for 20 years to a loving, supportive husband, Rob Drover, and together we have three handsome sons: Eddie, Noah, and TJ. Lori invited me to share my experience in designing and building a culturally responsive outdoor play space that incorporates land-based teaching.

Coming to Know: Conceptualizing and Creating

Biigtigong Nishnaabeg Centre's vision includes the understanding that coming to know is a "journey, a process, a quest for knowledge and understanding" of all relationships (Cajete, 2000, p. 66). Coming to know means being open to an intuitive connection with and showing respect for the land in which we live – recognizing that we need the land to support our health and well-being. The Earth is seen as "Mother Earth." We care, love, and hold the utmost respect for Mother Earth, and see the spirit in the living and non-living on earth. This "spirit is conscious and has awareness – the wind, water, stars, frogs, rocks, smoke, people, cedar trees, salmon, and killer whales possess a spirit" (Snively & Williams, 2016, p. 34).

Within an Indigenous worldview, a child is recognized as a sacred gift from the creator. As such, children are treated with the utmost respect, care, nurture, and dignity, and are raised to become people who honour and respect all living things. Children are part of a collective group, closely connected to and supported by extended family and community members. Traditional parenting involves the whole community, the immediate and extended family in connection with the land (Fenton, 2018). Accordingly, it was not only the IECEs at Biigtigong Nishnaabeg Centre who were involved in designing the outdoor play space. Community Elders, Knowledge Keepers, and the families of the children attending the centre met frequently with the IECEs to create shared visions of land-based education in early learning. This approach to planning is similar to that described by Wood (this volume) who found, "the common denominator of success has been early and regular consultation with specially gifted Elders who have a love for children" (p. 113).

Indigenous Knowledge varies across all Indigenous peoples as they incorporate ways of being and relationships with the land and other things within the local environment (Ball & Simpkins, 2004). As noted above, Biigtigong Nishnaabeg Centre is located on the Pic River, alongside sand dunes and spruce trees. The Pic River has been the focus of the Anishinaabek people's endeavours for at least 2,500 years. Although the river is known to community members as a means of transportation for industry, in the past, members relied on the river for trade with surrounding First Nations communities. They used the river as a route to reach inland lakes and hunting areas. Pic River Elders often describe the Pic River as a highway, with dog teams going up and down the river in the winter and canoes in the summer. From the late 1940s to the 1970s, the Marathon Paper Company used the river to move newly harvested boom logs to a nearby sawmill. The river was always full of pulpwood during the summer, limiting use by Anishinaabek hunters and fishermen. Today, now that the river is free of pulpwood, community members can use it once more. Spiritually, the river connects members to the ways in which their ancestors lived. Community members still recognize and use historical routes along the Pic River. As Cajete (2000) explains, Indigenous peoples have "interacted with the places in which they lived for such a long time that their landscapes became reflections of their very souls" (p. 183).

Well-being and spirituality are interconnected and reflect close connectivity with the natural environment – the land in Indigenous cultures. There are many sources of natural medicines found along the Pic River, such as cedar, that members rely on to support their well-being and spirituality. For example, community members drink cedar teas and prepare cedar in ceremony. At the child care centre, the presence of cedar trees enables educators to share the medicine teachings with the children.

In creating the outdoor play space, the relationships of everyone that came together and the knowledge that everyone contributed enhanced the vision and created momentum for the needed action. The educators and community members understand the land is the foundation of knowledge and that coming to know involves an exploration of complex relationships within nature and between nature and humans. Drawing on traditional teachings, the educators and community members recognize that, because of these interconnections, every interaction with others and with nature has a ripple effect. They also recognize that, in order to live in harmony and balance, it is important they give thanks for all life, striving not to take more than is needed from the land. They share with the children the teaching of offering tobacco on Mother Earth with prayers of gratitude for all living beings and the gifts they receive. The vision of supporting land-based teachings is one of "connections" in that it involves community members participating in activities that reflect the identity and history of the community, whether it is fishing on the Pic River, picking wild blueberries, or hunting and trapping. The child care centre supports all of these activities. The children and their families plan berry picking field trips and attend seasonal gatherings in the community where hunters prepare animals and fishers net fish on the river.

Since many Indigenous cultural activities do not align within the regulations of licensed child care centres, it is paramount to allow space for Indigenous educators to have flexibility in interpreting mainstream regulations to improve the quality of life for Indigenous families in a First Nation context.

Constraints on Outdoor Play Spaces in First Nation Communities

Children raised in First Nation communities do not just grow up in families, nor are they the sole responsibility of the family. Rather, the community shares the responsibility of raising children. Within traditional Indigenous ways of life and Indigenous scientific knowledge, there is "no physical separation between school and home" (Snively & Williams, 2016, p. 43). Learning, play, and living are interconnected, so there is no place for compartmentalizing knowledge.

Subsection 55 (3) of the Child Care and Early Years Act, 2014 (CCEYA) authorizes the Minister of Education to issue policy statements regarding programming and pedagogy for the purpose of guiding operators of child care and early years programs and services in developing their programs and services. This section of the CCEYA deals with program development and vision statements in connection with *How Does Learning Happen, Ontario's Pedagogy for the Early Years* (Ontario Ministry of Education, 2014), the guide to programming and teaching in licensed child care centres.

Biigtigong Nishnaabeg Centre's program statement is a shared vision of the professional and personal experiences of the educators and includes the teachings received from community Elders that support relationships with the land. The centre's IECEs have all been employed there for over 10 years, some up to 20 years; they share a strong commitment to supporting the children and families in their communities. The IECEs love what they do and value their contributions to the community.

To address the barriers of moving freely in the community with the children, the educators wrote the child care centre's program vision statement to reflect Indigenous culture and community. They ensured that the program statement outlined the community and cultural programming connected to services they provide in relation to the children's holistic development and well-being. The holistic development and well-being of children in the community of Pic River First Nation is built on appreciation of FN language, culture, and identity. The educators and staff believe that children should be encouraged to draw on the skills and knowledge they have developed and explore their environment freely. Traditionally, Indigenous children were expected to learn by doing instead of through formal instruction, and thus were not forbidden to try activities that, in today's risk-averse environment, might be considered dangerous. For example, in Indigenous culture, children climbing trees or sitting around a fire is customary, but fire is not permitted in licensed child care facilities.

Biigtigong Nishnaabeg Children & Family Learning Centre's Vision

> The Pic River Children and Family Learning Centre Program will ensure that all children have an opportunity to develop socially, mentally, physically, and spiritually. These skills will be fostered through a curriculum that addresses culture and language, health promotion, nutrition, social support, education, and parent involvement, and will be used as a tool for successful integration of our children into the school system. (*Parent Handbook*, p. 3)

Pic River Children and Family Learning Centre's Vision Connected to Community

1. Support of economic participation is only one purpose of the Children and Family Learning Centre in the Native community.
2. Children and Family Learning Centre is a service to the Native community and its purposes, not just a child service or a place of employment.

> The Native Family has suffered many assaults historically. Native childcare shares responsibility, along with other community resources, to promote the healing of children, and families. This will be done in concert with parents and other services, not as a separate initiative. (*Parent Handbook*, p. 4)

The Biigtigong Nishnaabeg Centre's vision statement supports the development of its program and services while maintaining Indigenous cultural ways of knowing and being, and serves as a model for many other licensed child care centres in FN communities. The Ministry of Education's approval of the centre's vision statement, with the clear understanding that the centre is very much community-based, provides educators with the flexibility to access surrounding bush lines and community gatherings. In an effort to share the program model and teachings, the centre has hosted Indigenous supervisors from all over northwestern Ontario.

The design and use of outdoor playgrounds in Ontario are regulated within the Child Care and Early Years Act, 2014. In the play space design at Biigtigong Nishnaabeg Centre, fixed play structures, including fallen trees, and traditional structures have to meet the requirements set out in the Canadian Standards Association standard CAN/CSA-Z614-14, "Children's play spaces and equipment" (Ontario Ministry of Education, 2018). Biigtigong Nishnaabeg Centre received approval for all structures in their outdoor play space. The original drawings of the play space were approved by the Ministry of Education and also approved by the provincial health inspector. The play space approved by the ministry is within the fenced area of the outdoor play space.

Access to outdoor learning is often compromised in northwestern Ontario by extreme weather conditions, predatory animals, and hordes of insects. Extreme cold temperatures in the winter result in minimal outdoor play. Wild animals, such as bears, wolves, and lynx, often roam the community within the dense bush lines surrounding the community. When animals are observed within community limits, community members inform others through posts on social media and phone calls to local programs and schools to ensure the children are kept inside and safe. Biigtigong Nishnaabeg Children & Family Learning Centre has had many situations in which a black bear has walked right up to the windows. Typically, bear sightings in the community occur in the springtime, when bears are looking for food after waking from hibernation. In such instances, the educators would share with the children the teachings of the bear waking up and looking for food. The children would then be encouraged to observe the bear's behaviour. There are many natural teachings and learning opportunities through which children gain knowledge of the animals in their area. Children are not raised to be scared of the bears in the community. Instead, they are raised to respect that the bears live there too and that everyone has to take safety precautions around wild animals. For the children at the child care centre the reality is that they live and play in safe proximity to black bears, foxes, and lynx within the community.

It is important to mention that, in a First Nations context, playgrounds belonging to early learning centres are often the only properties enclosed by a fence. Private homes and local schools are not fenced. For very young children, the fence can be a barrier to their seeing the surrounding community and a barrier to the interconnections of nature. Biigtigong Nishnaabeg Centre has a chain-link fence that allows children to see out. The centre has huge support from local members in maintaining the fence to meet licensing requirements, which state, "Fencing must be in good condition, e.g. no splintering, no rust, no sharp ends or edges. There should be no gaps between the fence and building structures to avoid injuries and form a safe boundary" (p. 13). Biigtigong Nishnaabeg Centre feels a strong need for a fence to act as an environmental barrier to animals. Based on Lori's experiences and from conversations with many IECEs, we can say that some centres have no playground access since the outdoor play spaces do not meet licensing requirements and are deemed unsafe. This is due in part to the fact that fences can be a challenge to maintain owing to a lack of building supplies and licensed carpenters.

The team at Biigtigong Nishnaabeg Children & Family Learning Centre is always looking for ways to improve and enhance their program for the families and children in their community. Prior to building the playground, they had been talking about using natural resources and community knowledge to make changes to their outdoor play space. The nearby city of Thunder Bay offered educators and program staff training on designing natural playgrounds. Staff members Esther Michano and Stephanie flagged the training, as it would provide them with further knowledge in implementing their vision. They attended the training in June 2011 and found it to be very informative and hands-on. It inspired them to begin the journey of designing an outdoor play space that would honour their community knowledges and culture.

Later that year, and towards the spring of 2012, Stephanie received a notice from Health Canada informing her of the availability of a one-time child care funding grant. Stephanie submitted a proposal to Health Canada for a new outdoor play space design. In her submission, Stephanie included detailed information on the need for an improved and enhanced play space and outlined descriptions of the child development program, the current challenges and barriers to the program, and the centre's vision. The main requirement for the new playground was that it was to be built within the natural environment of the existing treed area at the centre. The treed area is connected to the community, culture, and land, and provides the children with endless opportunities for enjoying land-based teachings. The outdoor playground would include a gathering space to allow for teachings and traditional ceremonies, as well as music, sensory, and dramatic play materials within designated spaces to support the children's play. The vision included utilizing local plants, some of which were already growing within the chosen area, and also planting a medicine garden to include the four traditional medicines. Many materials to support teaching Indigenous culture were also considered, for example, making and installing large wooden images of the seven grandfather animals along the chain-link fence, and incorporating traditional structures, such as a tipi and willow wigwam, for use as a gathering space and as a space for children to engage in dramatic play experiences. The detailed funding submission included draft designs and costs based on hiring local community members to build and to prepare the land.

Upon receiving the funding, the centre's staff set up team meetings with community members to build on their vision for the playground and implement the next action steps. To prepare the space within the tree-covered area, they worked alongside the maintenance crew, who were very knowledgeable about the land and able to read the environment, knowing what trees should be kept based on sunrise times and optimal shade during the day. Working from a shared understanding, Stephanie and her staff provided details and direction based on a draft sketch. This included the dramatic play centre, a music centre with tubing and drums, and an obstacle course made of natural materials. These spaces were open-ended and were designed to inspire children's creativity. They left many trees and shrubs in the space. When some of the trees were being cut down and the undercut brush was being cleaned out, Stephanie saw the potential of one fallen tree to become a balance beam and a gathering place for sitting together. The land started to naturally take shape along with the vision of how traditional teachings and play would come together in relation to licensing and provincial curriculum expectations.

Implementing Land-Based Teachings in the Play Space

As Sharla *Mskokii* Peltier states, "Land informs the knowledge of how we are to live in a particular Place" (this volume, p. 37). The outdoor space at the Biigtigong Nishnaabeg Child Care Centre provides children with opportunities for experiential learning from the land, their first teacher. The cultural teachings support Indigenous children's overall well-being by fostering positive Indigenous identity. From the entranceway of our building to the pathway of our playground, we have tried to create a welcoming and home-like environment for our families and children.

We want to provide the children with many possibilities to connect to the land and spirit by allowing them to engage with natural materials, gain the knowledge of the traditional territory, and be outside in the elements, and to provide them with many activities and experiences to holistically enhance their self-esteem and build on their development skills. For example, to encourage and support gross motor development and master new skills, we designed the natural obstacle course to circle around the outer edge of the entire playground.

The base of the large trees supports some of the main areas of interest for the children and the traditional teachings of land-based knowledge. Since many of the trees have exposed roots, educators can share knowledge of the tree's life cycle, and teach that the roots are connected to the water sources to feed the tree and that all trees need to be respected and treated with care. Such knowledge supports the children's deeper understanding of their connection to their own roots to the land. The tree roots also support the children's imagination. It is typical for the children to use small toys to create and pretend in their play experiences together. For example, they use the tree roots as small homes for animals and action figures and create roads embedded in the roots.

A parent volunteered to build a willow wigwam in the heart of the outdoor playground. The children use the wigwam as their house while engaging in dramatic play, and as a gathering place connected to the teachings they received of the wigwam.

The children and staff also use the walking trails located beside the centre. These trails allow for children to move freely and engage with the natural environment. The children and staff also walk to nearby community events, such as the fish harvest in spring, and visit local hunters when they are preparing moose, rabbit, geese, partridge, and fish. The children are involved in learning how to care for an animal once it has been killed for the purpose of providing food for the community. All the children have enjoyed traditional food as the main food source at the centre and in their homes. Given the teaching that everything has a purpose and there is no waste, children develop a clear understanding that hunting is connected to natural life cycles and sustainability.

Educators further support the healthy development of the children's identity by taking them on walks around the community and surrounding area to collect natural materials and medicines such as sweetgrass. Such experiences provide the children with opportunities to enhance their creativity, gain knowledge of their traditional territory, and be outside in the elements.

The educators and children have also explored the life cycles of butterflies, worm composting, and gardening (planting flowers, growing vegetables for the centre). Over the years, they have planted potatoes in stacked tires and used portable greenhouses. Children and staff tend to the gardens together, with the children actively engaged in planting the seeds, watering, weeding, and so on. This year the centre has a permanent greenhouse to support the teachings of growing food for the centre and living sustainably. The large greenhouse will support community and healing with the intention to share vegetables with Elders and families. The centre's educators have been building on the garden initiatives for years, with the knowledge that they are empowered through their connection with Mother Earth plants. The staff see the same empowerment in the young children when, after tending to the garden, they harvest food to share.

Place-Based Education

Place-based education includes learning about the specific environment (community) that we live in, as well as its history and stories. We believe it is important for all children and families to understand the culture(s) of the First Peoples of the area in which they live. In order to connect the children to their history and culture and, ultimately, to the plants, animals, waters, sand dunes, sun, moon, stars, and planets of their world, educators at the centre introduce the children to their community's teachings. They do this through teachings around the grandfather rocks, Father Sky, Mother Earth, and the night sun (the moon). Indigenous people's teachings deepen their connection to nature.

On the fence closest to the access road, where community members and visitors drive, the educators created silhouettes of the seven sacred teachings, also known as the grandfather's teachings. The seven grandfather teachings, Eagle (love), Buffalo (respect), Bear (courage), Sabe or Sasquatch (honesty), Beaver (wisdom), Wolf (humility), and Turtle (truth), are connected to living a good life, as the grandfather teachings provide guidance and wisdom for an individual's own actions in life and how to treat others. The teachings are not separate from each other and are meant to be used as one. The seven grandfather teachings are also displayed inside the learning environment for the children. To further support the children in reflecting on how they connect, the educators make reference to the animals that hold the value of each teaching. Additionally, with the children's help, the educators painted the teachings on rocks outside for use when sharing stories connected to the teachings. The children also use the painted rocks as props in their play.

Gisela Wajskop (this volume) described how Brazilian children attending the Escola do Bairro have "daily contact with nature" (p. 162).

Similarly, the educators and children at the Biigtigong Nishnaabeg Children & Family Learning Centre use some areas, such as the willow wigwam, the natural tree and stump sitting area, and the tipi, for gathering and sharing and as places to rest and reflect. While in the gathering areas, the educators share the teachings orally with the children. Children also use all areas for pretend and dramatic play.

The children's tipi has a ribbon with the four direction colours – black, red, yellow, and white – tied to the top. The four colours are represented in Indigenous teachings of the medicine wheel and connect to the many layers of representation and teachings of living holistically, with interconnections to all areas of development. The children also have the medicine wheel representing the four colours in other areas of their learning environment.

There are so many values, traditions, and experiences that our children gain from being on the land and from the spiritual connection to our Mother Earth. The staff provides a wide variety of experiences and opportunities that enhance the children's strengths and support areas for growth. These experiences help to build connections to the being, spirit, and land.

Deep, Respectful Observation, Learning, Listening, and Personal Reflections

Designing outdoor play spaces that combine land-based teachings with opportunities for children to explore and have the freedom to play requires collaboration between Elders, early learning teachers, parents, and community members. It begins with a political awareness and will to grant Indigenous communities permission to weave the provincial requirements into a culturally responsive, licensed child care centre built on a relational framework.

The story of Biigtigong Nishnaabeg Child & Family Learning Centre's outdoor play space, designed with input from the community, shows that traditional land-based teachings can be the foundation for children's outdoor learning, and can be achieved within a framework of provincially mandated program and policy regulations. We know that more support is needed for all educators trying to embed land-based teachings in the early years. The deepening of knowledge, histories, and pedagogies of Indigenous peoples will be transformative in educating young children. IECEs play an important role in sharing their lived experiences and stories to move the conversations and policies forward. Biigtigong Nishnaabeg Centre will continue to integrate its community's

Indigenous Knowledges with daily practice connected to the community and the provincial regulations.

Miigwech to our readers.

ACKNOWLEDGMENTS

We gratefully acknowledge and honour the territory and the lands on which the chapter originated, those of the Biigtigong Nishnaabeg First Nation and those of the Robinson-Superior Treaty, the land of the traditional territory of the Anishnaabeg, Thunder Bay, Ontario.

REFERENCES

Ball, J., & Simpkins, M. (2004). The community within the child: Integration of Indigenous knowledge into First Nations childcare process and practice. *American Indian Quarterly, 28*(3/4), 480–498.

Cajete, G. (2000). *Native science: Natural laws of interdependence.* Clear Light Publishers.

Fenton, A. (2018, February). *An Aboriginal resource guide for Indigenous early childhood education.* Shkoday Abinojiiwak Obimiwedoon Aboriginal Head Start.

Ontario Ministry of Education. (2014). *How does learning happen? Ontario's pedagogy for the early years.* Author. Found at https://files.ontario.ca/edu-how-does-learning-happen-en-2021-03-23.pdf

Ontario Ministry of Education. (2018). *Information on childcare and the early years.* Author. Found at http://www.edu.gov.on.ca/childcare.

Parent handbook. (2018). Biigtigong Nishnaabeg Children & Family Learning Centre.

Peltier, S. (2022). Seven Directions early learning for Indigenous land literacy wisdom. In S.S. Peterson & N. Friedrich (Eds.), *The role of place and play in young children's language and literacy* (pp. 33–51). University of Toronto Press.

Snively, G., & Williams, Wanosts'a7, L. (2016). *Knowing home: Braiding Indigenous science with Western science, Indigenous education, Book 1.* University of Victoria. Retrieved from https://greatbearrainforesttrust.org/wp-content/uploads/2018/05/Knowinghomebook1.pdf

Sutherland, D., & Swayze, N. (2012). Including Indigenous knowledges and pedagogies in science-based environmental education programs. *Canadian Journal of Environmental Education, 17,* 80–96. Retrieved from https://cjee.lakeheadu.ca

Wajskop, G. (2022). Children's engagement and inquiry in outdoors contexts as play and place-based learning. In S.S. Peterson & N. Friedrich (Eds.),

The role of place and play in young children's language and literacy (pp. 159–176). University of Toronto Press.

Wood, J. (2022). The importance of the land, language, culture, identity and learning in relation for Indigenous children. In S.S. Peterson & N. Friedrich (Eds.), *The role of place and play in young children's language and literacy* (pp. 109–126). University of Toronto Press.

7 Negotiating a Place to Belong in an Aotearoa New Zealand Playgroup

MARY M. JACOBS

Introduction

Fifteen-month-old Zacharias runs down the ramp and stops to look through the rails at the older children playing the drums in the school music room. He circles back and climbs two stairs. His mother, Meron, offers him a hand, but he doesn't take it and steps down one at a time, deliberately and carefully. "Baba! Baba!" he calls over and over again. Meron occasionally reminds Zacharias to be careful in Amharic, the language of their home. He goes up the stairs again and shouts to Meron each time as he steps down. "Baba! Baba!" Meron explains that Baba is what Zacharias calls his father. Zacharias repeats the cycle of up three stairs and down again a few more times. Zacharias balances himself on Meron's shoulder [Meron has taken a seat at the top of the stairs]. On one go, he walks around her and uses the handrail without prompting. Zacharias returns to the music room door to call out to the children a few more times. They giggle as he shouts for their attention and peers through the rails of the gate. Zacharias circles back to the stairs with a plastic spoon he has retrieved from the sandpit. Each time he repeats up and down the stairs again, he makes a mark with the spoon against the concrete as if to mark his accomplishment, like a long jumper. Each time he shouts for his father, who, Meron says, is visiting Ethiopia for two months. (fieldnotes, 8 August 2018)

The opening ethnographic snapshot takes place at a community playgroup on the grounds of a public school in Auckland, Aotearoa New Zealand's largest city. In this chapter, all names (pseudonyms) and pronouns were identified by adult participants for themselves and for their children. Meron, a newly settled mother who moved from Ethiopia in 2015, and her son, Zacharias, who was born in Aotearoa New Zealand in 2017, were enjoying an unusually dry and sunny winter day in the playgroup courtyard. Zacharias composed as he played through movement, words, and gestures. Zacharias's actions (using the stick, manoeuvring the stairs, and stopping to chat with the older children along his route), were punctuated with special words, embedded with meaning. Meron did not offer up an interpretation of what Zacharias was doing on the stairs with the spoon but, rather, shared the meaning of "Baba" and the information that his father was away in Ethiopia. Although any interpretation of Zacharias's play would likely fall short of the complexity of his representation of meaning, his social action and languaging were less likely to be trivialized because of Meron's presence at the playgroup.

This chapter draws on selected data from a year-long, multilingual, qualitative study to highlight how the participation of newly settled families in a community playgroup created space for the languages, cultural practices, and knowledges of their homes (González et al., 2005). Play is a social practice through which children represent and communicate meanings, allowing them to participate in the communities they belong to (Wohlwend, 2011). Children draw on the cultural practices and languages of their homes to read the worlds they inhabit and to compose in play (Souto-Manning & Yoon, 2018). Although Meron did not try to explicitly interpret the meaning of Zacharias's play, she offered glimpses of his world beyond the playgroup, making more visible what he represented and communicated through play. In this sense, Meron played a significant role in making space at the playgroup for the people that matter to Zacharias, shaping his sense of place and who he is in that place (Comber, 2016). In this chapter, I argue that the intercultural ethos of the playgroup and the focus on play positioned young children and families as *place makers* (Gruenewald, 2003), inviting them to draw on their family languages and literacies to contribute to the collective social and cultural practices of the playgroup community. I also highlight the integral role of family expertise to make visible children's meaning-making and to support children to negotiate new ways of knowing in the playgroup. In the following section I describe the playgroup context of the study.

Context: A Playgroup in Aotearoa New Zealand

Playgroups are one early childhood service in Aotearoa New Zealand available to families and their children, from newborn to 5 years old. According to the Ministry of Education (MoE) website, playgroups, which acknowledge the significance of the role of parents in early childhood education, may have a specific focus on a particular language, cultural affiliation, or philosophical approach. Playgroups can be set up to meet the needs of a particular community and to increase participation in early childhood education. Playgroups do not need to be licensed and may be less formal than other early childhood education options in Aotearoa New Zealand because there are fewer regulatory requirements involved in their establishment. Generally, playgroups in Aotearoa New Zealand are parent-led and held in a community space (MoE, 2014). While playgroups, by design, include the people most important to children, playgroups have the potential to be places where family knowledges and cultural practices are privileged as learning and teaching resources (Fleer & Hammer, 2014).

The playgroup that was the site for this study was available to families from 9:30 am to 12:30 pm, three days per week, through a larger educational organization with an employed playgroup leader. The playgroup was located on the grounds of a public primary school nestled in a neighbourhood where many newly settled families lived. While Matavaha, the playgroup leader, greeted families and was responsible for the day-to-day routines, adult family members accompanied their children to the playgroup and were expected to look after their children. Attendance was voluntary. The day's activities were not rigidly scheduled except when trips to nearby parks, museums, and other sites were decided upon by Matavaha and the families. Morning tea, a time when families shared food, occurred mid-morning each day. On some days before morning tea, Matavaha shared music and stories and invited families to share their own, during "mat time." Matavaha encouraged families to follow children's interests in play and to interact with their children in the languages of their homes, consistent with the vision of *Te Whāriki* (MoE, 2017), Aotearoa New Zealand's official bicultural early childhood curriculum.

A Bicultural Early Childhood Curriculum

Te Whāriki acknowledges the bicultural imperative of te Tiriti o Waitangi/ the Treaty of Waitangi, the founding document of Aotearoa New Zealand, privileging Indigenous Māori cultural practices, tikanga Māori, and language, te reo Māori, alongside dominant Western early childhood pedagogical approaches and English. In Aotearoa New Zealand, early childhood contexts that enact the bicultural commitment of *Te Whāriki*, have the potential to strengthen a sense of belonging for immigrant families and their children (Chan & Ritchie, 2019). Outlined in *Te Whāriki*, the principle (*Family and Community/Whānau tangata*) and three strands of learning and development (*Communication/Mana reo, Exploration/Mana aotūroa,* and *Belonging/Mana whenua*) are particularly relevant to this chapter.

The *Family and Community/Whānau tangata* principle emphasizes that "the wider world of family and community is an integral part of early childhood curriculum" (MoE, 2017, p. 20). The involvement of families in the playgroup was integral to understanding children's meaning-making in play. The *Communication/Mana reo* strand defines languages beyond spoken and written words to include "languages of sign, mathematics, visual imagery, art, dance, drama, rhythm, music and movement" (MoE, 2017, p. 41) that children use to think and communicate. *Te Whāriki* emphasizes that early childhood settings should acknowledge the languages and cultures of the children who attend and children's understandings of linguistic and cultural practices should be extended beyond their own. The *Exploration/Mana aotūroa* strand describes the early childhood environment as a place where children's "play is valued as meaningful learning and the importance of spontaneous play is recognised" (MoE, 2017, p. 25). The *Belonging/Mana whenua* strand states that children and families "know that they have a place" (MoE, 2017, p. 24), emphasizing that connections to families and the wider world in which children learn and grow should be affirmed and extended in the early childhood setting.

Sociocultural Theoretical Perspectives of Learning and Literacy

The *Te Whāriki* principle and strands referenced above are consistent with sociocultural theories that suggest learning occurs within valued social and cultural practices influenced by relationships with people, places, and things, including the material, social, and cultural contexts in which children play (Hedges & Cullen, 2011). Though not made explicit in *Te Whāriki*, the strands also align with sociocultural theoretical perspectives of early literacies that privilege multimodal meaning-making as children compose, read, represent, and communicate (Kress, 1997). Play, as an embodied action text, provides a window to understand how children draw on the expertise of their lived experiences, including their interests and family cultural resources, to interpret, create, and belong in early childhood settings (Wohlwend, 2017). These early literacies are linked closely to oral language and how it is taken up by young children in order to make sense of the social and cultural contexts in which they live (Halliday, 1975). The playgroup context provided an ideal setting for learning from the expertise of families about how children draw on what they know from their everyday experiences and negotiate new ways of knowing in play (Hedges et al., 2019). These theoretical underpinnings influenced my research activities in collaboration with families at the playgroup, detailed in the following section.

Participants, Data Collection, and Analysis

Matavaha, the playgroup leader, and 15 families who attended the playgroup were enrolled in the research study from which the data in this chapter were collected. The study focused primarily on nine newly settled families who moved to Auckland within six years of the beginning of the study in February 2018. This chapter features ethnographic snapshots of the multimodal meaning-making of children from newly settled families in the study to illustrate how the participation of their parents supported children to establish their place in the playgroup by drawing on the languages and literacies of their homes.

The qualitative design of the study involved the ethnographic data-collection methods of semi-structured interview conversations, photo-elicitation interview conversations, and fieldnote observations of families engaged in playgroup sessions (Saldaña & Omasta, 2017). Families had the option of participating in the interviews in the languages of their homes, supported by translators as co-researchers. The data highlighted in this chapter are predominantly from fieldnote observations and informal conversations in the playgroup setting that I recorded in English. I engaged in the everyday activities of the playgroup and took fieldnotes of my observations over a period of approximately 35 weeks. The fieldnotes were not restricted to observations, but deliberately engaged families as interpreters of their children's participation in the playgroup. Fieldnotes focused on family expertise of children's ways of knowing in the playgroup, how children's play reflected the cultural practices and knowledges of family homes, and how parents supported their children to negotiate new ways of knowing.

Although sociocultural theoretical perspectives influenced my researcher lens in the study, I engaged in an inductive and iterative data analysis process to identify themes in the data (Charmaz, 2014). Concepts derived from initial open-coding provided a larger meaningful unit of analysis to identify themes across the data set – each organized into subthemes. For the purpose of this chapter, I composed ethnographic snapshots that highlight two subthemes related to children's play and the playgroup as a culturally negotiated place: recognition of family knowledges, and children's early literacies across multiple modes, languages, and cultural practices. These ethnographic snapshots are moments in time that acknowledge the fluidity of the cultural-historical repertoires of practice of children and their families, shaped by their membership in multiple communities over time (Gutiérrez & Rogoff, 2003).

Because of the multi-layered outsiderness and institutional privileges associated with my positionality as an American monolingual speaker of English with European ancestry, I relied on family cultural insider perspectives to inform my observations of children's play. I often asked families to interpret what their children were saying and doing in play so I could learn from their expertise. This approach was important in establishing trust and acknowledging what families could contribute that I could not. In the following section, I share two more ethnographic snapshots to illustrate the playgroup as a culturally negotiated place influenced by Matavaha's recognition of family knowledges in the playgroup setting and children's multimodal representation and communication in play.

A Negotiated Place

The playgroup was a place saturated with meanings that children negotiated in play, in their interactions with other children, and with adults. Comber (2016) argues that place is not only material, but also "social, dynamic, and negotiated" (p. 39). People who belong to any one place also belong to other places. The people in the playgroup shaped the place and the playgroup shaped the people who participated. The recognition of multiple languages, national affiliations, and cultural practices in the playgroup contributed to a place that invited and represented the local and global communities of the families (Comber, 2016). Gruenewald (2003) wrote, "places are what people make of them – that people are place makers and that places are a primary artifact of human culture" (p. 627) and "places teach us about how the world works and how our lives fit into the spaces we occupy. Further, places make us: As occupants of particular places with particular attributes, our identity and our possibilities are shaped" (p. 628). The playgroup in this study was a culturally negotiated place where children could be confident communicators, readily drawing on the linguistic and cultural resources of their homes to negotiate new meanings in the company of their family members.

Recognition of Family Knowledges

Matavaha's invitations to families to share their cultural practices and languages encouraged families to shape a place representative of their multiple communities, homes, and histories. Matavaha, a Tongan New Zealander, explicitly encouraged families to talk with their children in the languages of their homes. Matavaha also invited families to share material objects such as written texts, artwork, photographs, favourite toys and books, and food from their homes. Displayed on the walls were texts in several languages, created, translated, and composed by parents. The display included a description of Ramadan, a children's song in Mandarin, a prayer in Tuvalu, and a song to say goodbye in te reo Māori. These texts, combined with photographs of children playing and families gathered together at the playgroup, contributed to a place that affirmed the languages and cultural knowledges of family homes and the communities important to them, both local and global.

Central to Matavaha's interactions with families was her recognition of family knowledges as unique to their lived experiences and her dismissal of deficit explanations for differences in early childhood.

> We have a multicultural playgroup and the parents and children have their own way of doing things and their own ways of being. Every time we are talking about the new entry problem, and what are the kinds of things we need to do to solve that problem. Sometimes we think we have to focus on what the kids don't know. (personal communication, 14 August 2018)

Matavaha's words, "parents and children have their own way of doing things and their own ways of being," highlight that her recognition of family knowledges stands in contrast to dominant deficit discourses embedded in discussions of school readiness and narrowly conceived measures of English language competence (García & Otheguy, 2017). As highlighted by Cooper and Hedges, "there are many possible opportunities in early childhood education centres for children to share their own languages and cultural values and interests that differ from the centre's dominant or instructional language/s, in this case English" (this volume, p. 75). Matavaha invited children and families to draw on their full communicative repertoires to participate in the playgroup community in meaningful ways. Perhaps because there was no set agenda outside of the structured times of occasional mat time and daily morning tea, it was not unusual for children to make choices about what to do upon arrival. The materials available to them and few scheduled activities provided ample opportunities for spontaneous play. In the following snapshot, Unaiza, a professional cake maker who transferred her skills from Pakistan when her family moved to Aotearoa New Zealand in 2017, discusses a cupcake order with Matavaha. Sana, her 3-year-old daughter, appears to enter the conversation through play.

Snapshot #2

> Sana moves to the table where her lunchbox is open. She takes out a cracker and sits down to feed the baby doll she is carrying. She says something to her

mother, Unaiza, in Urdu. Unaiza is discussing, in English, a cupcake order with Matavaha. Unaiza will make cupcakes for Matavaha's granddaughter's birthday. Sana appears to be listening closely to their conversation, occasionally inserting words, and then begins to prepare food in the nearby play kitchen with some urgency. She uses a combination of the pretend plastic food and playdough, working the dough with her hands and with the kitchen tools, stepping back to pause and look at her work. She shapes the dough on the plate and places it inside the oven. With one more quick movement, Sana turns the knob on the play stove, takes a deep breath, and wipes her brow, as if she is relieved to get the plate in the oven just in time. (fieldnotes, 21 August 2018)

Sana represented what she knows, composing an action text through listening, speaking, and movement. She used materials in the play kitchen to embody the everyday activities of her mother's work as a professional cake maker at home. The spontaneity of this moment is particularly important to consider as Sana was responding to, and entering into, a conversation in English between Unaiza and Matavaha. Sana composed this action text with confidence in a place where she was able to both respond to, and demonstrate her knowledge of, the practices of her home, listening in English, and responding in a combination of Urdu, gestures, and movement. Although the adults continued their conversation, Sana did not seem concerned with whether they acknowledged her, as she was representing her own thinking through play. Yet, Unaiza's presence at the playgroup, her relationship with Matavaha as someone who recognized and valued her mother's work, and Sana's freedom to choose what and how to play likely shaped Sana's decision-making. In this sense, the conversation between Unaiza and Matavaha may have prompted Sana's representation of what was important to her in that moment in that place.

Language learning is couched in the meanings children construct from the interactions, observations, and social action with people they know and trust, in the modes they choose to communicate, and in the places where they belong. Sana had to make sense of the context in which the communication was taking place in order to respond in a meaningful way. In this moment, Sana chose to engage through movement, with only limited words. Many of Sana's activities at the playgroup did not involve oral language, except for the interactions she had with Unaiza in Urdu. Although Sana did not choose to speak very often at the playgroup, her confident multimodal response to Unaiza and Matavaha's discussion of cupcakes suggests that too narrow a focus on oral language can diminish the myriad ways children represent and communicate. An even narrower focus on English-language competence promotes deficit perspectives about children who are learning to navigate more than one language. Recognition of play as place-making carves out space for children to draw on the languages and literacies of their homes to represent and communicate their worlds in multimodal action texts.

Early Literacies across Multiple Modes, Languages, and Cultural Practices

Family involvement in the playgroup created space for parents to speak in their languages, interpret their children's meaning-making, and to support children with negotiating the new social and cultural practices they encountered. For Sabine, mother of Hassan (4 years) and Amna (2 years, 3 months), who moved from Karachi, Pakistan, in 2018, Urdu was the window into what her children were making sense of and contributed to her sense of belonging at the playgroup. Although Hassan had attended kindergarten in Pakistan, Sabine chose an early childhood option that allowed her to attend with both her children so Hassan would continue to speak Urdu. Sabine acknowledged that Hassan and Amna understood more than one way to do things as they explored and communicated in the playgroup and noticed what was different from the Muslim practices of their home. Through movement, eye contact, gestures, and oral language communication in Urdu and English, Hassan and Amna carved out a space to belong in relationship with other people, supported by their mother. Sabine shared that her children negotiated new social and cultural practices in the playgroup, ones that required them to navigate the differences between Halal (allowed) and Haram (disallowed) food items during morning tea, differences in the way people dressed and greeted one another, and the ubiquitous presence of English.

Sabine acknowledged her children's learning as they expanded their understanding of language and cultural practices beyond their home. She explained that, when the family first arrived in Auckland, Hassan would become very frustrated when people were not speaking Urdu in public spaces. Sabine chuckled as she explained that Hassan wondered what was wrong with all the people who did not understand Urdu as people did in Karachi, where he spent his first three years. Sabine felt that coming to playgroup helped her children to adjust to hearing English, but also to hearing multiple languages in one place. Within weeks of attending playgroup, Hassan and Amna had begun to sprinkle English words in their multimodal communication with other children and adults, while continuing to speak Urdu with Sabine. Sabine often described what her children were doing in their activities to help people understand the trail of Urdu that accompanied their strokes with pens, their movements with blocks, puzzle pieces, dolls, and outdoor toys, and their handling of kitchen equipment and clay. The following snapshot shows how Sabine's intimate understanding of Amna's ways of communicating made more visible her representations of new learning and discoveries in play.

Snapshot #3

Amna sat at the small round table as she assembled a puzzle of shapes in various colors. She named each piece in Urdu before she secured it in place, occasionally in English if encouraged by Sabine. When she lifted the square-shaped piece, she looked from the piece to the table and exclaimed something in Urdu. She rested her head upon the table while tapping her finger underneath the table top. In this instance her mother confirmed what Amna was saying, "She is saying the table is a square too." As Amna communicated in Urdu to show her mother what she had discovered about the larger, square-shaped table in relation to the smaller, square-shaped puzzle piece, she understood that my presence as a listener required communication beyond words. Amna knew I could not understand Urdu. Looking up with her eyebrows arched as her head rested against the table whilst drawing attention to the table by tapping it with her finger, Amna showed me her thinking. Amna assembled the puzzle pieces several times, announcing "finished" (in English) each time she completed the puzzle. She called the point of the star "triangle" (in Urdu) and Sabine's raised eyebrows and wide smile showed pride in Amna's noticing as she praised her daughter in Urdu and translated Amna's Urdu to English. (fieldnotes, 25 September 2018)

Sabine's presence at the playgroup provided insights into Amna's and Hassan's meaning-making in play and how they were responding to the new cultural practices they encountered in public spaces. Sabine translated Amna's communication and representation in play to make clear the complexity of her thinking. Amna did not simply name puzzle shapes in Urdu, but communicated her considerable expertise of shapes and spatial relationships in play with a combination of modes that drew our attention to the relationship between the puzzle piece and the table. This snapshot also shows that Amna understood that she had to go beyond oral language to be understood in the playgroup setting where only a couple of other families spoke Urdu. Amna's simultaneous gesture to the table and eye contact in combination with Urdu demonstrate her recognition of language differences and the sophistication of her efforts to communicate with a monolingual English speaker. At their young ages, Hassan and Amna knew a great deal about negotiating differences in relationships with people whose everyday practices differed from their own. Sabine's invitations to Hassan and Amna to share what they understood in English and to participate in the playgroup were intertwined with her desire to support their transition to an English-dominant environment with new dominant cultural practices while sustaining the language that was a pathway to the valued knowledges and everyday cultural practices of their home.

Negotiating a Place to Belong

The snapshots in this chapter illustrate the sociolinguistic and sociocultural competence of young children, and their contributions to the playgroup community as a culturally negotiated place alongside their family members. Halliday's (1975) notion of "learning how to mean" suggests children are learning language, but are also learning *through language* and gathering the meanings of the social system in which they are situated. When children are encouraged to draw on and expand their knowledges to understand something new, these invitations shape a child's sense of belonging in a place and the place itself. The participation of families and Matavaha's strength-based approach made space for Zacharias, Sana, Amna, and Hassan to bring the familiarity of their homes into the playgroup. Meron, Unaiza, and Sabine supported their children to negotiate and understand the cultural and linguistic differences they encountered, nestled in the intimacy of their family languages and cultural practices.

The playgroup as a culturally negotiated place shaped children's languaging and social action, processes that reflected the knowledges of their family homes as well as their flexibility and openness to negotiating practices different from their own. Orellana and D'warte (2010) argued that the transcultural competencies and dispositions of young children who learn to navigate multiple languages and cultural practices flexibly should be legitimized as early literacies. The bicultural commitment of *Te Whāriki* has the potential to shape transcultural competencies and dispositions in early childhood settings. In this volume, Cooper and Hedges discuss the critical importance of prioritizing Indigenous Māori language and cultural practices, and valuing the ways of knowing and being of Pasifika peoples as foundational to enacting the principles of *Te Whāriki*. As Cooper and Hedges illustrate, these priorities shape early childhood settings that affirm the multiple heritages, histories, and places important to children, families, and teachers that might otherwise be restricted by monocultural dominance.

Children draw on the linguistic and cultural resources of their homes to represent and communicate multimodally and they attempt to expand these resources to understand other people, themselves, and the communities they participate in (Souto-Manning & Yoon, 2018). The presence of the families at the playgroup was invaluable to understanding children's multimodal communication and exploration in play. The cultural construction of place that was made for and through family languages and cultural practices shaped how children as place-makers represented their thinking and communicated in the playgroup (Gruenewald, 2003). The space to engage across languages and modes contributed to an ethos where children and family members could carry the knowledges of their homes and multiple communities into the playgroup and draw on these resources to negotiate new ways of knowing and being.

Early childhood settings that position the linguistic and cultural resources of young children's homes as assets invite children and their families to "know that they have a place" (MoE, 2017, p. 24). Narrow emphasis on phonological and grammatical aspects of oral language development in English, rather than a broader sense of language as described in *Te Whāriki* (MoE, 2017), detracts from the significance of children's multimodal meaning-making in play. Restrictions on what counts as language and early literacy, and restrictions on play itself, limit the potential of young children's play to support oral language and to lead to meaningful early experiences with reading and writing (Wohlwend, 2011). When young children are responded to as confident communicators as they play across modes and languages, they can see that their ways of communicating and representing are meaningful in the early childhood settings where they belong.

ACKNOWLEDGMENTS

Many thanks to the children, families, playgroup leader, and translators who generously contributed to this project. This research was supported by a post-doctoral research fellowship within the Marie Clay Research Centre, funding from the Faculty of Education and Social Work at the University of Auckland, and ethics approval from the University of Auckland Human Participants Ethics Committee.

REFERENCES

Chan, A., & Ritchie, J. (2019). Critical pedagogies of place: Some considerations for early childhood care and education in a superdiverse "bicultural" Aotearoa (New Zealand). *International Journal of Critical Pedagogy, 10*(1), 51–75. http://libjournal.uncg.edu/ijcp/article/view/1529

Charmaz, K. (2014). *Constructing grounded theory: A practical guide through qualitative analysis* (2nd ed.). Sage. https://doi.org/10.1002/9781405165518.wbeosg070.pub2

Comber, B. (2016). *Literacy, place, and pedagogies of possibility*. Routledge. https://doi.org/10.4324/9781315735658

Cooper, M., & Hedges, H. (2022). Young children exploring identities, languages and cultures in a multicultural place. In S.S. Peterson & N. Friedrich (Eds.), *The role of place and play in young children's language and literacy* (pp. 67–80). University of Toronto Press.

Fleer, M., & Hammer, M. (2014). Repertoires of cultural practices for enacting play and learning in a playgroup. *International Research in Early Childhood Education, 5*(1), 42–55. Retrieved from www.education.monash.edu.au/irecejournal/

García, O., & Otheguy, R. (2017). Interrogating the language gap of young bilingual and bidialectal students. *International Multilingual Research Journal, 11*(1), 52–65. https://doi.org/10.1080/19313152.2016.1258190

González, N., Moll, L.C., & Amanti, C. (2005). *Funds of knowledge: Theorizing practices in households, communities, and classrooms*. Routledge. https://doi.org/10.4324/9781410613462

Gruenewald, D.A. (2003). Foundations of place: A multidisciplinary framework for place-conscious education. *American Educational Research Journal, 40*(3), 619–654. https://doi.org/10.3102/00028312040003619

Gutiérrez, K.D., & Rogoff, B. (2003). Cultural ways of learning: Individual traits or repertoires of practice. *Educational Researcher, 32*(5), 19–25. https://doi.org/10.3102/0013189X032005019

Halliday, M.A.K. (1975). *Learning how to mean: Explorations in the development of language*. Edward Arnold. https://doi.org/10.1016/B978-0-12-443701-2.50025-1

Hedges, H., Cooper, M., & Weisz-Koves, T. (2019). Recognising and responding to family funds of knowledge. In S. Alcock & N. Stobbs (Eds.), *Rethinking play as pedagogy* (pp. 107–120). Routledge.

Hedges, H., & Cullen, J. (2011). Participatory learning theories: A framework for early childhood pedagogy. *Early Child Development and Care, 182*(7), 921–940. https://doi.org/10.1080/03004430.2011.597504

Kress, G. (1997). *Before writing: Rethinking the paths to literacy*. Routledge.

Ministry of Education (Aotearoa New Zealand). (2014). *Choices*. Retrieved from https://parents.education.govt.nz/assets/Parents/Documents/Early-Learning/ECE-Choices-Booklet.pdf

Ministry of Education (Aotearoa New Zealand). (2017). *Te whāriki. He whāriki mātauranga mō ngā mokopuna o Aotearoa: Early childhood curriculum.*

https://www.education.govt.nz/assets/Documents/Early-Childhood/Te-Whariki-Early-Childhood-Curriculum-ENG-Web.pdf

Orellana, M.F., & D'warte, J. (2010). Recognizing different kinds of "head starts." *Educational Researcher, 39*(4), 295–300. https://doi.org/10.3102/0013189X10369829

Saldaña, J., & Omasta, M. (2017). *Qualitative research: Analyzing life.* Sage.

Souto-Manning, M., & Yoon, H.S. (2018). *Rethinking early literacies: Reading and rewriting worlds.* Routledge. https://doi.org/10.4324/9781315650975

Wohlwend, K.E. (2011). *Playing their way into literacies: Reading, writing, and belonging in the early childhood classroom.* Teachers College Press.

Wohlwend, K.E. (2017). Who gets to play? Access, popular media, and participatory literacies. *Early Years, 37*(1), 62–76. https://10.1080/09575146.2016.1219699

8 The Importance of the Land, Language, Culture, Identity, and Learning in Relation for Indigenous Children

JEFFREY WOOD

We're taught that our language comes from the Creator, and that speaking it acknowledges our connection. We're taught that our voice is a sacred gift and that there is a lot of power in our words. When we speak, our words go around the world forever. (Dr. Sharla *Mskokii* Peltier in Ball, 2007, p. ii)

Over many years, efforts have been made by Canadian governments to assimilate First Nations peoples. These efforts can be seen in the residential school system, where First Nations children were punished for using their languages; the White Paper (Canada, Indian and Northern Affairs, 1969; Cardinal, 1999), where the government of Canada proposed making Indigenous people Canadians; foster care policies that discriminate against First Nations families, with Indigenous children being removed from their families as an assimilative practice (Blackstock et al., 2004); and the Indian Act (Milloy, 2008), whose provisions include placing Indigenous people on reservations, defining who is and who is not Indigenous, and ordering restrictions on the lives of Indigenous people in Canada. All of these assimilative practices have led to the loss of Indigenous languages. And, although Canada's Indigenous people are resourceful and resilient, with only a few exceptions, Indigenous languages in Canada are in danger of extinction (Neegan, 2005). (For further reading on the effects of these policies, see, for example, Battiste, 2013; Truth and Reconciliation Commission of Canada, 2015.)

In response to the decreasing numbers of fluent speakers (Corbiere, 2014), many First Nation communities have introduced language learning into their schools over the past 20 years. Despite these efforts, however, the number of fluent speakers has not increased dramatically (Statistics Canada, 2017). The ultimate goal of any First Nation language program is to create fluent First Nation speakers who are in touch with their culture and their own cultural identity. I argue that the failures are due to teaching approaches that view language from a grammatical, structuralist perspective, without considering the important relationship between language, culture, and the land.

I have the privilege of carrying out research with Indigenous teachers and children in their classrooms through my work as a university researcher and through my work with schools in Northern Ontario. Out of concern for the failure of a structuralist approach, the schools I have worked with (federally funded First Nation schools and provincially funded public schools) started to use a morphological and semantic place-based approach to First Nation language learning. I have, at times, been part of the committee designing the program and have also conducted research exploring the efficacy of language programs. Each school and community is unique, and each has taken a different approach to making their local Indigenous language foundational to their teaching. Their initiatives have shown remarkable results for the children and teachers.

Each initiative is based on a number of understandings, some obvious and others initially hidden, that have been learned from Elders, children, teachers, Knowledge Keepers, and fellow researchers. The most important understandings are that language comes from the land, culture comes from language, identity comes from culture, and all learning happens in relationship. These concepts are foundational to all educational practice with Indigenous children and all our work must flow from these principles. Also foundational to teaching are the principles of land, culture, identity, and relationship, including the understanding of "all my relations":

> "All my relations" is at first a reminder of who we are and of our relationship with both our family and our relatives. It also reminds us of the extended relationship we share with all human beings. But the relationships that Native people see go further, the web of kinship to animals, to the birds, to the fish, to the plants, to all the animate and inanimate forms that can be seen or imagined. (King, 1990, p. ix)

Yet, being in relation to language speakers and the land, and using the community's Indigenous language, are rare practices in schools. These principles are often treated as an add-on, if they are considered at all.

In developing these language programs, the participating teachers and I considered ways to include more language, as well as story, legends, traditions, and culture. Our guiding principle was that, to save the language, the process of learning needs to bring the language to life as organic, engaging, and playful. Language must be treated as something that is real and lived (that is, the different parts of the language are not

Land, Language, Culture, Identity, and Learning in Relation 111

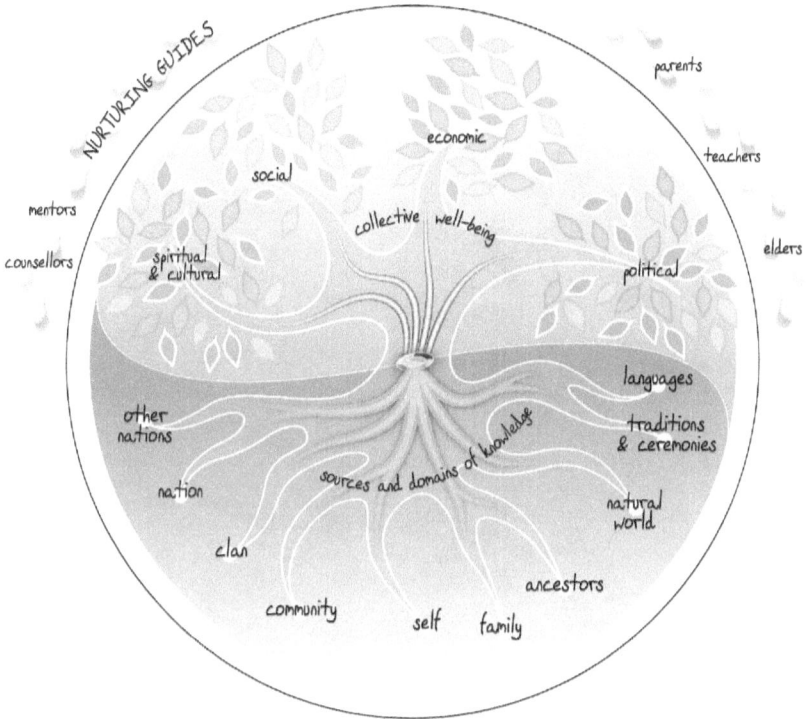

Figure 8.1 Nurturing Guides

Note: From *Redefining How Success is Measured in First Nations, Inuit and Métis Learning*, by the Canadian Council on Learning, 2007. Copyright 2007 by the Canadian Council on Learning.

taught synthetically in a step-by-step, isolated manner) and taught to the children in a way that is immersive, supportive, and holistic. Another important consideration we had was how to incorporate more time outside on the land in the process of language learning.

At the beginning of each project, the teachers and I took relationship for granted. We have slowly come to realize it is the most important part of learning, and even more so in an Indigenous context. Our work has dramatically shifted in recent years as we realized that relationship does not necessarily just happen and that it is the types of relationship that are established that matter most. When we talk about being in relation from an Indigenous perspective, there are multiple things that need to be considered. This includes how the child is in relation to various environments (indoors and outdoors), nature, materials, place, their family, the teachers, other children, the school, the community, their ancestors, the place they are in, and their community (see Figure 8.1).

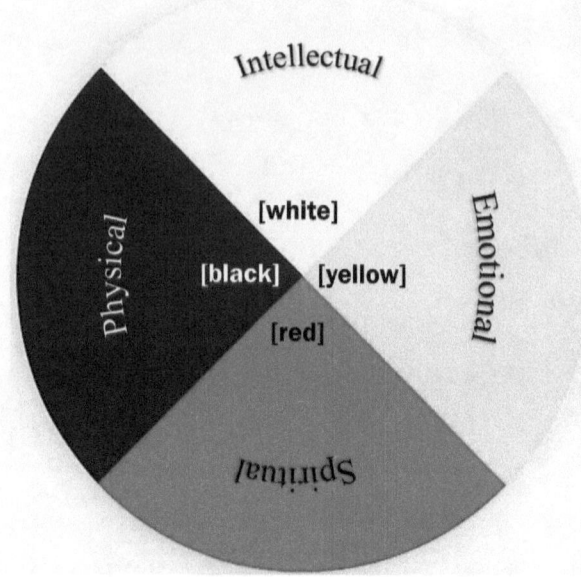

Figure 8.2 The Holistic View of the Child

Many theorists have talked about this as decentring the child (Spyrou, 2018). Our work is very focused on the children with whom we work. Decentring means that our lens is much broader and encompassing, including all our relations. Relationship, from an Indigenous perspective, goes beyond the children and teachers; it includes family and extended relatives and all human beings. We think about all our relations: the animals, birds and fish, the water, air and sky, our ancestors and future generations. We are a part of nature, not separate from it; we are all connected. From this inclusive perspective of relationship, we move away from centring on the child or the teacher and are far more inclusive about what we mean by being in relation. These relationships are sacred and ethical. We have also taken a holistic approach to our understanding of children, seeing them as spiritual, emotional, physical, and mental beings (Toulouse, 2016) (see Figure 8.2).

Sharla *Mskokii* Peltier (this volume) states, "an educator who works toward inclusivity and reconciliation values the child's life experience, relationships, and cultural knowledge systems such as the earth, family, and community" (p. 49). We see each child as unique and as having a contribution or gift to serve the community (Toulouse, 2016). We see them as active community members figuring out their place in the community. These beliefs have caused us to fundamentally change how we approach education. What is important has shifted away from the curriculum and skills towards an understanding of individual children, their needs, and their interactions across time, space, and materials. This approach turns our gaze onto the child as a unique member of the community, while also decentring the child by acknowledging the child as being holistically in relation to all places, materials, and people.

Setting Up a First Nations Language Program: Guiding Principles and Practices

What matters to Indigenous peoples in education is that children, youth, adults and Elders have the opportunity to develop their gifts in a respectful space ... It is about fostering identity, facilitating well-being, connecting to land, honouring language, infusing with teachings and recognizing the inherent right to self-determination. (Toulouse, 2016, p. 4)

The ultimate goal of these First Nation language programs is to create fluent First Nation speakers who are in touch with their culture and their own cultural identity. Because each of the schools I work with is in a different place, with different people, strengths, culture, language, environment, and so on, they each required a different approach to language teaching. Language comes from the land, culture comes from language, identity comes from culture, and all learning happens in relation, so it makes sense that each school would have different approach.

What follows are some general guidelines we have used to develop language programs across different schools. Many of these guidelines parallel practices for building and implementing outdoor play spaces in First Nations' communities as outlined in Huston and Michano-Drover (this volume).

Start by Consulting the Elders

Schools wishing to change their approach to First Nations language learning must first consult with Elders and the community, in particular Elders who are gifted with a passion for the language and a heart for children. These Elders will form the heart and lifeblood of the program. Some schools have relied on these Elders to design their First Nation language program, while others have relied on educators within the school in consultation with Elders to develop the program. The common denominator of success has been early and regular consultation with specially gifted

Elders who have a love for children. In communities where I have worked, this approach established the language program in a good way and focused the program on the local nuances of the language as well as on local culture. This part of the process takes time, often more than a year.

Recognize That Language Is Place-Based and Involves the Community

Being proud of who we are as a people is a very important aspect that must be conveyed to our younger generations. This will be accomplished by providing opportunities to understand our people more fully through developing resources and learning opportunities regarding our local history, traditions, and our local stories. (Corbiere, 2014, p. 12)

There are real differences between the language that is spoken in each Indigenous community, even when communities use the "same" language. Communities' stories are different, as they emphasize what is considered important locally. This is one of the reasons that consultation with Elders is so important. Language is tied to the land, and each community is on different land. Among the tragedies of the residential schools and forced relocation is a loss of connection to place. Connection to the land is an essential consideration in any Indigenous language program. The school and local band council need to collect the local stories for the children and the community. Language learning is not only about teaching the children; it is about implementing restorative practice in the community.

The language program should intentionally engage teachers, families, and community members in language learning. Because of the loss of language in First Nation communities, it is unreasonable to expect that children's family members will be fluent speakers of their language. Language learning should be made available to family and community members, and there should be support for school staff to learn the language as well. There should be regular communication with families outlining the language the students are learning and the cultural content that is being covered, so that families are engaged and the children's language learning can be supported.

Another essential component of language revitalization programs is regular invitations to the community to participate in school cultural activities, such as traditional feasts that are held every harvest. The schools provide traditional teachings on powwow, ceremony, and regalia; the clans system; the language; and traditional resources and tools, such as the drum and shaker. These elements, and the importance of tradition and spirituality, are also integrated throughout the school's daily lesson plans and school routines. This work can be seen as a response to the Truth and Reconciliation Commission of Canada's (2015) call for the development of culturally restorative practices (Simard & Blight, 2011). By incorporating culture, stories, and language into their daily teaching practices, schools create a space where Indigenous children feel accepted, confident in their identity, and able to share their families' cultures.

Take Up a Holistic Image of the Child

It's necessary that we believe that the child is very intelligent, that the child is strong and beautiful and has very ambitious desires and requests. This is the image of the child that we need to hold. (Malaguzzi, 1994, p. 56)

In order to be successful, a First Nation language program should be seen as a way of helping students develop a strong sense of identity. The schools I work with take a holistic approach to learning and the learner, emphasizing the student as capable, self-reliant, intelligent, curious, creative, and unique (Edwards et al., 1998; Project Zero & Reggio Children, 2001; Toulouse, 2016). These schools take an Indigenous holistic approach to our understanding of the spiritual, physical, emotional, and intellectual nature of children and people (Neegan, 2005).

The success of each of the Indigenous language programs I have worked with is largely due to the educators who have worked hard to engage in pedagogical listening (Rinaldi, 2001), and who have made tremendous efforts to show each child in the classroom respect and love. This simple yet effective act of empowerment is capable of transforming students' lives and represents a tangible step towards healing centuries of intentional subjugation. Much of this culturally restorative practice is not radical; rather, it is simply about showing love, being honest, and making a genuine attempt to connect to the real lives of children in relation. Most importantly, however, this approach values and acknowledges the culture and language the students actively or unconsciously bring to school with them. This approach allows educators to really engage with their students and to get to know them in deep, personal ways. In turn, these personal connections allow teachers to form strong relationships with their students; and it is these relationships that provide the basis for mutual trust and respect. This is critical, as trust is a necessary ingredient to learning for Indigenous children (Simard & Blight, 2011). Relationship is a foundation of all learning and needs to be intentional from the beginning of any language program.

Regard the Environment as a Third Teacher

These schools' approach to language learning also treats the environment as a "third teacher" (Edwards et al., 1998) and encourages teachers to strive to create learning environments that are comfortable, safe, and enhance the students' ability to learn. These spaces can be indoors, typically classrooms, or outdoors on the land. The educators need to be intentional about using the educational space, materials, and time to teach the children – whether inside or outside – while keeping in mind that the environment is used to teach the children and that being outdoors is essential in teaching the language.

The local place will influence the way in which the environment acts as a third teacher. In one of the communities I work with, life is governed by the river – there are six seasons, including "freeze up" and "breakup" – and by the harvest of moose and geese in the fall and spring. The calendar is necessarily different in this school, to reflect the culture of this place. It changes what the children, families, and the community value, what they see as interesting and important to know. Place is an important consideration in any Indigenous language program.

Identify and Support Champions of the Program

When creating programs for different Indigenous cultures and languages, it is of the utmost importance to consider the people who will create and direct them. What each program needs to be successful is a champion. Without a person who is excited and passionate about the language and culture, a First Nations language program will lose its way and be less successful. This is something we have observed acutely, as when champions have moved into other roles of leadership or have been unable to sustain their role for whatever reason. Language programs are demanding, and it has been my experience that the people delivering and administering any program make all the difference.

For example, I have seen language teachers who have stood out as champions. When in their role as language teachers, they were able to dedicate themselves to the development and implementation of the program, spending many extra hours promoting and supporting language in the community. In both these cases, these champions were recognized for their leadership in their school and moved to administrative positions (principal and vice principal respectively); in this new role, their time was divided among the many needs of the school and they were no longer able to champion the language program – and the language program suffered as a result. The right people matter and can make all the difference in the success of any language program.

Recognize Complexities in Finding and Supporting
Language Teachers

There is an obvious preference for immersion language teaching at the early grades; however there has been a consistent lack of teachers and fluent language speakers to support such programs in these schools. Consequently the schools have used language teaching as a planning time release for teachers, guaranteeing students 40 minutes a day of First Nation language instruction from a trained, fluent-speaking teacher. This is a pragmatic and sustainable decision; it is not better than an immersion program but is a good alternative when immersion is not a viable option. It is hoped that the students of the language programs will become future teachers and language teachers in their community, and that these communities will have more options in the future.

We have found that the usual training that First Nations language teachers are receiving is inadequate and that most require additional training. Many are taught to teach First Nations languages using a structuralist approach, which does not suit the needs of a comprehensive language program. In each case, we have needed to retrain our language teachers to use an approach that nurtures and supports students' interest in the language and culture – ideally by using a play-based approach imbedded in a cycle of inquiry (Berghoff et al., 2000), which is intended to motivate the students to explore and learn about the language and culture outside of their time at school. As described in the following section, we use storytelling as a methodology for teaching and learning the language.

The Language Program

To save Indigenous languages, the language needs to be taught as real, organic, and engaging. The language teaching model we have used is based on Arlene Stairs' concept of the Native language teacher as cultural broker (Stairs, 1991) (see Figure 8.3).

The programs are based on the belief that children need to have a strong sense of identity and pride in who they are in order to be able to learn effectively (Battiste, 2013; Toulouse, 2011). From an Indigenous education perspective, the schools draw upon six main tenets: the importance of Indigenous identity to the students as learners and individuals; the Medicine Wheel teachings; the importance of culture; the key First Nations teachings (which vary depending on community and place); time on the land; and learning in relation. The importance of being on the land cannot be understated: identity comes from the culture, culture comes from the language, and the language comes from the land. Learning is lifelong, complex and interrelated, and extends beyond the school.

118   Jeffrey Wood

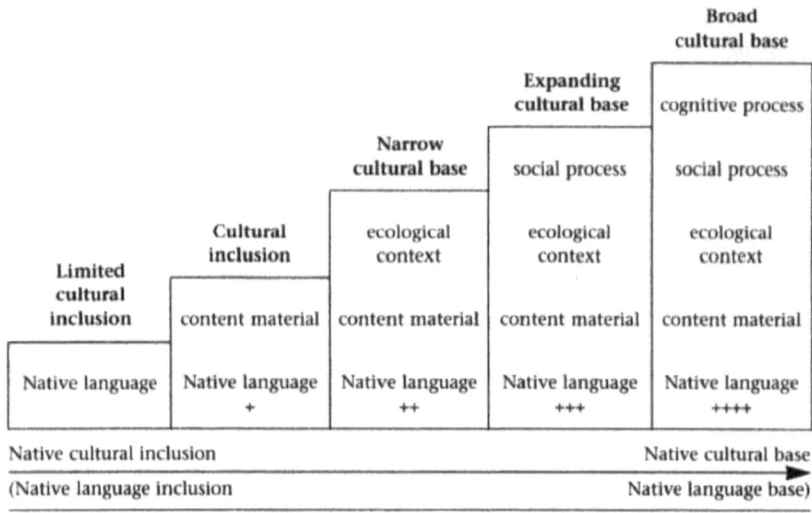

Figure 8.3 Native Language Teacher as Cultural Broker

Note: From "Learning Processes and Teaching Roles in Native Education: Cultural Base and Cultural Brokerage," by A. Stairs, 1991, *Canadian Modern Language Review,* 47(2).

In these programs, language, culture, and the land are connected and are learned together. Sharing the culture and storytelling out on the land brings the language to life for the children. Adding songs, games, and cultural experiences makes the language engaging and fun to learn and, more importantly, easier to remember. The language teachers use play to support and teach the language, creating spaces that are playful both inside and outside. As children are engaged in dramatic play, for example, the language teacher speaks to the children in the language, using and offering words and phrases within the context of the children's play. The same is true in any of the learning centres that are set up throughout the language classroom and in outdoor learning settings. The language teaching is organic and an extension of the children's play. The children have the opportunity to use puppets to retell legends and histories as well as to read and write in the language. They often sing the songs they learn in their language class during their play, in their home classrooms, in their community, and at home.

In each of the schools, the language teachers have intentionally avoided teaching the children about grammatical structures and terminology and yet, through using the language in real and holistic contexts, the children are learning and applying these concepts in their language

Land, Language, Culture, Identity, and Learning in Relation 119

Figure 8.4 Tipi

Note: Tipi used as an outdoor classroom to teach local cultural practice.

use. Language does not need to be broken down for children; instead, it needs to remain whole and complex so that they can learn.

The language needs to be taught and learned in a way that is comprehensive and intentional. Language teaching needs to scaffold the delivery of the language so the learning is always supported and contextualized. It is this semantic (meaning-based) structure that allows the children to access the language and retain what they are learning. Regardless of the pedagogical approaches used to teach the language, language teachers in these schools ensure that language learning is always supported and contextualized on the land, and is combined with cultural learning in relationship. Having said that, I think it is worth mentioning again that this approach is complex and requires competent, committed staff.

Measures of Success

At each of the schools, as a part of the implementation process, my research team (comprised of university, Indigenous, and local researchers) conducted research to help guide our teaching practice and to measure whether the language programs were successful (see Wood et al., 2019; Wood et al., 2018). We conducted interviews with students, family members, staff, and community members and surveyed the community. We also analysed provincial achievement test scores of the communities' Grades 3 and 6 students (administered by the Education Quality and Accountability Office of Ontario), as well as school-based reading and writing assessments, report card grades, and attendance records. These quantitative measures were contextualized with direct observation of language classes and grade-level classrooms.

What follows is a summary of the interview and survey comments and the report on academic measures, with reference to the themes arising from our analysis.

Increased Language Use and Enhanced Cultural Knowledge

The key metric that we sought to investigate was, Are the children speaking the language in their classrooms and outside of their classrooms? Students, family members, staff, and community members observed that the children were remembering the language lessons learned in their classes and were applying this learning throughout the school day, at home, and beyond. The sense of pride the children showed in their language, their culture, and who they are as First Nations people is remarkable, according to family members, staff, and community members.

Almost all of the children reported that they were speaking the language outside of school with friends and family, in addition to speaking the language in their classrooms. School-based adults verified this, stating, "It took about a year and then students started speaking the language in the halls and they were making connections between concepts." They also explained that "parents are reporting that children are speaking at home." Participating grandparents also provided evidence of this by saying, "My granddaughter would come home and share her wonderful [language and cultural experiences]," and "I love that my grandson is singing songs in Cree when I take care of him."

Positive Identities Created

Together with promoting children's increased fluency in speaking the language, the program fostered children's development of positive identities. One participant said, "The [language program] is getting students speaking and they are excited and enthusiastic to use [the language] and about who they are as [First Nation]." The Indigenous, culture-oriented approach improved the children's outlook on school, with 84% of students in one of the schools saying that they believe that the school "support[s] the best learning" for them. Significantly, just under 90% of the children that we surveyed said that they liked "learning about Cree and Cree culture at school."

Community Recognition

The language program benefits extended to community members and teachers as well. We heard: "It isn't just the students, it's the teachers in the school speaking the language." and "Teachers are speaking the language in the classroom." All of the interviewed teachers said that they were using the local First Nation language as a part of their teaching throughout the day. Their comments included, "I do use the language in my teaching – the things that I use every day," and "I do use the language in my teaching – just simple words and counting." Participating students provided further evidence, saying, "Miss D. speaks every day and then we know more." Lastly, in reference to some of the teachers, the Elders reported that "they really have learned."

The First Nation language programs have been universally recognized in each of the participating communities. In an interview, one community member explained, "It [First Nation language program] has created an awareness of the language in the community." Another participant valued the program because "the traditional practices are coming back to the school and the community." Each person that was interviewed about the First Nation language programs talked about hope – the hope that they now have for their language, their culture, and their community.

Academic Improvements

Across all schools, the students' Developmental Reading Assessment (DRA) scores showed an unprecedented improvement of 10 to 20 DRA reading levels in a single year. This is a finding that was universal across all schools involved, and has resulted in almost all students improving in their reading and general school performance. As a side note, all schools have also experienced a reduction in the number of students being sent to the office, improved school attendance rates, and fewer classroom disturbances. This seems to be the result of reduced stress and increased cultural identity, but these factors require further research to be understood fully.

Enthusiasm for the Teaching Approach

Participating children expressed their enjoyment of the program in interviews, with many children saying, "I love [the language program]!" They also showed great appreciation for learning their community's First Nation language and culture (e.g., "It is fun and I get to learn about my language and my culture," "I love learning about my culture!," and "I love speaking my language"). Figure 8.5 shows a boy who chose to write "speak Cree to me" during his play time.

Participating adults talked about past approaches that had not been successful in creating fluent speakers. One community member said, "I went through school; I didn't end up speaking the language outside of Ojibway class, it wasn't working." Another community member added, "We have been teaching the language for the past 20 years and we have fewer Anishinaabemowin speakers than we did then." Their assessment of the new program was noticeably different. "We need to engage students and make it more play-based; put them to work without making them feel like they were learning." "They learn faster and use the language in a natural way." "The kids love joining into the activities." Family, staff, and community members showed great support for the teaching approaches used in the language programs.

Children and adults also saw the importance of being on the land and how it relates to language learning. A common observation among participating children was "When I am [on the land], I just know the language, the words come easy." Similarly, the adults noted the land's tremendous impact on learning. One staff member observed that, when the children are learning from the land, "It is like [they] come alive." Other comments included "It is a far more organic way to learn the language, out on the land" and "The context is tied together, [the language is] not just random, but in ways that are connected and relevant back to the lives of the students."

It appears that the programs' focus on fostering a strong cultural identity, bringing in Elders, Knowledge Keepers, and community members, and spending time on the land has led to improved student success in school in general. The introduction of Indigenous language programs that focus on culture has significantly improved how the students view their school and their school performance. Ultimately these programs aim to improve students' academic success by engaging them in learning through culture and developing them into First Nations language speakers who are in touch with their culture and their Indigenous identity.

Figure 8.5 Student in One of the Language Programs

Concluding Thoughts

Language, culture, and the land are all connected and therefore must be learned together. The First Nations language programs taught in the past were structuralist in nature, which means that individuals were taught Indigenous languages in isolation from their real-world context. This approach only led to further colonization of the culture and language; language was treated as something to be memorized, rather than lived. In contrast, these new programs use local cultural teachings to bring the language to life for the children through play, songs, games, and experiences. As a result, the language component of the programs becomes more engaging and fun to learn, more hands-on, and easier to remember. The programs also help to connect these cultural teachings to the students' classrooms and to the school as a whole, making the language an integrated part of the students' daily lives at school rather than a mere 40-minute daily lesson.

Language comes from the land, culture comes from language, identity comes from culture, and all learning is done in relation. In order to save our Indigenous languages, they must be made real, organic, and engaging. Culture and language programs should take up new approaches that truly engage our children and that connect them to the land. First Nations language programs need to treat language as something that is real and lived, and teach children in a way that is supportive and holistic. In order to do the work of having fluent First Nations speakers who are in touch with their culture and who can create a vibrant language community, we need to have language programs that make a difference in the lives of our students and our communities – both now and in the future.

REFERENCES

Ball, J. (2007). *Aboriginal young children's language and literacy development: research evaluating progress, promising practices, and needs.* Canadian Language and Literacy Networked Centre of Excellence. http://www.ecdip.org/docs/pdf/CLLRNet%20Feb%202008.pdf

Battiste, M. (2013). *Decolonizing education: Nourishing the learning spirit.* Purich Publishing.

Berghoff, B., Egawa, K., Harste, J., & Hoonan, B. (2000). *Beyond reading and writing: Inquiry, curriculum, and multiple ways of knowing.* NCTE.

Blackstock, C., Clarke, S., Cullen, J., D'Hondt, J., & Formsma, J. (2004). *Keeping the promise: The Convention on the Rights of the Child and the lived experiences of First Nations children and youth.* First Nations Child and Family Caring Society of Canada. https://fncaringsociety.com/sites/default/files/docs/KeepingThePromise.pdf

Canada, Indian and Northern Affairs. (1969). *Statement of the Government of Canada on Indian Policy.* Ottawa: Department of Indian and Northern Affairs. http://epe.lac-bac.gc.ca/100/200/301/inac-ainc/indian_policy-e/cp1969_e.pdf

Canadian Council on Learning. (2007). *Redefining how success is measured in First Nations, Inuit and Métis learning.* Canadian Council on Learning.

Cardinal, H. (1999). *The unjust society.* Douglas & McIntyre.

Corbiere, A. (2014). *First Nation revival program framework for curriculum development.* Kenjgewin Teg.

Edwards, C., L. Gandini, & G. Forman. (1998). *The hundred languages of children: The Reggio Emilia approach advanced reflections*, 2nd ed. Ablex Publishing.

Huston, L., & Michano-Drover, S. (2022). Placing the child's hands on the land. In S.S. Peterson & N. Friedrich (Eds.), *The role of place and play in young children's language and literacy* (pp. 81–94). University of Toronto Press.

King, T. (Ed.). (1990). *All my relations: An anthology of contemporary Canadian Native Prose.* McClelland & Stewart.

Malaguzzi, L. (1994). Your image of the child: Where teaching begins. *Exchange* (3), 52–56.

Milloy, J. (2008). *Indian Act colonialism: A century of dishonour, 1869–1969.* Research paper for the National Centre for First Nations Governance. http://fngovernance.org/ncfng_research/milloy.pdf

Neegan, E. (2005). Excuse me: Who are the first peoples of Canada? A historical analysis of Aboriginal education in Canada then and now. *International Journal of Inclusive Education, 9*(1), 3–15. https://doi.org/10.1080/13603110420002 99757

Peltier, S. (2022). Seven Directions early learning for Indigenous land literacy wisdom. In S.S. Peterson & N. Friedrich (Eds.), *The role of place and play in young children's language and literacy* (pp. 33–51). University of Toronto Press.

Project Zero & Reggio Children. (2001). *Making learning visible: Children as individual and group learners.* Reggio Children.

Rinaldi, C. (2001). The pedagogy of listening: The listening perspective from Reggio Emilia. *Innovations in Early Education: The International Reggio Exchange, 8*(4), 1–4.

Simard, E., & Blight, S. (2011). Developing a culturally restorative approach to aboriginal child and youth development: Transitions to adulthood. *First Peoples Child & Family Review, 6*(1), 28–55. https://doi.org/10.7202/1068895ar

Spyrou, S. (2018). *Disclosing childhoods: Research and knowledge production for a critical childhood studies.* Palgrave Macmillan.

Stairs, A. (1991). Learning processes and teaching roles in native education: Cultural base and cultural brokerage. *Canadian Modern Language Review, 47*(2), 280–294. http://doi.org/10.3138/cmlr.47.2.280

Statistics Canada. (2017). *Census in brief: The Aboriginal languages of First Nations people, Métis and Inuit.* Catalogue no. 98-200-X2016022. https://www12.statcan.gc.ca/census-recensement/2016/as-sa/98-200-x/2016022/98-200-x2016022-eng.pdf

Toulouse, P. (2011). *Achieving Aboriginal student success: A guide for K to 8 classrooms.* Portage & Main Press.

Toulouse, P. (2016). *What matters in Indigenous education: Implementing a vision committed to holism, diversity and engagement.* People for Education.

Truth and Reconciliation Commission of Canada. (2015). *What we have learned: Principles of truth and reconciliation.* Truth and Reconciliation Commission of Canada, Winnipeg. Retrieved from www.trc.ca

Wood, J., Daviau, C., & Daviau, N. (2018). *Anishinaabemowin revival program.* Indspire Research Report. https://indspire.ca/education/educators/.

Wood, J., Daviau, C., & Gunner, B. (2019). *Enhancing Cree anguage with culture.* Indspire Research Report. https://indspire.ca/education/educators/.

9 If Writing Floats "on a Sea of Talk," How Best to Harness the Waves and Currents of Place and Play?

JUDY M. PARR

Introduction

Talk and writing share a common communicative intent; they are at once similar yet different. While almost all children learn to speak the language(s) around them, the acquisition of written language requires supportive instruction. The first part of the title of this chapter is a quote from James Britton (1970, p. 29) and is intended to emphasize the idea that talk is an essential underpinning of writing, especially for young children. The second part of the title foreshadows the argument of this chapter, namely, that there are ways of ensuring that the free form and perhaps a certain aimlessness implied by the notion of talk "floating" are given purpose and direction in the pursuit of supporting writing. Support in educational settings is commonly associated with the metaphor of scaffolding but, in this piece, the argument of Valsiner (1997) is invoked: the notion that teachers, through their active channelling of activity and deployment of resources, create a zone of promoted development, harnessing the waves and currents of the sea of talk, in particular in relation to the affordances of place and of play.

In this chapter, I consider how notions of place and play are viewed within the context of Aotearoa New Zealand, and how they may be stimulated, channelled, and directed, specifically to promote the development of writing as children progress through primary school. I examine these concepts as they are represented in culture, curricula, and research within the country. As part of this discussion, examples are presented of some of the myriad ways in which the country's teachers, particularly of younger and primary school aged children, actively employ and deploy talk, notions of place and belonging, and playful practices, often in concert, to enhance the development of children's writing. The way in which teachers do this is explored through glimpses of classroom practice and from teacher and student views drawn from research work in writing classrooms and from other relevant data from research projects. The efficacy of these means is discussed with reference to theory and the existing research literature.

The Aotearoa New Zealand Context

Aotearoa New Zealand is a small country. The Māori people were colonized by settlers of largely British origin; today Aotearoa New Zealand is a bicultural nation with an increasingly multicultural population. The largest city, Auckland, home to about a third of the nation's people, rivals Toronto (widely considered the most multi-ethnic city in the world) in terms of the range of ethnicities who reside there. Aotearoa New Zealand, about the size of Norway or Scotland, or a small US state like Vermont, is one educational jurisdiction. There are about 2,000 state-funded primary schools, including Māori-medium, where the medium of instruction is te reo Māori, the Indigenous language of Aotearoa New Zealand, and some special character schools, plus a small private system. About 17,000 students are in Māori-medium teaching (where te reo is used more than 50% of the time) and 147,500 in English medium but where the Māori language is used 50% or less of the time. The latter are largely bilingual units within schools; there are also some Samoan and Tongan (the largest Pacific nation groups) units. In early childhood or preschool education, the current participation rate (of 4-year-old children) averages 96%. There are full immersion *kohanga reo* (preschools) and a number of preschools where Māori is spoken half or less of the time. Language nests (largely Pasifika languages) are funded where, for 50% plus of the time, the target language is used.

Aotearoa New Zealand enjoys a broad, non-prescriptive national curriculum in compulsory schooling (Ministry of Education, 2007), which identifies overall outcomes for learners, but not the content that is taught. Schools function autonomously and are encouraged to situate the curriculum objectives within their local context and to set their own goals for student learning. Teaching is viewed, within the curriculum, as a process of inquiry into how best to meet the learning needs of each student. This is consistent with a tradition of teaching the individual, recognizing that students take different paths to common outcomes (Clay, 1998), rather than teaching a content-prescriptive curriculum. Regard for the professionalism of teachers is a core principle and this is reflected in assessment policy and practice. In Aotearoa New Zealand there is no mandatory testing until the national qualification, in the last three years of schooling, where students are aged approximately 16–18 years. Before this, professional judgment, informed by a range of strategies and tools, is used to establish and describe student performance. Assessment in Aotearoa New Zealand is viewed as predominantly in the service of learning. Both teachers and schools use data that they collect about their students in their classrooms to evaluate how well they are serving their students and community, to communicate this to their community, and to self-identify teaching and learning issues that need to be addressed.

Employing and Deploying Talk, Place, and Playful Practices in Writing

Situating the discussion within the Aotearoa New Zealand context, I explore how the active channelling of activity and deployment of resources by teachers engages students in writing. How do the waves of place and play feature? In junior classrooms oral language, reading, and writing often merge seamlessly within activities or are deliberately linked to literacy and across the curriculum. While choice or agency, interest, and fun align with concepts of play, and will be considered in this light, place in our context has strong historical and cultural, as well as location or landscape-based, connections.

Foregrounding Place in Writing

The place where you belong, *tūrangawaewae (domicile, literally where you have the right to stand)*, where you come from, is central to Indigenous Māori culture. When a person is formally received by a community, introductions (*mihi*) speak of place. In introducing yourself, you share a little about where you come from and who you are in relation to your place of origin. This often includes significant parts of your *whakapapa (genealogy)*, your connections to people, and your relationships with them. You literally create a base through your connection to lands and to ancestry. It is your identity: your place in a wider context, your links to land, sea, and sky, and to tribal groupings, and to the *mana* (prestige and power) of those groupings. Pakeha (non-Māori) Aotearoa New Zealanders come to appreciate the significance of identifying their river/lake/sea and their mountain as indicators of the place where they are from or where they belong; the *waka* (canoe) on which they or their ancestors came to the island (their means of travel); as well as their kin, their immediate family members.

The recent Early Childhood Curriculum, *Te Whāriki* (Ministry of Education, 2017), like its earlier edition, has been developed and framed using concepts drawn from te ao Māori. It provides the principles for curriculum development; its strands describe valued learning, goals relating to the provision of a supportive learning environment, and learning outcomes. Like other national curriculum, it is expected that it will be "the basis for local curriculum of valued learning, taking into consideration also the aspirations and learning priorities of hapū, iwi and community" (p. 8). The *whāriki*, or woven mat, is used as a metaphor, whereby four curriculum principles are interwoven with five curriculum strands. Principle 4, *Ngā hononga*, acknowledges that children learn through responsive and reciprocal relationships with people, places, and things, while a goal of the strand, *Mana whenua* (belonging), is that children know they belong and have a sense of connection to others and the environment.

This centrality of place in terms of cultural and linguistic belonging is further recognized by acknowledging and drawing upon the situated experiences of students, particularly those experiences within their immediate environment, to enhance their communication abilities. The organic methods of a renowned early Aotearoa New Zealand educator, Sylvia Ashton-Warner (1958, 1963), who worked with Māori students in isolated areas from the 1930s, involved listening to students and using what was most important to them, what emerged from the context, as the material for teaching and learning. Her students, from a culture rich in oracy, struggled with the concept of the printed word as representing something. Ashton-Warner reasoned that Māori children generally could not identify with features of the landscape and lifestyle represented in the United Kingdom's reading primers. She wrote with passion about the need for literacy to be meaningful to children and taught vocabulary through associating the written word with each child's personal, emotion-laden mental images; this supplied the meaning of the word to Māori children.

The organic teaching methods of Ashton-Warner are generally seen to have given rise in Aotearoa New Zealand to the idea of language experience. Language experience is essentially a planned, joint meaning-making activity involving talking, reading, and writing. The teacher sets up this language experience; it revolves around an interesting, perhaps novel, event, essentially one that draws on the lived experience, language, and culture of the child as the point for literacy development. The activity is often connected to the outdoor flora and fauna or to aspects of everyday life like cooking and growing plants, although sometimes teachers take advantage of a serendipitous happening like a fire engine arriving for a fire drill or a formal welcoming of a visitor to the school. In language experience, children engage in the activity, talk with one another and as a group about the experience, incidentally and deliberately learn vocabulary associated with it, and then read and write about it or similar experiences.

This is but one means by which Aotearoa New Zealand teachers support writing development through promoting talk related to familiar experiences in the child's own environment. As primary schools have considerable freedom as to content taught to achieve curriculum objectives, some primary schools organize learning on a thematic basis; the notion of place in terms of the local environment is a common choice of topic or theme.

Aotearoa New Zealand teachers of primary-aged children view reading and writing as closely linked, and writing often springboards from the books being read and the resources used. Ashton-Warner devised her own resources to enable children to construct meaning through familiar contexts and concepts. In this regard, the Ministry of Education has a proud history of leading the production of local resources for literacy teaching, resources produced by Aotearoa New Zealanders and reflecting the country's landscape and culture. The book *A Nest of Singing Birds* (O'Brien, 2007) celebrates 100 years of the ministry's publication of *The School Journal*, said to be the longest-running children's serial publication in the world. And, while publications such as the *Journal* have been criticized at times, such as in its early days for its pejorative representation of Māori culture, they have come to represent content, illustrations (some of the country's foremost artists have produced illustrations for the *Journal*) and style that are uniquely bound to Aotearoa New Zealand. Our research (McDowall & Parr, 2012) explored the principles underpinning the production of local literacy resource materials, using the *School Journal* as an example. One of the guiding principles was providing rich texts and tasks to support strategic instruction and build student capacities to meet the literacy (reading and writing in particular) demands of the curriculum. Other principles were promoting wider notions of place and belonging, recognizing the diversity of students, and supporting Māori students to achieve success as Māori. We analysed the journals and teacher resources, observed how they were used in classes, and talked with teachers about them.

Our analysis of the then current *School Journal* texts examined the extent to which Māori ways of knowing and being in the world (*Ka hiktatea*, Ministry of Education, 2009) were represented and also how the teacher support materials that accompanied the texts exhibited features of a culturally responsive pedagogy of relations (Bishop et al., 2007). We found that the then publisher had in place processes to ensure that the *School Journal* texts focused not just on characters and contexts familiar to Māori students, but also provided a space for representing who they are in the contexts of their *whānau* (extended family), *hapū* (clan), and *iwi* (tribe) lived experiences. This resonates with descriptions of what Graham did in his elementary classroom at Tipiyimisiw school, where he worked to ensure that Indigenous students could see themselves reflected authentically within the classroom (see Eppley et al., this volume). For the *School Journal*, these processes included the engagement of Māori writers, illustrators, and photographers; Māori advisers to check the representation of Māori; and Māori editors who were responsible for the production of texts targeting Māori students. Our analysis found many texts in the *School Journal* that had been written by Māori authors, writing from such lived experiences. Some of these experiences would be familiar to New Zealand students from a wide range of backgrounds. Others written by these authors touch on experiences and worldviews that fewer students would likely be familiar with, providing an opportunity for students with such experiences and views to share their knowledge with others.

In this research, we also analysed how teachers used the *School Journal* and accompanying resources in the classroom. We talked with them about their views. The teachers we interviewed considered that the texts in the *School Journal* supported them in providing their Māori students with opportunities to experience success as Māori:

> I think what [the publishers have] done is they have begun to create New Zealand as it is and they've tried to identify, from what I can see, that Māori and Pacific identity which I think in the past was missing. So that makes [these texts] different to other texts that come from out of New Zealand.

From the classroom observations in our research (McDowall & Parr, 2012), we share the example of a teacher whose practice illustrates a way of working with students and with written texts that is consistent with what the research literature suggests is likely to support Māori students in achieving success as Māori. The teacher concerned was from a school where approximately one-third of the students were Māori; he described how important it was for his students to see themselves, including their place of belonging, in text. He was very much aware of the need to build on their world of experience:

> There's a lot of good New Zealand stuff in there too with the journals, that's what I like about them. There's stuff that the kids would probably have a lot of experience with. They will be able to draw on some of that prior knowledge and some of the experiences because they've actually experienced that ... It's really hard for some of these kids when they're reading a story and they haven't experienced it.

This teacher began all of the lessons we observed with opportunities for students to share their interests, knowledge, and also values in relation to the topic of the text being introduced. They did this in pairs and then as a whole group. We saw him using his knowledge of the text and of the students to enrich discussions. With reference to his pedagogy and philosophy, this teacher noted that he was prepared to engage in extended discussions with students around texts, and he saw this as a quality that comes with being a more experienced teacher. These sharing times were a means to connect with his students by showing interest in their views and experiences as well as sharing his own.

In all of the lessons we observed, the teacher co-constructed the learning by modelling a particular process or skill and then giving students the opportunity to try it themselves with less teacher support. There was a clear example of this in preparing the students to write a brief report. First, the class worked together, led by the teacher, to write a report on the All Black rugby player they had talked about previously, Mils Muliaina. They also used the information from an interview with him reported in an article in one of the *School Journal*s, and some further information from an Internet clip about him. The teacher then let students choose their own sports hero about whom to write. The nature of the writing task was negotiable and students had opportunities to shape their learning. The following example illustrates how the teacher makes it clear that students can make the writing their own:

> Miles has asked me a very good question, so listen carefully. Miles said can we write the facts in all different boxes. Those boxes might be very good for you to start planning out where to put each of the facts so, for example, anything about his position or about the game you might put in one box.

The teacher used different strategies to empower students as peer teachers and to use this as a means of learning with which Māori and Pasifika students could readily identify. As Eppley et al. (this volume) note, with respect to the teachers described in their vignettes, positive identities can be developed by affirming social practices that are part of everyday experience in the students' communities. In the current case, this teacher used more expert peers to help less able readers (a pedagogy known as *tuakana teina*: more expert helping less expert or, in traditional Māori culture, an older relative helping a younger) to access text that would be too difficult for them to read on their own. He described how he sometimes matched text difficulty with students' reading levels and how, at other times, he used the text with the whole class:

> I don't worry too much about the reading ages and that sort of thing ... It's more sort of the context or whatever the genre is [talking of what is important in selecting text]. And because we're doing it within the whole class, you know, some of those lower readers are still able to access [the text] because I am doing the reading or the more high-ability kids are doing the reading.

He provided many opportunities for students to work with others to co-construct the meaning of certain aspects of text:

> Okay now, I want you ... can you guys just have a chat with the person next to you. I want you to talk to your neighbour and find out what has been important so far in the text, what has been important so far since you've been reading? Have a good chat with your neighbour.

This teacher not only thought deeply about means to connect with his students' experiences and interests so that they could see themselves and their world in the texts they read and the topics they wrote about, but he employed pedagogies that were culturally sustaining.

Playful Practices in Writing

> Play takes a primary role in the research, theory, curriculum, and pedagogy of ECE in many western countries because it is viewed as a way that young children participate in learning about social and cultural practices, and as a way for children to express and practice creative ideas and thinking that can lead to later academic learning. (Hedges et al., 2018, p. 12)

Play is recognized in *Te Whariki*, the Early Years Curriculum (Ministry of Education, 2017), as an important means of learning; the curriculum addresses a rich array of primarily play-based experiences (p. 15). Play is generally viewed as informal learning. The potential of play as informal learning is that it is relevant to children's life experiences; it involves intrinsically motivated interests and initiative on the part of the child (Rogoff et al., 2016). However, play that is effective for learning also involves supportive actions on the part of adults to ensure an optimal zone of promoted development (Valsiner, 1997), to ensure appropriate play provision (Wood, 2014a). The potential for learning from play is enhanced when teachers utilize it in a way that is cognizant of children's motivations and interest (Hedges & Cooper, 2014).

The notion that children progress from play-based learning to formal learning denies that play-based pedagogy is potentially appropriate for all learners (Hedges, 2018). Here, rather than consider the modes of play in terms of the pedagogy-play interface (Wood, 2014b) or, for example, games, which are commonly used within primary school curricula, as a form of play (Lai et al., 2018), I broaden the notion of play-based pedagogy to consider how the defining characteristics of play-based or informal learning might be utilized in writing pedagogy as children progress through primary school. Writing is a social and cultural practice that, like play, children use to express ideas and to think and to learn.

One hallmark of play is that it involves initiative on the part of the child. Regarding this initiative or initiation of activity as part of a wider notion of student participation in their learning, the research literature suggests that students "should be afforded opportunities to actively shape their education" (Cook-Sather, 2006, p. 359) and that such activity is associated with engagement in learning and schooling more generally. Dissatisfaction of those students who remain on the periphery of the literacy classroom has been shown to be related to a perceived lack of autonomy (Fisher, 2014). Initiating a task or activity of their own volition as opposed to doing what is set for them (this is considered to be work!) in writing would involve, for example, students having some say or choice in the writing tasks to be undertaken and/or in how the task would be approached and the outcome presented.

So, having agency around the task or the purpose for writing and how they engage with it is key for students. It likely also involves ideas discussed above; the notion of being able to see themselves in text or, in the case of writing, being able to see themselves as writers. Informal learning and play are characterized as being relevant to children's experiences (Rogoff et al., 2016). Much has been written on the need for authentic writing tasks. Writing topics that have meaning and purpose within the world of the student foster engagement and a sense of ownership. Recently, we used an online, anonymous survey of students in upper primary (449 students aged 10–13) (Gadd et al., 2019) to help teachers with whom we worked collaboratively to get a sense of the range of viewpoints that their students held about writing. From this we gained some insight into these notions of agency and purpose or relevance. We asked questions that examined attitudes to writing, self-efficacy beliefs, and reactions to teachers' instructional strategies. Responses as to why students did or did not like writing suggest that seeing a purpose, personal or social, is important. One student wrote that s/he could not see the point of writing in his/her world. "I don't like it because I feel that it is unnecessary. I just don't see the use in it." One response that was a cause for much teacher reflection around purpose and audience but also ownership was from a boy who did not consider himself to be good at writing because "I can never come up with an idea, one that makes the teacher happy anyway." For other students it was clear that, for them, writing did not relate to their experiences or interests. "I don't like writing – I have no interest in it," wrote one, while another reflected the lack of real interest for him in school writing: "You have to write on boring topics." In contrast, among responses as to why they liked writing were those reflecting deep feelings of engagement and satisfaction. "I live for writing," wrote one student, while others liked writing "because I can create my own little world" or "it expresses my creativity and makes me feel happy." "I love being able to captivate my audience through my writing" – was a sophisticated response from a 12-year-old about the purpose of writing for her. One student was very specific about the conditions under which he liked writing: "I like writing if I have a choice in what I write and the topic is one I enjoy." This theme of choice was reiterated in responses to a question that asked students to nominate up to three things that their teachers did that made writing easier for them. Here, the most frequently nominated (on all four occasions the survey was completed over two years) of eight actions was selecting a topic to write about that was of interest to the student, followed closely by the idea that the teacher gave them some choice in topic or how they wrote about it.

In primary school writing contexts, characteristics similar to those seen in play that stimulates learning include initiation, choice, and a say in what is happening. The notion of intrinsic motivation is also a characteristic of play or informal learning. Research shows that children who enjoy writing and are motivated to write are much more likely to achieve academic success (Clark & Teravainen, 2017). Play, arguably, also includes interest (linked to relevance) and, relatedly, elements of fun or enjoyment and satisfaction. The specific sources of these in writing are many and varied and will be different for individual writers in different contexts. The comments from some of the students in our survey, quoted above, provide insight into these sources. Young (2019) argues that enjoyment and satisfaction are two types of pleasure in writing, namely, writing *as* pleasure (enjoyment) and writing *for* pleasure (satisfaction). The former includes feeling a need to write, and experiencing enjoyment in practising the craft of writing; feeling confident and content when engaging in the different processes of writing and enjoying being part of a writing community; and discussing their own writing and how it feels to be a writer. The latter (writing for pleasure) includes having a sense of purpose fulfilled; the expectation of a response; sharing something to be proud of; feeling you have achieved something significant; and discovering your own writing voice.

Drawing on our work on the practices of effective teachers of writing (e.g., Gadd, 2014; Gadd & Parr, 2017; Parr, 2017; Parr & Limbrick, 2009) and the recent work of Young (2019), it is possible to identify the teacher actions which are most likely to promote writing as a pleasurable act. As Young (2019) noted, effective teachers, seen as such because their students consistently exceed normative expectations, employ practices that increase children's enjoyment, agency, satisfaction, volition, self-efficacy, self-regulation, writer-identity, motivation, and thus their pleasure in writing. The practices include fostering a sense of community of writers who are engaged in meaningful practices; ensuring purposeful and relevant writing activities or tasks; promoting agency, for example, through choice and involving students in setting their learning goals; regarding writing as a social act and providing opportunities for dialogic talk; allowing sustained time for deep engagement with and practising of the craft; building self-efficacy in the writer through providing instructional input at the point of need; encouraging students to draw on their own funds of knowledge and ensuring supports that help students to become self-regulating; and linking reading and writing, including volitional reading to volitional writing.

To illustrate how the learning-enabling characteristics of play might be utilized for learning in the later primary years, an example is drawn from our research (Parr & Gadd, 2019). It was inspired by an article in our national newspaper that recalled for me a very powerful means by which a teacher in our research had described combining elements of interest, fun, enjoyment, and, relatedly, elements drawing on the students' cultural background, so that they perceived themselves as able communicators. The newspaper article (*NZ Herald*, 19 May 2019) featured four teens who had been invited to the world's largest slam poetry contest, the Brave New Voices Festival in Las Vegas. They were the first Australasian poets ever invited. Slam poetry is spoken word performance art, like rap without music, as one of them described it. The actions of the teacher in our research had targeted the same "genre" with her class. In this class, she had a number of boys who were reluctant writers. Many of them were of Pacific nations heritage, nations which possess a vibrant singing and rhythmic dancing culture, together with an oral tradition that requires accurate memorizing of stories and events of significance. The students had been undertaking a poetry unit in their schoolwork; they had been exploring rhyme, emphasis, and patterns in poetry, and were reading and studying examples that appealed to them. They could see the links to the rap and hip-hop music lyrics which they both identified with and enjoyed in their leisure time. The students wanted to write their own poems; these were a type of hybrid rap poem. Our sense was that, rather than regarding the pop culture of rap as an assimilative force as the Elders in Eppley et al. (this volume) did, the students and teacher (who was of Pacific nations heritage) brought to bear their own cultural knowledge and skills and appropriated hip-hop culture! They were very proud of their efforts as their classmates had reacted so positively to their compositions, so much so that they were prepared to "perform" the "poems," using their own style of voice and movement, for other peers outside their own class, even at a whole school assembly. As the teacher explained to us, this activity was a deliberate effort to connect to the interests of the students. She had hoped to find a way into writing that was fun for them. And, with their help, she had identified a means that would allow these often reluctant writers to showcase and build on strengths, in this case writing song or rap lyrics, an ability to memorize text, and to deliver engaging performance art. Performing their poems unquestionably helped students to see themselves as creators of meaning, as writers.

Conclusion

Writing is enabled by talk and notions of place and play, deliberately and judiciously employed and deployed by teachers aiming to develop writing and their writers. In this chapter, I have tried to illustrate the interplay of talk, place, and play in a way that reflects the Aotearoa New Zealand context. The historical and philosophical underpinnings of curricula involving notions of teaching the individual, teaching as inquiry, adapting pedagogy to meet the needs of individuals, and assessment as learning go some way in explaining that talk is a key means of knowing the developing writer, as expressed by teachers in our recent research (Parr & Gadd, 2019). The bicultural nature of Aotearoa New Zealand and its increasingly multicultural population add complexity in terms of teachers knowing the writer, including their linguistic and cultural background, knowledge, and experiences.

If a writer's identification with the context of writing and with the activities or tasks is central for writing and writer development, then enabling students to "see" themselves as participants in, and their world as germane to, writing, particularly the writing within schooling, is key. To do this, teachers need to gain an appreciation of the background of the student, particularly as it relates to language, heritage, and experience. For teachers, engagement in professional learning, inquiry, and reflection are essential to be able to glean and to utilize optimally the knowledge of the writers and their writing.

In each of the descriptions of classroom practice, the concepts of talk, place, and play – the latter in its sense of authentic, agentic action – are interwoven. It is fitting to conclude with an abridged version of a quote from a teacher (in the research of Si'ilata, 2014, p. 85). This is a teacher who proactively sought to know her class of 5-year-olds in order to use talk, place, and play to build bridges between the linguistic and cultural worlds that they inhabited. She deftly tapped into an experience the class had just shared, Cook Island dancing performed at the recent school gala day. She supported, through observations and genuine questions, one of the young performers to recreate it for the class, who joined the teacher in following the young girl as she expertly danced and explained what she was doing. This was a powerful springboard for writing.

> Basically, the shift I've made is that of knowing my learner ... [the process] has been huge for me and that involves building relationships as well. So it's knowing my learner and building relationships as a result of that and so, if I know my learner – I know who they are, I know where they are academically but I also know about them and their family and the history and the narrative that comes in with them ...

REFERENCES

Ashton-Warner, S. (1958). *Spinster*. London: Secker and Warburg.

Ashton-Warner, S. (1963). *Teacher*. London: Secker and Warburg.

Bishop, R., Berryman, M., Cavanagh, T., & Teddy, L. (2007). *Te Kōtahitanga phase 3 whānaungatanga: Establishing a culturally responsive pedagogy of relations in mainstream secondary school classrooms*. Report to the Ministry of Education. New Zealand Ministry of Education.

Britton, J. (1970). *Language and learning*. Penguin Books.

Clark, C., & Teravainen, A. (2017). *Writing for enjoyment and its link to wider writing*. National Literacy Trust.

Clay, M.M. (1998). *By different paths to common outcomes*. Stenhouse.

Cook-Sather, A. (2006). Sound, presence and power: Student voice in educational research and reform. *Curriculum Inquiry, 34*, 359–390. https://doi.org/10.1111/j.1467-873X.2006.00363.x

Eppley, K., Peterson, S.S., & Heppner, D. (2022). Valuing rural and Indigenous social practices: Play as placed learning in kindergarten classrooms. In S.S. Peterson & N. Friedrich (Eds.), *The role of place and play in young children's language and literacy* (pp. 17–31). University of Toronto Press.

Fisher, H. (2014). Using pupil perception in the primary classroom: An exploration of potential issues. *Research Papers in Education, 4,* 390–409. https://doi.org/10.1080/02671522.2013.776624

Gadd, M.O. (2014). *What is critical in the effective teaching of writing? A study of the classroom practice of some Year 5 to 8 teachers in the New Zealand context.* Unpublished doctoral thesis, University of Auckland.

Gadd, M.O., & Parr, J.M. (2017). Practices of effective writing teachers. *Reading and Writing, 30*(7), 1551–1574. https://doi.org/10.1007/s11145-017-9737-1

Gadd, M.O., Parr, J.M., et al. (2019). Portrait of the student as a young writer: Some student survey findings about attitudes to writing and self-efficacy as writers. *Literacy 53*(4), 226–235. https://doi.org/10.1111/lit.12178

Hedges, H. (2018). Play-based learning: Questions and invitations from early childhood education. *SET, 3,* 60–64.

Hedges, H., & Cooper, M. (2014). Engaging with holistic curriculum outcomes: Deconstructing "working theories." *International Journal of Early Years Education, 22*(4), 395–408. https://doi.org/10.1080/09669760.2014.968531

Lai, N.K., Ang, T.F., Por, L.Y., & Liew, C.S. (2018) The impact of play on child development – a literature review. *European Early Childhood Education Research Journal, 26*(5), 625–643. https://doi.org/10.1080/1350293X.2018.1522479

McDowall, S., & Parr, J.M. (2012). *Deliberate design: An analysis of the 2010–11 school journals and teacher support materials.* Report to the Ministry of Education. New Zealand Council for Educational Research.

Ministry of Education. (2007). *The New Zealand curriculum.* Learning Media.

Ministry of Education. (2009). *Ka hikitia: Managing for success.* Ministry of Education.

Ministry of Education. (2017). *Te Whāriki: The early childhood curriculum.* Ministry of Education.

O'Brien, G. (2007). *A nest of singing birds: 100 years of the New Zealand School Journal.* Learning Media.

Parr, J.M. (2017). Accelerating student progress in writing: Examining practices effective in New Zealand primary school classrooms. In E. Ortlieb, E.H. Cheek, & W. Verlaan (Eds.), *Writing instruction to support literacy success: Literacy research, practice and evaluation* (Vol. 7, pp. 41–64). Emerald Press.

Parr, J.M., & Gadd, M. (2019). *Generating positive outcomes by Year 5 to 8 priority learners in writing: An inquiry into effective teacher practice.* Final Report of TLRI Project. http://www.tlri.org.nz/tlri-research/research-completed/school-sector/generating-positive-outcomes-year-5-8-priority

Parr, J.M., & Limbrick, E. (2009). Contextualising practice: Hallmarks of effective teachers of writing. *Teaching and Teacher Education, 26*, 583–590. https://doi.org/10.1016/j.tate.2009.09.004

Rogoff, B., Callanan, M., Gutierrez, K.D., & Erickson, F. (2016). The organization of informal learning. *Review of Research in Education, 40*, 356–401. https://doi.org/10.3102/0091732X16680994

Si'ilata, R (2014). *Va'a Tele: Pasifika learners riding the success wave on linguistically and culturally responsive pedagogies.* Unpublished PhD thesis, University of Auckland.

Valsiner, J. (1997). *Culture and the development of children's action: A theory of human development* (2nd ed.). Wiley.

Wood, E. (2014a). Free choice and free play in early childhood: Troubling the discourse. *International Journal of Early Years Education, 22*(1), 4–18. https://doi.org/10.1080/09669760.2013.830562

Wood, E. (2014b). The play-pedagogy interface in contemporary debates. In L. Brooker, M. Blaise, & S. Edwards (Eds.), *The Sage handbook of play and learning in early childhood* (pp. 145–156). Sage.

Young, R. (2019). *What is it that writing for pleasure teachers do that makes the difference? What it means to write for pleasure.* Final Report to Goldsmith's Company, United Kingdom Literacy Association and the University of Sussex.

10 Scaffolding Community Literacy Practices in Kindergarten Classrooms

NICOLA FRIEDRICH

Tamara (all names are pseudonyms) and her students sit on camp chairs around a cardboard box wrapped in white paper. Tamara asks who has been ice fishing. Two of the children raise their hands. She brings out a small stick to which she attached a piece of string. She points to the small piece of plastic affixed to the end and explains that this is the "lure" used to attract fish. Tamara casts her line into the hole and, moments later, reels in a small fish, identifying it as a bass. While fishing, the students talk with Tamara about ice fishing. She shows them a slotted ladle and asks them what it might be used for. One student correctly identifies it as a tool to scoop slush from the ice hole. Tamara encourages them to take turns scooping out the slush from the hole. Once all of the fish are caught, Tamara asks the students to place their fish on top of the box. She picks them up one by one and points to the label printed on the back. She reads the name, asking the students to read it back to her. She then takes out a measuring tape and demonstrates how to measure its length. Tamara encourages each student to measure their fish using the measuring tape and read out the measurement to the group.

This vignette introduces us to a community-inspired play context within a kindergarten classroom in a rural town in Northern Ontario, Canada. Tamara is a participant in the Northern Oral Language and Writing through Play (NOW Play) project, a partnership between university researchers, classroom teachers, and early childhood educators (ECEs). Tamara initiated the ice-fishing context as one of her NOW Play action research projects. This vignette demonstrates her use of modelling and guided participation to support students' literacy and other learning in a place-based play context.

Researchers have expressed concern with the literacy scores of young rural children upon entering school (e.g., Durham & Smith, 2006) and questioned rural teachers' capacities to support their literacy learning (e.g., Stockard, 2011). The belief underlying such research is that literacy is a measurable skill and can be developed directly through teaching. My purpose in writing this chapter is to demonstrate rural teachers' ability to support young children's literacy and other learning by describing teacher-initiated, student-directed, community-inspired play contexts. I argue that, by combining elements from the pedagogical practices of guided play and place-based education, kindergarten teachers can move beyond scaffolding their students' emergent writing skills and towards fostering in them an understanding of text types and their uses in the community. The following questions guided my analysis:

- What play contexts did the educators initiate? What inspired the educators to initiate these contexts? How did the educators support the children's learning in these contexts?
- How did the children respond to the various types of informal scaffolding initiated by the educators in these contexts?
- What learning did these contexts support?

I have organized this chapter as follows: I begin by identifying the theoretical framework guiding my work and reviewing literature highlighting learning outcomes from the pedagogical approaches of guided play and place-based education. Next, I present a brief description of the NOW Play project and my research methodology. I then report the findings and discuss the significance and implications of the study for theory and practice.

Framework

Informing my approach are constructs from within the sociocultural perspective of learning and literacy (Vygotsky, 1978), whereby learning is understood as a lifelong process. Initially, adults transfer culturally specific ways of knowing and doing directly by guiding children's active participation in shared activities (Rogoff, 1990). Rogoff uses the metaphor of the *scaffold* to describe the type of guidance adults provide. Much like the temporary structures work crews use to extend their reach during construction, Rogoff suggests an adult's conscious structuring of tasks allows children to increasingly extend their level of knowledge and skills. Throughout their lifespan, through their ongoing participation in local communities of practice (Lave & Wenger, 1991), children continue to acquire diverse sets of cultural knowledge and performance capacities and skills (Erickson, 2002). As such, children learn to use tools from within their community, such as reading and writing, for their own purposes (Wertsch, 1998). Children develop understandings of and hypotheses about the form and function of print through their continued engagement in the act of writing (Harste et al., 1984; Teale & Sulzby, 1986).

Dramatic play acts as a stimulus for young children's developmental processes (Vygotsky, 1978). Role play is a form of activity through which children come to understand their surroundings (Elkonin, 2005). However, not all dramatic play events foster cognitive development. Children need to reach a level of *mature play*, where their individual roles and the sequence of their play actions are well defined (Elkonin, 2005). This level of play in early childhood classrooms is made possible through adult mediation (Bodrova & Leong, 2015).

Guided play blends adult initiation with child direction to achieve specific learning objectives (Wasik & Jacobi-Vessels, 2017; Weisberg et al., 2015). The extent of adult involvement in guided play varies. Adults may design and prepare the play environment to achieve a particular learning goal or simply observe child-directed activities and then extend their actions as the play unfolds over time (Weisberg et al., 2016).

Also guiding my work are tenets from within the sociocultural view of literacy. Within this view, literacy is understood as a set of social practices that individuals develop rather than as a measurable, independent skill (Street, 1984). Literacy practices, or the types of texts and the ways individuals use them (Barton & Hamilton, 2000), reflect the physical and cultural conditions of communities and inform children's early understanding of print (Corbett & Donehower, 2017; Eppley & Corbett, 2012; Purcell-Gates, 2013). Barton and Hamilton (2000) suggest literacy practices be inferred from literacy events which they define as "activities in which literacy plays a role. Usually there is written text or texts, central to the activity and there may be talk around the text" (p. 8).

Finally, I draw from concepts within the field of place-based education, which emphasize the rural context (Gruenewald, 2003a) and conceptualize the role of education as one of inquiry and action. Gruenewald (2003b) suggests teachers turn to one of three educational traditions to support their practice: natural history, cultural journalism (local history), and action research. These *pedagogies of place* can help guide teachers in identifying community features and resources that provide students with opportunities to engage in literacy-related activities to meet curricular standards (Lester, 2012). Thus teachers become brokers of community resources to support students as they create knowledge through their own lived experience (Smith, 2002).

In this chapter, I understand the educators' scaffolding, in the form of their structuring of tasks before and during play-based projects, as a pedagogical tool to support young children's developing hypotheses about print and to mediate their understanding of texts and their use within the community.

Related Literature

SUPPORTING LEARNING THROUGH PLACE-BASED EDUCATION

A small body of research demonstrates how teachers successfully use place-related texts to develop students' understanding of place. In these studies, teachers of students in younger grades had chosen picture books with strong settings (e.g., Wason-Ellam, 2010) and rural-based stories from basal readers (e.g., Waller & Barrentine, 2015), while teachers of middle and high school students had selected song lyrics, poems, and novels (e.g., Azano, 2010; Bishop, 2004; Hodges, 2004).

In addition to contributing to a child's developing sense of place, this research demonstrates how place-based pedagogy supports rural students' language development. Donovan (2016) conducted a descriptive case study to investigate the impact of place-based writing practices on her rural middle school students' use of language. Donovan co-created a unit to engage students in independent and interactive writing tasks around place in response to teacher read-alouds and formal classroom debates. From her analysis of student work samples, transcripts of interviews with the teachers and students, and her own field notes from classroom observation, Donovan concluded that this place-based approach to writing developed in students a valuing of place, which led to their creating more complex texts (i.e., increased text length, fewer grammatical issues).

SUPPORTING LEARNING THROUGH GUIDED PLAY

To determine the efficacy of guided play as a pedagogical practice, recent research drew data from researcher-designed interventions to support young children's vocabulary development. In the first of their two studies, Toub et al. (2018) trained intervention specialists (IS) to introduce low-income preschool children to target words during scripted 10-minute book-reading sessions. Each session was followed by a 10-minute play period. They randomly assigned children to three play conditions each differing in the level of scripted language use. In the second study, the teachers led book-reading sessions during which they taught the target words, followed by either a hybrid (guided/directed) play session or a picture card review session. Based on the children's gains as indicated by pre- and post-receptive and expressive vocabulary tests, Toub et al. concluded that adult-supported play provides unique benefits for young children's early vocabulary growth.

In contrast, Dickinson et al. (2018) found no statistically significant differences in children's vocabulary gains between their two experimental conditions of Reading Only and Reading + Play. In this study, participating Head Start and pre-kindergarten classrooms were randomly assigned to one of the two conditions. In both conditions, teachers led children in a group book reading, where they taught the children vocabulary. In the Reading + Play condition, teachers added a review of the target vocabulary during two play sessions with story-related figurines. Following the intervention, the researchers tested each child individually for expressive and receptive vocabulary, finding that children in both groups showed large effects for target words as compared to control words.

My interpretation of the scant literature on scaffolding children's learning through place-based education and guided play is that teachers can support their students' developing language skills and sense of place by encouraging them to read and respond to place-based texts. However, measured benefits to young children's vocabulary development from short periods of adult-assisted play in structured contexts are unclear.

NOW PLAY PROJECT

This project aims to support, through play, the oral and written language development of young children living in northern rural and Indigenous communities. We visited quarterly with educators in their classrooms to discuss possible action research (Cohen et al., 2005) projects to support students' learning through play. Based on these discussions, the educators initiated their own activities, themes, and scenarios, video recorded their students' participation, and took photos of any texts the children created during their participation in the initiative. We watched the videos and examined images of texts prior to revisiting the site. Then, during action research meetings, we discussed the recordings and artefacts. Together, we developed theoretical understandings of what the children's interactions revealed about their language, literacy, and social learning before brainstorming new initiatives. During the fifth year, we challenged educators to incorporate place-based learning within their projects. Data for this chapter were drawn from this set of projects.

Research within the NOW Play project has identified language (Peterson, 2015) and literacy (Friedrich & Portier, 2020; Peterson & Portier, 2016) outcomes associated with young children's dramatic play as well as how teachers successfully emphasized academics while maximizing play (Portier et al., 2019). For the latter study, we reviewed 41 of the action research projects for patterns in how the teachers supported their students' learning when they combined curricular outcomes with student-directed play. We found that each project espoused the spirit of guided play in that the primary role of the teacher was to observe and respond to their students' activity. In general, they supported student-led interactions by providing resources or by suggesting ways the students might collaborate to complete an activity, and scaffolding their literacy learning during individual writing events. For the most part, children directed their own participation within each project. They collaborated with others to shape and extend individual activities and storylines during dramatic play, explored ways to creatively express their ideas, and created written texts, often in collaboration with others. Within every project, we found evidence of literacy and other curricular learning.

Given these findings, I understand educators' place- and play-based educational practices as scaffolding young children's learning. In their chapter, Eppley et al. (this volume), described how Polly, a kindergarten teacher in northern rural Alberta, incorporated rural and blue-collar work in her play-based classroom. Similarly, Portier (this volume) illustrated how three Grade 1 teachers drew from their own connections to place to engage their students in meaningful learning through guided play. In this chapter, I demonstrate the capacity of rural educators in supporting their students' early literacy development and understandings of place by describing community-inspired, adult-initiated, student-directed, play-based projects in three kindergarten classrooms.

Methodology

Site and Participants

The kindergarten program in Ontario is a two-year program for children aged 3–5 years. A teacher and an ECE teach each class. Data informing this paper were drawn from three kindergarten classrooms in two schools in a small English-speaking service town (population 8,000) in Northern Ontario. Three teachers and two ECEs participated in the research; all spoke English and lived in the town.

Data Sources

Data sources included videotapes totalling 215 minutes of the children engaging in classroom activities related to the educators' action research projects, multiple pages of field notes from my action research meetings with the educators, and 41 samples of the children's texts created as part of the projects.

Data Analysis

After gathering the data, I watched the videos, noting the activity of the educators and children, specifically their actions at the beginning, middle, and end of the initiative. I read and reread these notes as well as notes from our action research meetings to identify patterns in relation to my research questions. I reviewed the textual artefacts and organized them according to their text type. In the following section, I present findings from this analysis. I begin by describing each individual project and highlighting the roles of the educators and students. I then discuss the instructional approach and demonstrate how this approach combines elements from two pedagogical traditions, guided play and place-based education.

Place-Based Learning through Guided Play

In response to our suggestion, the educators initiated projects based on elements from within the community. In each project, they guided their students' play and situated their writing within community-inspired play centres and during individual theme-related activities. Within the sociocultural contexts and during activities associated with the overall project, students enacted community roles that broadened their understanding of elements of place, and created different types of texts that extended their developing hypotheses about print and increased their awareness of how texts are used in the community.

Farmer's Market

Jennifer and Leslie's project was based on a community experience. The farmer's market, which Jennifer remembered visiting as a child, had been a mainstay in the community. The formal market no longer existed, although individuals could still pick up produce and other farm-related products from market stalls around the region. Jennifer and Leslie thought they would recreate the experience for their students in the classroom. To create the market centre, they repurposed the puppet stand as a market stall and brought in a small wooden gate. They sent out requests for pumpkins and brought in bags of leaves and sunflowers to scatter around the room. To supplement their pumpkin collection, they and their students stuffed small orange bags with tissue paper. Jennifer and Leslie initiated the project during a whole class read-aloud. Rather than sharing picture books with a strong local setting (Wason-Ellam,

2010) or target vocabulary (Dickinson et al., 2018; Toub et al., 2018), they stimulated their students' interest by reading fall-related books.

Throughout the month-long project, Jennifer and Leslie observed their students' actions and responded to their needs (Weisberg et al., 2016). At times, they provided the students with materials and resources to create props associated with the cultural practice they were enacting (e.g., a pie crust template to facilitate their making of pies). At other times, they prompted the children to collaborate while creating materials or while enacting roles at the market stall (e.g., suggesting reasonable time limits for students' role playing). Jennifer and Leslie also entered in role to extend their students' opportunity to write (e.g., taking on the role of a customer wanting to order a pumpkin). Finally, they stepped in to assist students individually during writing events (e.g., assisting with the sounding out of words).

Initially, the students responded by taking part in the group read-alouds, asking questions about pumpkins, making suggestions as to how to solve small issues that arose during the setting up of the market centre, and initiating writing activities to support their play in the centre. For example, the students created banners, signs, price lists, and product labels, and copied recipes. Throughout the month, they participated in dramatic play at the market stall centre by taking on roles such as selling pumpkins, making and selling pies, and ordering and purchasing pumpkins and pies. Their role playing afforded them the opportunity to engage in community literacy practices (Barton & Hamilton, 2000). For example, when enacting the role of farmer, they recorded their customers' orders, listed items available for purchase, and labelled items and objects on shelves. In their role as bakers, they recorded recipes on cardstock prior to their making of pies. Finally, when enacting the role of customer, they filled out order forms and signed their name.

Flower Shop

In recognition of the importance of the local greenhouse and market garden to their community, Dawn and Anna selected a flower shop as their project. Dawn shared that many teachers, herself included, scheduled annual class field trips to the greenhouse. In preparation for this year's field trip, she and Anna set up a flower shop centre in the classroom. They positioned a bookshelf and small table to replicate the front counter and added resources including artificial flowers and flower pots, watering cans and spray bottles, blank cards, ribbon, and tissue paper. They provided a toy phone, cash register, and play money along with clipboards and pens. Thus, rather than stocking the centres with materials to recreate a specific story and achieve a specific learning outcome (see Dickinson et al., 2018; Toub et al., 2018), Dawn and Anna included materials to mediate the students' enactment of roles related to the flower shop. Once the centre was in place, rather than reading a place-based text (see Wason-Ellam, 2010), they led a class discussion about activities within a flower shop and modelled (Rogoff, 1990) the roles of florist, salesperson, and customer.

Throughout the month, Dawn and Anna observed their students' activities and responded accordingly (Weisberg et al., 2016). For example, they supported the students' individual writing by providing materials (e.g., folded paper and markers for cards) and assisting with their writing attempts (e.g., pointing to individual words around the classroom, sounding out words for or with the student). At times, they extended their students' participation by initiating whole group activities. For example, they read flower-themed books during group read-alouds and directed whole class inquiries (Gruenewald, 2003a) to investigate flowers (e.g., learning how to plant flowers, understanding the life cycle of flowers, recognizing the different parts of a flower).

The students responded to the educators' initiatives and direction throughout the project. They actively participated (Gruenewald, 2003a) in group discussions and volunteered for roles during the educators' role-playing events. In preparation for play, they created money using scrap pieces of paper and coloured pens. Then, drawing from the educators' modelling, during free play in the classroom, they took up literacy practices (Barton & Hamilton, 2000) in their role of buyer and seller at the flower shop. As florist, they recorded orders on scraps of paper and composed messages in the folded cards. They also calculated the cost of an order and collected the money from the customer, and assembled and delivered flower orders. As customers, they placed orders, either over the phone or in person, and paid for the order at the counter.

Ice Fishing

Ice fishing is a popular winter activity in the north. Fishers set up huts on frozen rivers and lakes and drill holes through the ice. Since many of these huts were visible from her classroom window, Tamara decided to initiate a week-long ice-fishing theme in her classroom. Rather than creating a centre to support her students' dramatic play, Tamara aimed to achieve a specific learning goal (Weisberg et al., 2016) by initiating a series of activities to simulate the cultural practice of ice fishing (Smith, 2002).

Tamara stocked a corner of the classroom with a frozen lake (cardboard box covered in white paper with a hole cut into the top), fishing rods (strings tied to magnets and attached to sticks), and fish (printed images of fish on cardstock glued to small magnets). She placed child-sized lawn chairs around the lake and measuring tapes near the lake. She also provided students with a template of a fishing licence. First, she printed a picture of each student and then guided them through the process of completing the license. For example, the children printed their name, the date the licence was issued, and the date the licence would expire. They also included personal information such as their date of birth and their eye colour.

As demonstrated in the opening vignette, Tamara, working with small groups of students, introduced the children to the act of catching fish through a hole in the ice. The goal of this activity was to actively engage the students in the fishing experience. Ideally, this place-based experience would have involved field trips (Wason-Ellam, 2010) to ice-fishing huts on the frozen lake. However, for safety reasons, she decided to recreate the experience in her classroom. Next, she demonstrated how to measure the fish using either the measuring tape on-site or measuring it against the scale she had pinned to the wall. Again, for safety reasons, rather than having the students use knives in the classroom, she invited a guest to demonstrate how to clean fresh fish and identify the different parts of the fish. She ended the week with an inquiry project involving a cooking demonstration and fish tasting. She also set up and stocked a writing table where students could share their ice-fishing experiences with others.

Tamara's students responded to the various small and large group activities related to the ice-fishing theme and took up the various cultural practices related to ice fishing (Rogoff, 1990). For example, they filled out their fishing licences; caught, identified, and measured laminated images of fish; and tasted different varieties of cooked fish, offering their opinion as to which tasted the best. They also observed cultural practices related to ice fishing. For example, they observed their guest cleaning the fresh fish and Tamara preparing and cooking the fish.

In sum, Leslie, Jennifer, Dawn, Anna, and Tamara initiated student-directed, community-inspired projects that fostered in their students an appreciation of community practices and broadened their understanding of texts and how they are used in the community. I conclude this chapter with a discussion of the unique form of pedagogical practice underlying these projects. I argue that this pedagogical practice afforded the educators opportunities to scaffold cultural and school-like practices during play initiatives. In so doing, the educators supported their students' overall literacy development.

Discussion

Guided play, a form of play that combines child autonomy and adult guidance (Weisberg et al., 2016), is considered developmentally appropriate pedagogy (Weisberg et al., 2013). Research has demonstrated the effect of guided play as a pedagogical condition on young children's understanding of shape (Fisher et al., 2013) and expressive vocabulary (Toub et al., 2018). The goal of place-based education is, according to Smith (2002), "to ground learning in local phenomena and students' lived experience" (p. 586). Teachers can successfully initiate playful, collaborative classroom activities that support students' natural ways of interacting with their local place (Portier, this volume). And, as Wason-Ellam (2010) demonstrated, through their engagement with place-related texts and their participation in experiential learning, both in and outside of the classroom, "students find a *place* in their communities" (p. 291, italics in original).

In response to research that questions the literacy abilities of rural children (e.g., Durham & Smith, 2006) and views the literacy teaching capacities of rural teachers (e.g., Stockard, 2011) as lacking, in this chapter, based on my analysis of activities and their texts, I created descriptions of three educator-initiated projects: Farmer's Market, Flower Shop, and Ice Fishing. Each description served to demonstrate how these rural educators drew elements from both guided play and place-based education to scaffold their students' social and cognitive learning. Specifically, they structured and initiated community-inspired play-based contexts that afforded students the opportunity to direct their own participation in activities, providing support only when needed. In so doing, I suggest this unique pedagogical practice scaffolded the students learning, specifically their learning about community and their learning of literacies.

Learning about Community

The purpose of both a farmer's market and flower shop is to provide local goods to the community; thus the people who work in these businesses are considered part of the service sector. Through their recreation of these contexts within the classroom, Leslie, Jennifer, Dawn, and Anna were able to scaffold their students' active engagement in service-related activities mediated by texts. After designing and preparing the classroom environment (Weisberg et al., 2016), they modelled cultural practices so that students could create knowledge through their own lived experiences (Smith, 2002). Based on their observations of their students' activity (Weisberg et al., 2016), the educators further supported their students' learning about community by entering the students' play in role or by providing opportunities for them to reflect in writing on the various activities.

The freshwater lake adjacent to Tamara's town supports a number of recreational activities including fishing. Much of the town's population engages in the seasonal practice of ice fishing. Tamara recreated elements from this practice to simulate the ice-fishing experience for small groups of students. She also designed and implemented whole group inquiries (Gruenewald, 2003a) to scaffold their learning about fish and about the practice of fishing, including bringing in a guest to demonstrate how to clean fish and challenging her students to distinguish the taste of different fish.

Learning Literacies

Students in all three classrooms demonstrated literacy and other learning-related behaviours as they created texts to mediate their participation in activities within the various community-inspired contexts (Wertsch, 1998). Specifically, they recorded customer orders on forms and recipes on cardstock, and composed messages in cards and narratives on printed templates. They listed on paper items available for purchase and labelled on cardstock or sticky notes items and objects on shelves. They filled out forms, cards, and licences, and signed their names. I suggest that, as active participants in these writing events, the students further developed their growing hypotheses about print (Harste et al., 1982; Teale & Sulzby, 1986).

Moreover, the students' guided participation in the various role-playing opportunities within these contexts scaffolded their take-up of numerous community literacy practices mediated by cultural texts (Rogoff, 1990). For example, they created signs and banners to inform others of items available for sale, designed cards to share specific sentiments and forms to organize information, and made their own money so they could purchase items. In light of their active engagement, I suggest the children learned the social purposes of and features specific to each genre of community text (Corbett & Donehower, 2017; Eppley & Corbett, 2012; Purcell-Gates, 2013).

Conclusion

My purpose in writing this chapter is to offer a differing view of literacy education in the rural context by demonstrating the capacity of a small group of northern rural educators to support their students' literacy learning and foster in them an understanding of place through community-inspired, guided play activities in their classrooms. It is my hope that this small descriptive study will encourage other rural educators to adopt a broader understanding of literacy, one that includes an understanding of texts and the community practices they mediate, and then scaffold their students' literacy learning by actively engaging them in place-based, playful activities in the classroom.

REFERENCES

Azano, A. (2010). The possibility of place: One teacher's use of place-based instruction for English students in a rural high school. *Journal of Research in Rural Education, 26*(10), 1–12. Retrieved from http://jrre.psu.edu/articles/26-10.pdf

Barton, D., & Hamilton, M. (2000). Literacy practices. In D. Barton, M. Hamilton, & R. Ivanic (Eds.), *Situated literacies: Reading and writing in context* (pp. 7–15). London: Routledge.

Bishop, S. (2004). The power of place. *The English Journal, 93*(6), 65–69. https://doi.org/10.2307/4128896

Bodrova, E., & Leong, D. J. (2015). Vygotskian and post-Vygotskian views on children's play. *American Journal of Play, 7*(3), 371–388. Retrieved from https://files.eric.ed.gov/fulltext/EJ1070266.pdf

Cohen, L., Manion, L., & Morrison, K. (2005). *Research methods in education* (5th ed.). Routledge Falmer.

Corbett, M., & Donehower, K. (2017). Rural literacies: Toward social cartography. *Journal of Research in Rural Education, 32*(5), 1–13.

Dickinson, D.K., Collins, M.F., Nesbitt, K., Toub, T.S., Hassinger-Das, B., Hadley, E. B., . . . Golinkoff, R.M. (2018). Effects of teacher-delivered book reading and play on vocabulary learning and self-regulation among low-income preschool children. *Journal of Cognition and Development*. https://doi.org/10.1080/15248372.2018.1483373

Donovan, E. (2016). Learning the language of home: Using place-based writing practice to help rural students connect to their communities. *The Rural Educator, 37*(2). https://doi.org/10.35608/ruraled.v37i2.267

Durham, R.E., & Smith, P.J. (2006). Nonmetropolitan status and kindergarteners' early literacy skills: Is there a rural disadvantage? *Rural Sociology, 71*(4), 625–662. https://doi.org/10.1526/003601106781262052

Elkonin, D.B. (2005). The subject of our research: The developed form of play. *Journal of Russian and East European Psychology, 43*(1), 22–48. https://doi.org/10.1080/10610405.2005.11059242

Eppley, K., & Corbett, M. (2012). I'll see that when I believe it: A dialogue on epistemological difference and rural literacies. *Journal of Research in Rural Education, 27*(1), 1–9.

Eppley, K., Peterson, S. S., & Heppner, D. (2022). Valuing rural and Indigenous social practices: Play as placed learning in kindergarten classrooms. In S.S. Peterson & N. Friedrich (Eds.), *The role of place and play in young children's language and literacy* (pp. 17–31). University of Toronto Press.

Erickson, F. (2002). Culture and human development. *Human Development, 45*, 299–306. https://doi.org/10.1159/000064993

Fisher, K.R., Hirsh-Pasek, K., Newcombe, N., & Golinkoff, R.M. (2013). Taking shape: Supporting preschoolers' acquisition of geometric knowledge through guided play. *Child Development, 84*(6), 1872–1878. https://doi.org/10.1111/cdev.12091

Friedrich, N., & Portier, C. (2020). Let's go to the movies: Children's textual practices before and during a play-based classroom initiative. *Texas Journal of Literacy Education, 8*(1), 38–55. http://talejournal.com/index.php/TJLE/article/view/41/16.

Gruenewald, D.A. (2003a). The best of both worlds: A critical pedagogy of place. *Educational Researcher, 32*(4), 3–12. https://doi.org/10.3102%2F0013189X032004003

Gruenewald, D.A. (2003b). Foundations of place: A multidisciplinary framework for place-conscious education. *American Educational Research Journal, 40*(3), 619–654. https://doi.org/10.3102%2F00028312040003619

Harste, J.C., Burke, C.L., & Woodward, V.A. (1982). Children's language and world: Initial encounters with print. In J.A. Langer & M.T. Smith-Burke (Eds.), *Reader meets author/Bridging the gap: A psycholinguistic and sociolinguistic perspective* (pp. 105–131). International Reading Association.

Hodges, V.P. (2004). Using a sense of place to teach at-risk rural students. *The English Journal, 93*(6), 27–30. https://doi.org/10.2307/4128889

Lave, J., & Wenger, E. (1991). *Situated learning: Legitimate peripheral participation.* Cambridge University Press.

Lester, L. (2012). Putting rural readers on the map: Strategies for rural literacy. *The Reading Teacher, 66*(6), 407–415. https://doi.org/10.1002/TRTR.01062

Peterson, S.S. (2015). Supporting primary students' writing through reading, talk, and literate dramatic play in primary classrooms. *The Oklahoma Reader, 5*(1). https://now-play.org/publications/

Peterson, S.S., & Portier, C. (2016). Teaching vocabulary and writing in kindergarten through dramatic play centres. *Colorado Reading Journal, 27*, 25–32.

Portier, C. (2022). Enriching learning with the richness around us. In S.S. Peterson & N. Friedrich (Eds.), *The role of place and play in young children's language and literacy* (pp. 177–193). University of Toronto Press.

Portier, C., Friedrich, N., & Peterson, S.S. (2019). Play(ful) pedagogical practices for creative collaborative literacy. *The Reading Teacher, 73*(1), 17–27. https://doi.org/10.1002/trtr.1795

Purcell-Gates, V. (2013). Literacy worlds of children of migrant farmworker communities participating in a Migrant Head Start program. *Research in the Teaching of English, 48*(1), 68–97.

Rogoff, B. (1990). *Apprenticeship in thinking.* Oxford University Press.

Smith, G.A. (2002). Place-based education: Learning to be where we are. *Phi Delta Kappan, 83,* 584–594. https://doi.org/10.1177%2F003172170208300806

Stockard, J. (2011). Increasing reading skills in rural areas: An analysis of three school districts. *Journal of Research in Rural Education, 26*(8), 1–19. http://jrre.psu.edu/articles/26-8.pdf

Street, B. (1984). *Literacy in theory and practice.* Cambridge University Press.

Teale, W.H., & Sulzby, E. (1986). Emergent literacy as a perspective for examining how young children become writers and readers. In W.H. Teale & E. Sulzby (Eds.), *Emergent literacy: Writing and reading* (pp. vii–xxv). Ablex Publishing.

Toub, T.S., Hassinger-Das, B., Nesbitt, K.T., Ilgaz, H., Weisberg, D.S., Hirsh-Pasek, K., ... Dickinson, D.K. (2018). The language of play: Developing preschool vocabulary through play following shared book-reading. *Early Childhood Research Quarterly, 45*(2018), 1–17. https://doi.org/10.1016/j.ecresq.2018.01.010

Vygotsky, L. (1978). *Mind in society.* Harvard University Press.

Waller, R., & Barrentine, S.J. (2015). Rural elementary teachers and place-based connections to text during reading instruction. *Journal of Research in Rural Education, 30*(7), 1–13.

Wasik, B.A., & Jacobi-Vessels, J.L. (2017). Word play: Scaffolding language development through child-directed play. *Early Childhood Education Journal, 45,* 769–776. https://doi.org/10.1007/s10643-016-0827-5

Wason-Ellam, L. (2010). Children's literature as a springboard to place-embodied learning. *Environmental Education Research, 16*(3–4), 279–294. https://doi.org/10.1080/13504620903549771

Weisberg, D.S., Hirsh-Pasek, K., Golinkoff, R.M., Kittredge, A.K., & Klahr, D. (2016). Guided play: Principles and practices. *Current Directions in Psychological Science, 25*(3), 177–182. https://doi.org/10.1177/0963721416645512

Weisberg, D.S., Kittredge, A.K., Hirsh-Pasek, K., Golinkoff, R.M., & Klahr, D. (2015). Making play work for education. *Phi Delta Kappan, 96*(8), 8–13. https://doi.org/10.1177%2F0031721715583955

Wertsch, J. (1998). *Mind as action.* Oxford University Press.

11 Children's Engagement and Inquiry in Outdoors Contexts as Play- and Place-Based Learning

GISELA WAJSKOP

WITH THE ASSISTANCE OF DEBORA MACLEAN
AND BEATRIZ GOZZI

São Paulo Social and Schooling Contexts

São Paulo, the largest financial and economic centre in Brazil, is among the most populous cities in the world, with numerous cultural institutions and a rich architectural tradition. With an estimated population of 12,252,023 inhabitants, it has only 107 municipal parks. Only 74.8% of its streets have trees, and those are in middle- and upper-class neighbourhoods. Neighbourhoods in the urban fringes – to which the poor are relegated – fare much worse. Thus, poor children do not benefit from the natural environments within the city.

The current configuration of the city of São Paulo reflects a history of socio-spatial segregation throughout the twentieth century, which deepened in the 1980s. It has been described by Caldeira (2003) as the "city of walls." A culture of fear separates the different social groups in a drastic way through the use of walls, private security technologies, and differential access to public spaces. Children of the most privileged neighbourhoods are raised in closed condos, with no freedom to walk through the streets or squares. They are "kept safe" in schools or in their homes. Poor children do not live in communities with walls or gates, so they have ready access to the street as a leisure and play space. Thus, they can enjoy the freedom and autonomy that children in the most privileged neighbourhoods are denied (Nosek, 2018). This freedom, however, exposes them to all types of urban violence such as aggression, abandonment, exploitation, and frequent contact with drugs. Only 5% of São Paulo residents who participated in a recent survey (Instituto Brasileiro de Opinião Pública e Estatística, 2019) felt that public squares and parks are very safe, and 7% felt that sports courts are very safe. Thirty-four per cent consider no public spaces to be safe. Because of the fear of violence, Brazilian children are highly dependent on adults to go out in public, further distancing them from the spontaneous exploration of public spaces, mainly squares and parks.

As I show in this chapter, schools can provide an experiential alternative in relation to the safety and contact of children with open places and nature. I first situate the experience of an inquiry unit, taking place in outdoors spaces in a lab school in São Paolo, within broader education in Brazil.

Public education is mandatory for children from 4 to 18 years of age in Brazil. Basic Education is made up of early childhood education (daycare centres and preschools), elementary/primary school (children ages 6 to 10 years old), secondary school (11 to 15 years old), and high school (16 to 18 years old). In 2019 (Brazil, 2019), 67.6% of the 15,018,498 students between the ages of 6 and 10 years were attending schools within the municipal network of schools. In Brazil, the municipal network has the main responsibility for the provision of daycare centres, preschools, and primary schools. Nineteen per cent of students attend schools in private networks.

Since 1999, schools have been required to develop environmental education projects (Brazil, 1999). However, according to data from the last School Census (Brazil, 2019), most Brazilian public and private daycare centres and preschools do not have natural spaces, such as parks, gardens, and other recreational areas, in their infrastructure. Only 28.9% of municipal early childhood centres have natural spaces and in private schools this percentage is also low (33.2%). In elementary schools for children aged 6 to 10 years, resources associated with sports and leisure activities, such as sports courts and patios (covered or uncovered), are also in short supply, with 31.4% of municipal schools having sports courts and leisure spaces and 64.7% having sports courts and patios. In private schools, this percentage increases slightly to 59.9% (sports and leisure) and 89.6% (sports courts and patios). The situation is very similar in the city of São Paulo (Qedu, 2020). In 2018, only 49% of the 29,245 Basic Education schools in São Paulo had sports courts. Access to nature in daycare centres and schools is scarce, and little encouragement and few resources are provided for teachers to teach about the natural world and create a sense of place (Pereira & Benati, 2019).

The challenges to creating a sense of place are compounded by the absence of play as a valued pedagogical practice in São Paulo schools. Despite the continuous efforts of curriculum and policy developers to insert play in official programs (São Paulo, 2017; Brazil, 2017), research shows that time for play has been decreasing in daycare centres and preschools (Barros, 2008; Wajskop, 2012) and in primary schools (Ciardella,

2019; Palma, 2017; Rocha & Ribeiro, 2017), as pedagogical practices take a "banking education" perspective (Freire, 1996) that is geared towards children's future formal literacy learning. Play is sometimes conceived as recreation, and is thus viewed as a waste of time in relation to abstract learning, literacy exercises, and moral education. Commercial materials, such as textbooks, have been replacing direct experiences with nature and with others.

In this chapter, I report on an investigative unit developed over a semester in one of the combined kindergarten/Grade 1 classes of a lab school in São Paulo – Escola do Bairro. I situate the inquiry within the school's conceptualizations of the intrinsic relationship between nature and culture, and within sociocultural theoretical foundations about inquiry, play, and learning.

Escola do Bairro and a Sense of Place

Escola do Bairro is located in Vila Mariana, a middle-class residential neighbourhood in São Paulo; it was initially populated by Asian and Jewish immigrants and now has residents from diverse cultural backgrounds. The school was designed to be welcoming and to provide a sense of community within the neighbourhood for families, students, teaching professionals, and employees. The school offers daycare, preschool, and primary school for children from 1 to 10 years old. The location of the school was strategically chosen to allow for the use of the many public spaces, such as parks, museums, libraries, communities, and cultural centres, in the neighbourhood.

Escola do Bairro (translated literally as "school of the neighbourhood") is both a name and a concept. Inspired by Santos (1999), the school is conceived as place delimited in time and space but which is defined by use, that is, by the relationships and interdependence of those who occupy it. Children's and adults' daily interactions help them to build a sense of belonging as citizens of a neighbourhood and perhaps of city. As Santos (1999) explains, our notion of space or territory is "something that is in process ... that constitutes the link between the immediate past and the future" (p. 17). Taking up this perspective, teachers in Escola do Bairro consider the school as a place of choice with ties to the broader geographic and natural world and to the neighbourhood's history, all of which can be explored through inquiry. Our school, thus, can be a possible site of ethical and political action through inquiry that recognizes the importance of neighbourhood and community. The inquiry also promotes connections between past and present; it acknowledges the influences of geography, topography, flora, and fauna, and is framed by an understanding of the importance of cultural human production and relationships (Duncan et al., 2016).

In the backyard of Escola do Bairro, the four elements – earth, water, air, and fire – are present daily. There are several biomes of Brazilian flora which attract native fauna, especially birds and garden animals. Children have daily contact with nature, and are part of whole-school initiatives to preserve the natural elements. A strategically placed pond of ornamental fish and tadpoles, an open-air worm farm, and specimens of banana trees and coffee trees show the children a typical Brazilian environment. There is also a treehouse equipped with pulleys, ropes, and all sorts of loose parts, a wooden house built by Grade 2 in 2018, and herbal spirals in structures that invite children and adults to think about the role of the environment in their lives.

Play- and Place-Based Learning as a School Social Context for Inquiry

Escola do Bairro's program is based on a view that learning occurs in social contexts and that classroom talk is a cultural tool for more than communication (Elkonin, 1998; Goncü, 1999; Vygotsky, 1979). Through talk, children and adults make sense of and organize their world. Teachers structure a safe learning climate, based on trust, for children to use talk to get things done and to find out about the world in which they live.

As a messy and inconclusive process, talk in children's play is talk in use; "real talk" that is meaningful, exploratory, and engaging (Boyd & Galda, 2011). As they assume different roles or characters and incorporate known or unfamiliar objects in their play, children access and use what they know about the subject of the play, about the use of objects, about the place in which they are playing, and about language itself. To adapt the use of objects to make-believe, children need some meta-representational cognitive skills that are built through free play and improvised social exchanges (Smith, 2007). Thus, talk in play supports children's abstract learning at the same time as it supports their language development.

In their play, children use explicit language, metalanguage, and narrative language, which are important in early literacy (Pellegrini & Galda, 2000). Children select, develop, and put into practice their imagination, talk, and knowledge without direct adult intervention. Indeed, recent research shows that children's play may be more developed in the presence of peers than in the presence of adults. This allows children to think about and to solve problems free from the situational pressures of their immediate reality (Vygotsky, 1979).

When children play with open and unstructured heuristic (without explicit form) toys, they develop abstract thinking that supports literacy because they have to think, communicate, and negotiate with peers using language (Pellegrini & Galda, 2000). On the other hand, when playing with realistic toys, they use real talk to negotiate the meaning of the objects' use in play, drawing on their everyday-life concepts, procedures, and values. Observing and listening to children talking in their play and exploration provides teachers with a window into children's knowledge of everyday life.

Classroom environments can be set up intentionally for inquiry and the learning of scientific concepts through play. In these environments, children explore, listen, record, and explain ideas and theories about natural and sociocultural phenomena. According to Vygotsky (1979), children develop understandings of concepts through concrete experiences with their world. However, they are not aware of the act of thinking about them until they have words to give shape to the understandings and ideas. Scientific concepts begin with their verbal definition and are used in non-spontaneous and intentional operations and in response to contact with information sources. In this movement that goes from play to science through teacher mediation, children develop and incorporate scientific concepts into their funds of knowledge in a deliberate and conscious way.

As Kristina Belancic (this volume) points out, the notion of place consciousness is important in research and practice, "as both culture and place are constructive to human understanding and to students' academic achievement." As she indicates, previous research focusing on place-based learning, has shown that "outdoor play and learning are significant contributors to children's overall development and learning" (p. 55).

Teachers at Escola do Bairro take up a play- and place-based pedagogical approach. Through real talk (Boyd & Galda, 2011), teachers provide children with opportunities to observe, ask questions, and explore ideas, as they create and modify their provisional and spontaneous theories (Vygotsky, 1979). We can see a sample of this process in a K-1 teacher's classroom. I introduce the physical space of the classroom and then describe two inquiry projects, one at the fish pond and the other at the tree with pulleys.

Classroom Context and Inquiry Process

The inquiry described in this chapter takes place in a classroom of 14 children between the ages of 5 and 6 years old in a combined kindergarten and Grade 1 (K-1) class. Living, playing, and learning in a multi-age group allow the children to learn from classmates with varying levels of experience. The children attend school for six hours every day.

The classroom contains a sink and materials for both wet learning activities, such as ink and water experiments, and dry activities, such as reading and writing. The children spend much time engaged in outdoor learning activities as well. The outdoor learning is considered to be of equal pedagogical importance to indoor learning. In addition, the children have classes in capoeira, music, and English. (Capoeira is an Afro-Brazilian martial art, developed by enslaved Africans in Brazil in the early sixteenth century, that combines elements of combat, dance, and music.) The children also have a snack and have dinner together before their family members pick them up to go home.

The front of the classroom overlooks the backyard, where there is a fish pond, sand tank, and treehouse. The treehouse has a pulley system intentionally installed to stimulate questions among the children (see Figure 11.1).

The inquiry practices of teachers in our school start with careful observation and attentive listening to the children's actions and talk and by creating environments with real-life materials related to the local community. Teachers provide space for the children to explore, talk, and think about everyday concepts, procedures, and values. They stand back and watch what the children do with materials, observing the children's movements, the types of things they gravitate towards, and the things they ignore. They reflect on their observations by asking:

1. What do the children's actions and talk tell us?
2. Can we provide other materials and information to deepen and transform the children's knowledge?
3. Does considering what the children are showing us – through their talk and actions in play – about what they want to know broaden our perspective and expectations?
4. How can we help the children explore answers to big questions, such as, How does the world work? How does my community interact? What are my family values?

Observing, creating questions, and inviting children to compare, analyse, explain, and communicate are at the heart of the inquiries, as demonstrated in the following two examples of inquiries at Escola do Bairro.

Engagement and Inquiry in Outdoors Contexts   165

Figure 11.1 Children play at the Escola do Bairro's backyard
Source: Escola do Bairro

Fish Pond Inquiry

As shown in Figure 11.2, the fish pond is planted with tropical plants from the Brazilian rainforest. Over a vacation period, the plants were changed. When the children returned from the vacation, the K-1 teacher and her students walked around and sat beside the fish pond. The teacher invited the children to observe, talk, and then draw what they noticed was the same and what had been changed in and around the pond. The children noticed the number of new plants.

166 Gisela Wajskop

Figure 11.2 Children looking at the pond surrounded by tropical plants from the Brazilian rainforest

The teacher then asked the children what they would have to do to keep the fish pond environment alive. Several theories were made explicit by the children in their talk:

- "To keep the plants alive, we need to feed them with water";
- "Since plants are living things, we can't remove the leaves because they are the plants' veins";
- "Teacher, how are we going to care for the plants we don't know?" (showing that they have identified a specific type of knowledge needed in order to solve the problem)

After listening to the children explore ideas about keeping living things alive, the teacher initiated an inquiry by asking, "If you needed to tell someone about these new school plants, which one would you choose?" This inquiry led the children to create a catalogue of plants. The children deepened their knowledge by consulting source materials, both in botany and in the visual arts. The teacher also invited the children to draw, paint, and write, incorporating the tools of sociocultural knowledge into learning activities.

This place-based inquiry led the children to learn about the history and the cultural importance of various plants, enriching their experience with the plants. In this inquiry, natural phenomena in the children's daily life were the subject of exploration through concrete experience, reading, drawing, writing, and talk. Throughout the learning process, the children's subjective reality was maintained, and also was modified and reconstructed (Berger & Luckman, 1985).

Creating learning opportunities for children through place-based inquiry requires that teachers listen attentively to children's talk and observe closely what children do. Teachers must also be curious, acting as co-apprentices as they learn together with children. This involves asking questions to find out about children's understandings and perspectives, and then using what they learn in order to create and organize teaching and learning activities.

Treehouse Pulleys Inquiry

At the end of summer, the children began investigating weights and measures while experimenting and playing with ropes and wires suspended from one of the pulleys fixed to the treehouse (see Figure 11.3). Initially, the pulleys, inspired by Leonardo da Vinci's gear wheels, were installed to transport objects from the sand tank to the house.

While playing with the pulleys, one of the children connected the end of the pulley rope to the wire rope, generating a kind of balance. A new use of the pulley system emerged from this experimentation. For days after, the children turned the contraption they had created into a small elevator, trying to raise each other from the backyard up to the second level of the treehouse. They began an investigation into the mechanics of objects and the relationship between weight and human strength. In their play, which simulates aspects of real life, provisional and everyday-life concepts or pre-scientific theories (Vygotsky, 1979) guided the children's play and reflections.

The teacher mediated the children's learning of scientific concepts by suggesting that they record with chalk on the backyard wall the relationship between the number of children needed to raise

Figure 11.3 Children play with the treehouse pulleys in Escola do Bairro's backyard

various classmates from the backyard to the second level of the treehouse. She offered to be part of the scientific process by asking, "How many children are needed to lift me?" According to Boyd & Galda (2011), with this question the teacher provided "a collaborative environment, valuing students as knowledgeable and interesting human beings, and providing opportunities for extended explorations of ideas through talk" (p. 14), creating conditions for effective discussions.

As shown in Figures 11.4 and 11.5, their inquiry process involved playful exploration, using their bodies and their thinking to answer the questions that guided their inquiry.

While the children played, they talked and thought about their findings, sharing their own opinions and everyday-life concepts. Some days after this activity took place, the teacher stimulated further inquiry by asking an open-ended question: "Do children the same size have the same weight?" This time, the children were to write with a peer their responses to the question. Samples of their writing are found in Figure 11.6 and Figure 11.7. The English translation of the children's writing is below the figure.

The children's different hypotheses reflect the ways in which they made meaning from their shared experiences in the place-based inquiry. They used everyday experiences and concepts such as age, dress, weight, and strength to discuss important scientific topics. In regard to such shared experience, Kristina Belancic indicates that children "identify the schoolyard as a cultural and geographical place that provides them with the opportunity to draw on their cultural knowledge; as the children realize that those who are more competent have to support the less competent, they value the friendship of peers, and they create a space where it is acceptable and safe to use any language" (this volume, p. 60).

At the beginning of the inquiry, the children used only the words known from their everyday-life repertoire, naming the materials as rope, weight, and wheel. Noting the need to expand the scientific vocabulary, the teacher brought a video that presented the internal workings of an elevator and some reference books on the same subject. In addition, she showed the children the mechanical workings of the school's internal elevator and asked the children to draw what they observed. The children began to integrate the concepts of weight and balance, calling the rope and wheel by their more specific and scientifically oriented names: pulleys and steel cables.

The next step was the construction, in pairs and groups of three, of an elevator prototype. The children used materials made available by the teacher: scissors, string, construction pieces, adhesive tape, and wooden toothpicks. The development of small elevators consolidated the assimilation of the concepts of physics that were part of the inquiry. The children created the cabins and attached them to the rope that was also connected to the counterweight and the pulleys, thus allowing their movement. The children explained the operation of their elevators, suggesting that the weight of the cabin and the counterweight could balance, descend, and rise with the weight of the elevator passengers. The group learned

Figure 11.4 Children trying out the pulley to raise a girl in the rope seat.

the scientific concepts and language, as we can see in their statements: "Teacher, I will make the pulleys with the Lego car wheel," "The string will be the steel cable," "I chose a stone in the garden to be my balance."

Discussion

The children were completely engaged in these two outdoor contexts. Their play encouraged creativity and problem solving, leading to their construction of scientific knowledge (Roskos & Christie, 2007). The teacher aimed to make the children aware of the physical concepts of

Engagement and Inquiry in Outdoors Contexts   171

Figure 11.5 Children measuring how many children are needed to pull up a boy.

force and weight through experiences with their bodies. The children then transferred experience and action (Dewey, 2010) to the realm of language, as they built knowledge collaboratively. From Vygotsky's sociohistorical perspective, this social context is viewed as an integral aspect of learning and development (Neuman, 2007).

Outdoor inquiries through play support children's investigative thinking, leading them to deepen scientific knowledge and concepts about relationships in their social and natural worlds. The children's thoughts still mixed diverse everyday-life concepts, ideas, and values. The teacher presented them with other opportunities to increase their knowledge

Figure 11.6 Writing and drawing about the attempt to raise a child using the pulley

Note: "Valentina has more weight." "Clothes change people's weight." "The lightest are Arthur and Luiza."

through scientific information and questions that required the children to explain their ideas. When the teacher created opportunities for the children to be knowers, they also became askers, as their growing knowledge led them to ask questions for further examination.

Through their meaningful use of objects, spaces, and language in these specific cultural contexts, the children learned about the expectations, meanings, values, and perspectives of the culture in which they

Engagement and Inquiry in Outdoors Contexts 173

Figure 11.7 Writing and drawing about the attempt to raise a child using the pulley

Note: (Helena) "Lozenzo couldn't lift her." "Valentina is the heaviest." "Joaquim was the heaviest." "Those who have the same weight, have the same size."

live. Thus, they learned far more than basic vocabulary, grammar, phonology, and semantics (Elkonin, 1998; Goncü, 1999; Vygotsky, 1979). It is important for teachers to draw upon the affordances of the local place, to make explicit the complexities of social and cultural perspectives and relationships with elements of place. Through play in the natural world, children may learn more complex ways of understanding these relationships than can be found in textbooks or handouts.

Play and place-based learning are continuous and provisional learning processes in which children negotiate their theories based on real experience.

The elevator play encouraged the children's exploratory talk about force and weight. The children tried out new scientific words that became part of their oral vocabulary. Embedded within the words they used were historically constructed science concepts. Using the scientific language allowed the children to gain a deeper understanding of the historically constructed concepts. In this way, outdoor play advanced the development of the children's mental representations (Elkonin, 1998). This play involved the children's mastery of cultural tools, a process that led to the subsequent transformation of their mental functioning. The outdoor play, with peers and their teacher to support exploratory talk and action, provided a context that facilitated the children's acquisition of these tools, including written language (Bodrova & Leong, 2007).

Through their play and writing, K-1 children in Escola do Bairro learned that literacy is more than knowing the alphabet or being aware of phonemes. It requires a complex set of underlying cognitive skills in real and significant contexts:

> "Play is, in fact, the best context for developing skills necessary for both learning literacy and creating conditions in which teachers can support the development of mental tools. Using make-believe play allows teachers to maximize their impact on their students' developing literacy skills at the same time supporting their other critical competencies in cognitive, scientific, linguistic, and socio-cultural areas. (Bodrova & Leong, 2007, p. 199)

Our observations of play and place-based learning have confirmed that teachers and other adults can play an active role throughout the process by creating a cultural and physical environment that provides many opportunities for children's experiments and playful explorations. As adults respectfully listen to and challenge children's pre-scientific theories, children are invited to test and refine them. Learning through place-based play is mediated by attentive teachers who draw on what is known about affective, emotional, cognitive, and social developmental processes, and about cultural and human knowledge in general.

REFERENCES

Barros, F.C.O.M. (2008). *Cadê o brincar?* Da educação infantil para o ensino fundamental. Master's dissertation, Universidade Estadual Paulista.

Belancic, K. (2022). Sámi children's language use, play, and the outdoors through teachers' lens. In S.S. Peterson & N. Friedrich (Eds.), *The role of place and play in young children's language and literacy* (pp. 53–66). University of Toronto Press

Berger, P.L., Luckmann, T. (1985). *A construção social da realidade* (2nd ed.). Editora Vozes.

Bodrova, E., & Leong, D.J. (2007). Play and early literacy: A Vygotskian approach. In K. A. Roskos & J. F. Christie (Eds.), *Play and literacy in early childhood: Research from multiple perspectives* (2nd ed., pp. 185–200). Routledge.

Boyd, M.P., & Galda, L. (2011). *Real talk in elementary classrooms: Effective oral language practice.* Guilford.

Brazil, Ministry of Education. (2017). *Base Nacional Comum Curricular.* Retrieved 5 June 2020 from http://basenacionalcomum.mec.gov.br/

Brazil, Ministry of Education, Inep. (2019). *Resumo técnico* – Censo da Educação Básica. Retrieved 11 June 2020 from http://portal.inep.gov.br/informacao-da-publicacao/-/asset_publisher/6JYIsGMAMkW1/document/id/6874720

Brazil, Presidência da República Casa Civil. Subchefia para Assuntos Jurídicos. (1999). Lei No 9.795, 27 April 1999. Retrieved 10 June 2020 from http://www.planalto.gov.br/ccivil_03/leis/l9795.htm

Caldeira, T.P. do R. (2003). *Cidade de muros: Crime, segregação e cidadania em São Paulo* (2nd ed.). Editora 34/Edusp.

Ciardella, T.M. (2019). *"As escolas são tudo igual – só muda as criança": O ensino fundamental fotografado pelos alunos.* Master's dissertation, Universidade de São Paulo. https://doi.org/10.11606/D.48.2019.tde-03102019-123443. Retrieved 12 July 2020 from www.teses.usp.br

Dewey, J. (2010). *Experiência e educação: Coleção: Textos fundantes em educação.* Ed. Vozes.

Duncan, S., Martin, J., & Kreth, R. (2016). *Rethinking the classroom landscape – Creating environments that connect young children, families, and communities.* Gryphon House.

Elkonin, D.B. (1998). *Psicologia do Jogo.* Martins Fontes.

Freire, P. (1996). *Pedagogia do oprimido.* Paz e Terra.

Goncü, A. (1999). *Children's engagement in the world – Sociocultural perspectives.* Cambridge University Press.

Instituto Brasileiro de Opinião Pública e Estatística. (2019). *Pesquisa de opinião pública – Viver em São Paulo: Criança* – OB0170/2019, São Paulo. Retrieved 11 July 2020 from https://www.nossasaopaulo.org.br/2019/09/30/pesquisa-viver-em-sao-paulo-crianca-sera-lancada-no-dia-15-de-outubro/

Neuman, S.B. (2007). Social contexts for literacy development: A family literacy program. In K. A. Roskos, & J. F. Christie (Eds.), *Play and literacy in early childhood: Research from multiple perspectives* (pp. 151–168). Routledge.

Nosek, H.S. (2018). *A criança no espaço público da cidade de São Paulo: Diferenças e aproximações entre dois bairros: Jardim Lapenna e Itaim Bibi*. Dissertation, Universidade Presbiteriana Mackenzie, São Paulo.

Palma, M.S. (2017). Representações das crianças sobre o brincar na escola. *Revista Portuguesa de Educação, 30*(2), 203–221. https://doi.org/10.21814/rpe.8243

Pellegrini, A., & Galda, L. (2000). Children's pretend play and literacy. In D.S. Strickland & L.M. Morrow (Eds.), *Beginning reading and writing* (pp. 58–65). Teachers College Press.

Pereira, R.T., & Benati, K.R. (2019). O estudo da educação ambiental com práticas pedagógicas nas escolas: Um olhar para os desafios encontrados. *Revista Monografias Ambientais, 18*(1), e8. https://doi.org/10.5902/2236130838756

QEdu. (2020). *QEdu*. Retrieved 9 July 2020 from https://www.qedu.org.br/brasil/censo-escolar?year=2018&dependence=0&localization=0&education_stage=0&item=

Rocha, M. & Ribeiro, R. (2017). A vida cotidiana e as brincadeiras no primeiro ano do ensino fundamental. *Cadernos CEDES, 37*, 237–258. https://doi.org/10.1590/cc0101-32622017173572

Roskos, K.A., & Christie, J.F. (2007). Play in the context of the new preschool basics. In K.A. Roskos and J.F. Christie (Eds.), *Play and literacy in early childhood: Research from multiple perspectives* (2nd ed., pp. 83–100). Routledge.

Santos. M. (1999). O Território e o Saber Local: Algumas categorias de análise. *Cadernos IPPUR, Rio de Janeiro, 13*(2), 7–12.

São Paulo. (2017). *Currículo da Cidade*. https://curriculo.sme.prefeitura.sp.gov.br/. Accessed 10/06/2020

Smith, P. (2007). Pretend play and children's cognitive and literacy development: Sources of evidence and some lesson from the past. In K.A. Roskos and J.F. Christie (Eds.), *Play and literacy in early childhood: Research from multiple perspectives* (2nd ed., pp. 3–19). Routledge.

Vygotsky, L.S. (1979). *Pensamento e linguagem*. Edições Antídoto.

Wajskop, G. (2012). *O Brincar na educação infantil: Uma história que se repete* (9th ed.). Cortez Editora.

12 Enriching Learning with the Richness around Us

CHRISTINE PORTIER

In this chapter, I illustrate concepts about place-based education using examples drawn from the classroom initiatives of three northern rural Alberta teachers. These teachers drew from their own and their students' relationships with local places to initiate playful and collaborative classroom learning projects that evoked the spirit of guided play (Weisberg et al., 2016). By grounding learning in the familiar, they created space for their students to contribute to project activities and developments in ways that followed children's natural ways of interacting with the environment and community.

Place-based education begins with what children know and extends outward in a way that "reconnects the school to the world in personal, cultural and contextual ways" (Nichols et al., 2016, p. 29), and consequently deepens children's connections to learning and the curriculum (Demarest, 2015). Place-based learning is an approach to teaching that organizes programs around local relationships and embeds the curriculum in relevant community contexts and in what children know about places (Anderson, 2017; Demarest, 2015; Shamah & McTavish, 2009). The focus on relationships is key. Rather than viewing place as a static background, we can explore and develop the reciprocal relationships that we have with places: our thoughts and actions mediate our experiences of places, yet places are the products of our choices, actions, and decisions (Gruenewald, 2003). Places become pedagogical through our relationships within them, and through our relationship with any given place, we learn about its workings and about ourselves. Children develop feelings and affections, and sometimes a sense of belonging, for the places where they live, and, in turn, these places contribute to the foundation of their identities (Hay, 1998). As educators, we can develop pedagogies with places that will emphasize a view of place not as a passive background to children's activities but rather as "a rich interactive relationship in which place nurtures and stimulates children's development through interactions of play, exploration, sensory stimulation, and emotional regulation" (Morgan, 2010, p. 14).

By observing children's *natural* interactions with natural places, Sobel (2008) identifies several "play motifs" and suggests that educators can translate these motifs into themes to help shape place- and play-based learning projects and activities. I draw from the three Alberta teachers' initiatives to illustrate Sobel's (2008) motifs of small worlds, adventures in movement, maps and paths, gathering and collecting, animal allies, and fantasy and imagination. I begin my descriptions of the teachers' initiatives with reflections on their personal relationships with place, and then describe how place relationships served as starting points for their initiatives, specifically their and their students' interactions with the natural environment, the human-created environment, and local activities and events.

The NOW Play Partnership Project

The Alberta teachers' initiatives developed within the context of the Northern Oral Language and Writing through Play (NOW Play) project. This partnership project engaged northern Canadian rural and Indigenous educators in developing play-based classroom learning opportunities to enhance students' oral language and writing interactions. Our work within this project showed that parents supported play activities if they were related to curriculum learning (Peterson et al., 2017). The views expressed by these northern Canadian rural parents corresponded with the increasing validation for play in education frameworks, especially when play supports curriculum outcomes (e.g., Wood, 2013; Broadhead et al., 2010). With this in mind, the participating Grade 1 and 2 teachers of the NOW Play project designed ways to integrate more *playful* activities into their programs, often by relating collaborative writing, drama, and art activities to their literacy and social studies curriculum goals. Over the course of the partnership project, we examined these initiatives for patterns in how they met learning processes and products through playful activities (Portier et al., 2019), and how they brought together the child-directed nature of play with adult-scaffolded learning (Weisberg et al., 2013).

I draw from the projects designed and implemented by three of the Grade 1 teachers in Alberta. Some data are taken from my observations and notes recorded during regular visits to their classrooms. At these times, we would talk about the new directions their projects took, the new activities they envisioned, and the children's learning as part of the projects. Further data come from videos and photos the teachers sent to us in between our in-person meetings. I also draw from audio recordings of the semi-structured interviews that took place during a spring conference organized to bring all project researchers and educators together.

A Personal Relationship with Place

Adrianna, Marcel, and Janice live in Eagle County, a rich landscape spanned by tributaries that branch off the Eagle River. This river feeds a corridor of forests, grasslands, hills, and valleys that provide a lush habitat for an abundance of wildlife. Branching off Eagle River is the smaller Earnest River, along which the village of Deerview (pop. 400) is situated. Not far away is Aspen (pop. 2,700), a town located along highway and railway junctions.

All three teachers drew from these local places to develop learning projects with their students, and in turn, these places provided content and context for learning. Part of their motivation to take a place-based approach came from the personal meanings that they drew from the land, the community, and the people (Scannell & Gifford, 2010).

Adrianna grew up in a town of about 5,000 yet she is very fond of her home in the smaller community of Deerview. She explains, "There's just something special about our community. Everyone knows each other, and there is a genuine connection between people, which I really enjoy." Adrianna enjoys seeing the children, whom she taught in kindergarten, grow into adulthood and move on to university or remain in the village to start families. In her words, "It's really neat to see everyone's individual life stories."

Marcel feels at home in Aspen, where he has lived and taught for over 10 years. His love of nature developed from his own childhood experiences on the east coast of Canada. As he puts it, "There were trees everywhere, and there were lakes and rivers and so much to do ... I know how important nature is to children's learning." In Aspen, Marcel is surrounded by nature, where "you can travel for hours and hours and barely see anything [built] there."

Janice has lived most of her life in rural communities, including her childhood years along the west coast of Canada. As she explains, "I grew up in a beautiful community. We lived in the mountains and it was gorgeous. It was a small rural community, close-knit, and everyone knew each other. We had lots of community functions ... and there were so many outdoor things, like rafting down rivers, and just living and experiencing the outdoors." Janice now lives in the "very close-knit community" of Aspen, where her relationship with others and the outdoors is prominent.

Adrianna, Marcel, and Janice do not view physical spaces as something separate from themselves. For them, local places serve as the "unfolding backdrop(s) for ongoing personal and social events" (Devine-Wright & Clayton, 2010, p. 268) with a personal sense of place developed through their relationships to their places. Listening to all three teachers talk about their communities, it is not surprising all three used familiar places as starting points for many of their classroom projects and created a space in their programming where they could draw from their own and their students' unique place relationships.

Starting Initiatives with Place Relationships

Researchers have reported on and suggested ways to help educators shift from separating school from children's lives to embedding school within children's home and community places (e.g., Cochran-Smith & Lytle, 2009; Smith, 2002). To do this, teachers can take advantage of the opportunities afforded by features of, or changes within, their natural and (human) built environments, as well as the community interactions that they and the children experience.

Interacting with the Natural Environment

Smith (2002) proposes that teachers tap into the natural curiosity that children have for their physical world with natural explorations that can "serve as the foundation on which investigations of more distant or abstract phenomena can be constructed (p. 588). Natural inquiries can give shape to classroom projects.

Adrianna and Janice began projects with local nature walks through their neighbourhoods. While on one excursion, to develop a collaborative knowledge base of local wildlife, the children in Adrianna's class made observations of animals and talked about the animals that did not appear. From this outing and the children's observations, Adrianna initiated a wildlife project, which the students soon directed to include fiction and nonfiction comparisons, graphing, puppet plays, and story and script writing. Janice also began a project with an outdoor excursion, engaging the students in a kind of scavenger hunt to search for clues that spring had sprung. They used some natural items that they collected to create murals, and this served to launch further inquiries. The students followed Janice's plans for research, and, over the weeks, thought of their own creative ways to express their learning, for example, through models of animal habitats and dramatizations about seasonal changes.

Enriching Learning with the Richness around Us   181

Interacting with the Local Human-Built Environment

Children's curiosity for the natural environment extends to the interesting ways that we shape our communities in relation to the land (Sobel, 1998). Human-built environments connect us to one another and influence how we pattern our lives (Proshansky & Fabian, 1987). Children construct meaning in these settings, and much like natural places, local-built environments can serve as starting points from which projects and creative play develop (Wilson, 2007).

Drawing from outings in Deerview and in the larger Eagle County, Adrianna designed a community mapping project. She developed the project through classroom discussions about the natural and human-built features the children encountered in their daily lives. The children began by drawing their favourite community places, and then combined these drawings to form a large mural-map. They used art materials to connect places and represent community features on the map. The children wrote the names of places on the map; however, they really dove into writing when Adrianna placed a little wooden door at the edge of the map to serve as a "magic" portal to whisk them away to imagined places.

Marcel's onster (not *m*onster) school project did not begin with place, but rather evolved to draw in the children's community activities. Marcel initiated an activity where the children explored *character* by creating and drawing creatures called onsters and presenting onster *actions* through small dramatizations. They combined their onster characters onto a large mural around which they developed *settings* by adding features of both natural and human-built places. The children transposed ideas from within the mural into written stories and the project came to a natural end. However, in the spring, construction began on the children's new school across the road, and so Marcel engaged the students in explorations about local buildings, community services, and the roles of the different workers associated with the construction process. Unexpectedly, the children insisted on bringing their school construction knowledge into the world of imagination, so they relaunched the onster project and sent the onsters to school.

Interacting with Local Activities and Events

We live our lives in places, and, "as centers of experience, places can also be said to hold our culture" (Gruenewald, 2003, p. 625). Nicola Friedrich (this volume) describes how teachers brought cultural and community practices (e.g., ice fishing, farmer's market, and flower shop) into the classroom to give shape to the children's play activities. Teachers can draw upon community events and cultural practices to help children learn about these practices, address community concerns, and even contribute to events within the community.

Each year, the community of Deerview holds a Festival of Trees event where community members donate lavishly decorated Christmas trees as auction items to raise money for the local women's shelter. Adrianna made use of this event as an opportunity to introduce her students to issues around violence prevention and family safety, and how the festival addressed these concerns. From photographs of the festival, we can see that community members (adults) have a great deal of fun decorating, donating, and bidding on trees. Adrianna thought of a way to have her students participate in the event. In collaborative groups, they developed plans, prepared material lists, collected items, and decorated little trees, which they then donated to the festival.

Adrianna, Marcel, and Janice grounded their students' learning in the familiar by using local natural and human-built environments and community events as starting points for classroom projects. Although they drew from their own relationships with place to initiate projects, they inspired their students to respond by means of their own unique relationships to the communities. The teachers made space in the projects for the students to direct their learning as they shaped the evolution of activities by means of their own "natural inclinations" towards places (Sobel, 2008).

Interacting with Place through Play Motifs

Adrianna, Marcel, and Janice planned, organized, and set up the activities that began place-based projects. Upon reflection, they discovered similarities in how their projects developed. First, because their projects began from the children's particular relationships and interactions with the local communities, the teachers found that they were unable to fully plan project activities in advance (Smith, 2002; Smith & Sobel, 2010). Although they planned for activities, they needed to alter plans or create new opportunities in response to the (often unexpected) directions taken in the students' learning. Second, by grounding the children in familiar local content, the teachers noticed that the children had plenty to say. The children readily collaborated and shared their learning and started suggesting directions for their learning. The teachers realized that they needed to let go of the need to "be in charge" and embrace the notion of "child autonomy" (Weisberg et al., 2016). They reset learning agendas (Wanich, 2006) by welcoming suggestions made by their students and developing ideas made collaboratively with their students. In place-based education, educators often find that spaces need to be made in project planning for children to voice their ideas and make contributions (Smith, 2002).

Smith (2002) suggests that when teachers let their roles shift from "director" to "experienced guides" they can work with students to collaboratively shape project activities. In this way, learning projects are not only grounded in familiar *content* for learning, but can also be grounded in familiar *processes* of learning. Sobel (2008) reminds us that children have natural interests and natural ways of interacting with their environments, which educators can tap into "to structure learning experiences" (p. 20). Drawing from Sobel's (2008) descriptions of play-motifs, we can see how Adrianna, Marcel, and Janice cultivated their students' natural ways of interacting with the environment in their projects.

Small Worlds

Children "love to create miniature worlds" (Sobel, 2008, p. 45), where, to develop understandings of abstract ideas from the larger world, they piece together concrete materials in simpler ways. Janice's students showed particular interest in the small creatures that emerged in the spring in Eagle County, so they adapted her planned research activity to focus on these creatures. As they researched, Janice overheard them talking about building a world for these creatures. Together, they explored this idea further and decided to combine classroom art materials (e.g., plasticine, paper, paint) with items collected on their nature walk (e.g., sand, rocks, pine needles) to form diorama habitats for their researched insects and amphibians. Using their research notes and their own local observations, the children created "small worlds" through which they came to understand the relationships between animals and the environment (see Figure 12.1).

Children can also develop small *imaginative* worlds. Marcel designed an irate (not *p*irate) island project that was based on a local place from his childhood, but then evolved to take place entirely within the realm of the imagination. The children created their own island maps; these became small worlds in which they explored features of natural (e.g., palm trees, mountains, grasslands, sand, caves, diamonds, gold, flowers, sharks, fish) and human-built (e.g., fences, fortresses, huts, ships, dungeons, bridges, signs, tipis) environments. Through discussions, they navigated the nooks and crannies of their small island worlds.

Teachers can tap into this way of learning by providing opportunities for their students to create small worlds. These worlds can help children concretely figure out ideas from their subject area learning and, in turn,

Figure 12.1 Small Worlds

Note: Children combine nature and art materials to create small worlds.

teachers can use these small worlds to draw attention to key relationships, for example, how animals relate to their environments (e.g., in the spring, frogs lay eggs in ponds). The farmer's market and flower shop projects described by Nicola Friedrich (this volume) provided a way for the young children to recreate, in miniature, events from their communities, and gave them opportunities to explore the roles that community members enact in relation to one another and in relation to their places.

Adventures in Movement

Sobel (2008) identifies physical movement and adventure as another motif in children's environmental interactions. Children integrate action and thinking to develop meaning (Stolz, 2015). Some form of kinaesthetic adventure can easily find its way into project designs, especially if educators bring children outside to explore local places. Although the children in Adrianna's class did not see all the local wildlife on their walk, the very act of walking through familiar places reminded them of other adventures with family and friends and the animals they had seen on those occasions. Upon returning to the classroom, they were able to create a long list of animals, and from there they suggested ways to learn more about local wildlife.

When Janice's students explored familiar surroundings through a scavenger hunt for signs of spring, they darted around, peeked under, probed into, scooped up, crouched closer to, and grasped the natural environment. Janice had the children recreate their outdoor adventure when they returned to the classroom.

Places may also *inspire* expression through movement. Through embodied learning, educators can move beyond the concept of environment as *content* to one which integrates the environment with the kinaesthetic. In her spring project, Janice continued to foster learning through dramatic expression. The students used pantomime to enact the human changes they observed with the arrival of spring; they portrayed activities such as swimming, horse riding, climbing hills and trees, riding bikes, planting gardens, quadding with all-terrain vehicles, feeding birds, digging, and hiking. The children were excited by this foray into drama and suggested a springtime "talk show" dramatization as a culminating learning activity. Janice guided the students in the development of roles (e.g., host, guests, and audience members) and dialogues (e.g., questions, responses) for their performance.

Marcel integrated movement activities into all his projects, whether large or small. Following a local charity run, the students collaborated to find ways to express their experiences to one another through movement. In their onster project, they dramatized imagined ways that onsters might move, sound, and behave. They later connected their movement adventures to the building of the local school, as they used drama to understand the roles, actions, and materials observed in the local school construction process.

Maps and Paths

When out and about in local spaces, children tend to follow their own pathways and seem to "have an inborn desire to explore local geographies" (Sobel, 2008, p. 34). Alone or together, they search corners and crevices to discover real and imagined treasures. Teachers can design project elements that give expression to this natural process of environmental learning.

Adrianna grounded her mapping project in the children's community. When they began piecing together their large map, they used art materials to create pathways to follow that would lead them from one map area to the next, from one building to another, and to connect the elements of the natural and human-built environment. The students moved their hands around the map to follow imagined paths as they talked to one another, for example:

- "This is an off-roading ramp. You can ride off. And then you have to go back around."
- "Grass roads everywhere."
- "I'm doing grass bridges, so you can connect your places."
- "You need a road bridge."
- "Look, I put a dock right here. You could stop and fish."

Gathering and Collecting

When outdoors, children love to gather and collect, so educators might find ways to design project activities that afford children these opportunities (Sobel, 2008). The search for and gathering of physical items might later become the questions and the search for answers that lie at the heart of inquiry-based learning. This activity might be viewed as a physical expression of a deep and fundamental human intellectual activity – the search for meaning.

On their nature walk, Janice's students did more than search for signs of spring, they also collected samples (e.g., sand, pine needles, grass blades, branches with buds) to bring back to the classroom for murals (see Figure 12.2). They later applied their inclination for gathering physical items to ideas as they worked in small groups to record questions to guide their inquiry (e.g., "I wonder what the mommy and the daddy birds do with their babies in spring?" and "I wonder if cubs are looking for food?"). The fruits of their intellectual gatherings came to bear on the question-response format of their final class performance, as they asked and responded to these types of questions in role play as talk-show host, guests, and audience members.

Adrianna integrated a gathering and collecting activity into their little trees project, as the students located items to fit the Christmas carol theme of each tree. Throughout the week, the students searched the school, their homes, and other community sources for the desired human-made (e.g., playing cards, metal shapes, ceramic tiles, wire) and naturally occurring (e.g., pinecones, cork, wood) items (see Figure 12.3).

Animal Allies

Children are drawn to animals, and developing relationships with animals may serve to foster in children feelings of kinship with the larger

Enriching Learning with the Richness around Us 187

Figure 12.2 Spring Murals
Note: Children create spring murals using items gathered from nature.

Figure 12.3 Little Trees
Note: Children use stones and wood to decorate their little tree.

188 Christine Portier

Figure 12.4 Wildlife Puppets
Note: Children dramatize with the wildlife puppets that they made.

natural world and a willingness to care for the creatures with whom we share the world (Sobel, 2008). After talking about the wildlife that they had seen drinking from the river, wandering in the woods, and strolling through their village, the natural curiosity in Adrianna's students drove the project activities towards animal puppet play. They searched online for images that could be used to create wildlife puppets (see Figure 12.4).

The children's first interactions with the puppets primarily involved picking them up one by one and repeating the names of the animals. This developed into short, unscripted explorations of animal behaviours and sounds, and interactions through dialogue. For example:

HALEY: I am hoooo hooooo [*flies owl to top of theatre*]
BRIAN: Get down from there Hoo Hoo! [*moves fox to top of theatre but immediately brings it back down*]
HALEY: Why?
BRIAN: Tarrrrrgh [*makes fox noise*] 'Cause you can fall.
HALEY: No, I'm not.
BRIAN: Yes, you will.

HALEY: I can fly, see. Swoooooooosh, I can fly. [*makes flying sound as she moves the owl*]
BRIAN: Beeeoonnng! I can't [*tries to make fox fly but shows that it cannot*]

Their puppet play evolved from simple "realistic" animal behaviours to include imaginative activities from their lives (e.g., "You want to play hide-and-go-seek? Okay, Mister Bear, you're it"), books they have read (e.g., "Hi, I'm Scaredy Squirrel"), and family scenarios (e.g., "Where's my baby?"). They sometimes talked in role as an animal (e.g., "Where's all my friends?" and "Get out of here, frog!"), and often stepped out of role to narrate actions (e.g., "The frog fell" and "I'm attacking you") and direct interactions (e.g., "Move it back a bit" and "You stay here and keep the show going"). They later turned their written animal stories into scripts for their puppet play, as in this snippet:

MOOSE: It's my mother.
NARRATOR: He saw a bush wiggling. The moose started running suddenly he bumped into something big! It was his mother!
MOOSE: Mother!!
NARRATOR: They started running toward the woods. The little girl was sad. The mother and the little girl played tag and then they went home.

Fantasy and Imagination

Day (2007) suggests children perceive the world through their eyes yet *see* with their imaginations, where "single rooms, gardens or behind-the-shed forgotten places can be whole palettes of mood, whole geographies of mountains and jungles, harbours and shops" (p. 4). Children have a knack for taking ordinary items and constructing special places, often in ways that even the adults in their lives don't anticipate (Green, 2013). Sobel (2008) posits that, as educators, "we need to structure programs like dramatic play; we need to create simulations in which students can live the challenges rather than just study them" (p. 24). Teachers can build on children's familiar places in simple ways that will spark their imaginations.

Adrianna helped the children enter the realm of fantasy with the simple addition of a small "magic" door placed at the edge of the community map. She called them together for a short visualization:

We are going to transport ourselves, so everyone, gather around. Take a little bit of magic dust with you. Do you have some? Now I would like you to close your eyes. Imagine that you are transported through the door. I

Figure 12.5 Island Maps

Note: Children draw and label island maps.

want you to imagine what it might look like on the other side of the door. Will it look the same as our community? Or will it look like something different? What might you see? Open your eyes and gather some magic dust again. We're going to pop through this door and when we emerge on the other side ...

This portal allowed the children to move freely between the real-world places within their community and the places in their imaginations. They drew pictures of magic doors and new places and talked about what they might see on the other side (e.g., "the door is just in plain sky ... you have to stand on the clouds and jump in," "mine is going to be a way darker world").

To initiate the irate island project, Marcel played ocean sounds as he guided the students through a visualization exercise. He explained that the recordings were from an island off the coast of his childhood home, where stories abound about the "irates" that visit the island. Removing the "p" from the word "pirates" gave the children the freedom to leave preconceived notions of pirates and follow their imaginations. From a simple blackline shape, the children designed island maps (see Figure 12.5) and developed portraits and biographies of the irates who might inhabit their islands. Sobel (1998) suggests that map-making might begin much like early drawing begins, as representations and expressions of what is important to children, saying that "in the beginning, children's maps represent their experiences of beauty, secrecy, adventure and comfort" (p. 5).

Conclusion

Adrianna, Marcel, and Janice engaged their students in learning projects by being open to the natural ways that children interact with the environment and community. Much like the kindergarten teachers in Nicola Friedrich's (this volume) chapter, these Grade 1 teachers made space in their practices for place interactions to shape learning processes and activities. In so doing, they worked with their students to co-evolve the projects, embracing new child-led practices (Weisberg et al., 2013; Wood, 2010). All three teachers responded to their students' suggestions by keeping the curriculum objectives in mind and shifting into the role of guide to help them organize, focus, and follow new lines of inquiry (Peterson et al., 2017; Weisberg et al., 2013). Being Grade 1 teachers, they did not open their programs to *free play*, as sometimes occurs in their colleagues' kindergarten classrooms. Instead, by following their students' interests and motivations during the familiar, place-based beginnings of each project, they demonstrated their high regard for the exploratory aspect of play (Hedges et al., 2018; Wood, 2010).

My intention for this chapter was to illustrate ways that educators can ground their students' learning in the familiar by building on their students' experiences with local places and moving from there into the curriculum. Place experiences can easily give shape to or be integrated into playful learning activities and classroom projects. Children's natural curiosity for and interactions with their environments (Sobel, 1998, 2008) are harmonious with the qualities of play (Wood, 2013) and help in the development of their socio-affective and communicative skills and processes, investigation, exploration, and problem-solving skills and processes, and creative and imaginative skills and processes (Wood, 2013). When students embrace the places they live, "they will be more likely to commit themselves to the difficult but rewarding work of making their communities good places to live. Even when they move to new communities, they will at least have a sense of the importance of social capital and may become more likely to make sure they cultivate relationships similar to those they encountered in the places where they grew up" (Smith & Sobel, 2010, p. 47). Drawing from their affinity with local natural environments and rural communities, Adrianna, Marcel, and Janice were able to explore place-based projects, with naturally embedded play motifs, to engage their students in meaningful learning and to nurture the children's relationships with the richness around them.

REFERENCES

Anderson, D. (2017). *Natural curiosity: A resource for educators: The importance of Indigenous perspectives in children's environmental inquiry.* Laboratory School at the Dr. Eric Jackman Institute of Child Study.

Broadhead, P., Howard, J., & Wood, E. (2010). *Play and learning in the early years: From research to practice.* Sage.

Cochran-Smith, M. & Lytle, S. (2009). *Inquiry as stance: Practitioner research for the next generation.* Teachers College Press.

Day, C. (2007). *Environment and children: Passive lessons from the everyday environment.* Routledge.

Demarest, A.B. (2015). *Place-based curriculum design: Exceeding standards through local investigations.* Routledge.

Devine-Wright, P., & Clayton, S. (2010). Introduction of the special issue: Place, identity and environment. *Journal of Environmental Psychology, 30*(3), 267–270. https://doi.org/10.1016/S0272-4944(10)00078-2

Friedrich, N. (2022). Scaffolding community literacy practices in kindergarten classrooms. In S.S. Peterson & N. Friedrich (Eds.) *The role of place and play in young children's language and literacy* (pp. 143–157). University of Toronto Press.

Green, C. (2013) A sense of autonomy in young children's special places. *International Journal for Early Childhood Environmental Education, 1*(1), 8–30.

Gruenewald, D.A. (2003). Foundations of place: A multidisciplinary framework for place-conscious education. *American Educational Research Journal, 40*(3), 619–654. https://doi.org/10.3102%2F00028312040003619

Hay, R. (1998). Sense of place in a developmental context. *Journal of Environmental Psychology, 18*(1), 5–29. https://doi.org/10.1006/jevp.1997.0060

Hedges, H., Peterson, S.S., & Wajskop, G. (2018). Modes of play in early childhood curricular documents in Brazil, New Zealand and Ontario. *International Journal of Play, 7*(1), 11–26. https://doi.org/10.1080/21594937.2018.1437379

Morgan, P. (2010). Towards a developmental theory of place attachment. *Journal of Environmental Psychology, 30*, 11–22. https://doi.org/10.1016/j.jenvp.2009.07.001

Nichols, J.B., Howson, P.H., Mulrey, B.C., Ackerman, A., & Gately, S.E. (2016). Promise of place: Using place-based education principles to enhance learning. *International Journal of Pedagogy and Curriculum, 23*(2), 27–41. https://doi.org/10.18848/2327-7963/CGP/v23i02/27-41

Peterson, S.S., Portier, C., & Murray, A. (2017). The role of play at home and in kindergarten and grade one: Parents' perceptions. *Journal of Childhood Studies, 42*(1), 1–10. https://doi.org/10.18357/jcs.v42i1.16882

Portier, C., Friedrich, N., & Peterson, S.S. (2019). Play(ful) pedagogical practices for creative collaborative literacy. *The Reading Teacher, 73*(1), 17–27. https://doi.org/10.1002/trtr.1795

Proshansky, H.M., & Fabian, A.K. (1987). The development of place identity in the child. In C. S. Weinstein, & T.G. David, (Eds.), *Spaces for children: The built environment and child development* (pp. 21–40). Plenum Press.

Scannell, L., & Gifford, R. (2010). Defining place attachment: A tripartite organizing framework. *Journal of Environmental Psychology, 30*(1), 1–10. https://doi.org/10.1016/j.jenvp.2009.09.006

Shamah, D., & McTavish, K.A. (2009). Rural research brief: Making room for place-based knowledge in rural classrooms. *The Rural Educator, 30*(2), 1–4.

Smith, G. (2002). Place-based education: Learning to be where we are. *Phi Delta Kappan, 83*(8), 584–594. https://doi.org/10.1177%2F003172170208300806

Smith, G.A., & Sobel, D. (2010). *Place- and community-based education in schools.* Taylor & Francis.

Sobel, D. (1998). *Mapmaking with children: Sense of place education for the elementary years.* Heinemann.

Sobel, D. (2008). *Childhood and nature: Design principles for educators.* Stenhouse Publishers.

Stolz, S.A. (2015). Embodied learning. *Educational Philosophy and Theory, 47*(5), 474–487. https://doi.org/10.1080/00131857.2013.879694

Wanich, W. (2006). *Place-based education in the United States and Thailand: With implications for mathematics education* (Working Paper No. 33). Ohio University: Appalachian Collaborative Center for Learning, Assessment and Instruction in Mathematics. https://pdfs.semanticscholar.org/16c4/82dd0f5a683556067292a015d7299a5d7af2.pdf

Weisberg, D.S., Hirsh-Pasek, K., Golinkoff, R.M., Kittredge, A.K., & Klahr, D. (2016). Guided play: Principles and practices. *Current Directions in Psychological Science, 25*(3), 177–182. https://doi.org/10.1177%2F0963721416645512

Weisberg, D.S., Zosh, J.M., Hirsh-Pasek, K., & Golinkoff, R.M. (2013). Talking it up: Play, language development, and the role of adult support. *American Journal of Play, 6,* 39–54.

Wilson, R. (2007). *Nature and young children: Encouraging creative play and learning in natural environments.* Routledge.

Wood, E. (2013). *Play, learning and the early childhood curriculum* (3rd ed.). Sage.

13 Exploring Urban Place-Based Play as a Stimulus for "Language in Action" and "Language as Reflection"

JANET SCULL AND KIM O'GRADY

In this chapter, we explore the ways teachers might orchestrate multiple opportunities for children to experience the various forms and functions of language though engaging in urban place-based play and by participating in interactions beyond the immediacy of play contexts.

The study was conducted in an urban city school and surrounding area; on a daily basis the children would leave the school either by foot, tram, or train to play in local parks, borrow a book from the city library, work in community gardens, or volunteer at the local animal hospital. Children attending the school were highly motivated to conserve the environment and enhance the lives of others, both locally and globally, and were deeply connected to their "place in space." The children would frequently draw upon what was known to them in order to create contexts for play and topics of inquiry based on their daily interactions with the local environment. The possibilities to enrich and extend their learning were endless; for instance, the children became engaged in a mission to solve homelessness in the city. At times a single idea would spontaneously evolve into something spectacular like the quest to add a flying tram to the transportation system.

At the most general level, this study examined intersections between children's language development and the impact of imaginative place-based play as "language in action" and children's subsequent teacher-facilitated discussions about their play as "language as reflection" (Jones, 1996). It also looked at how teacher input mediates the challenges of context-reduced language for school-aged language learners. More specifically, the study was intended to provide a close and careful analysis of young children's control over content, vocabulary, syntax, and register in both language learning contexts.

Play, Place, and Language Learning

Play affords young children the means to experiment with oral language in a context that is intrinsically motivating (Hill, 2010; Van Hoorn et al., 1993). The symbolic nature of pretend play, whereby a cardboard box can be used to represent a house, a car, or a pirate ship, is replicated in the symbolic nature of spoken language, as phonemic sequences are used to represent a semantic meaning (Stagnitti & Lewis, 2015). It is during these role-play scenarios that children are encouraged to grapple with more complex grammatical structures, new vocabulary, and narrative language more broadly (Stagnitti et al., 2016), specific to the language registers associated with the various sociocultural practice(s) underpinning the play (Van Oers & Duijker, 2013). Rich imaginative pretend play-based experiences provide opportunities for young children to engage in sustained symbolic thinking that involves the use of language to narrate, hypothesize, inform, imagine, and reflect (Fleer, 2015).

Children frequently improvise and pretend by creating their own context for play, while the mediating role of adults in children's play, in creating play contexts, is also acknowledged. Neuman and Roskos (1990) note that "context" can have a powerful influence on language and literacy, as teachers scaffold language and literacy through creating situations where appropriate props and provocations for play and learning are provided. These enriched contexts for play include grounding learning in a sense of place with strong connections to children's own lives and communities (Smith, 2002; Woodhouse & Knapp, 2000). When drawing on ideas of place-based pedagogies, educators plan for "learning and communication experiences around the things that are most meaningful to their students: their own places, people and popular culture and concerns" (Comber et al., 2007, p. 14). Children are then able to build on familiar contexts and experiences to explore role relationships and situated language practices, a concept which McIntyre et al. (this volume) explore in-depth through their "Little Green Thumbs" action research project.

"Language in Action" and "Language as Reflection"

From an early age, children understand that language is used and constructed in different ways for different purposes, and will vary their language use flexibly to suit the context (Halliday, 1975; Schleppegrell, 2012). This ability to use language appropriately in different contexts suggests that children have control over a range of language registers. Gee (2004) defines different language registers and introduces the notion that vernacular and specialist varieties of language coexist and are reciprocal in nature. He contends that all children acquire a vernacular version of their native language, which is connected to their family and community and is used in daily life. Specialist varieties of language build from these familiar contexts, as it is the specialist language that makes the content accessible, while the content gives meaning to that form of language (Gee, 2004).

In play, children explore and experiment with oral language naturally; most of this occurs in a familiar context that helps the child to understand what the language is about, or it is supported by paralinguistic gestures. The familiarity of the play context, and contextualized use of the language interactions, are supportive of children's language use, with lexical, grammatical, and register choices often appropriate to "language accompanying action" (Jones, 1996; Martin, 1985). While play provides an authentic communicative context for children to use language in pursuit of their own goals, Hoff (2006) argues that "the evidence suggests that peer interaction alone is not a sufficient context for language acquisition" (p. 71). Acknowledging the rich affordances of adult interactions in children's play settings (Fleer, 2015; Peterson & Greenberg, 2017), scholars have shown that play also provides an authentic shared experience for reflection and discussion (Van Oers & Duijkers, 2013). Engaging children as active interlocuters after play allows teachers to scaffold language in ways that enable them to express ideas, independent of the immediate context (Bridges et al., 1981), and communicate information to a wider range of audiences at a distance (Raban, 2014; Snow, 1991).

Success in literacy learning is predicated on extended and decontextualized discourse forms and academic language registers, where children need to "understand language apart from a physical context and focus more on the ideational context that a more sophisticated language user can provide" (Raban, 2014, p. 2). This can be achieved through encouraging a shift to using "language as reflection" (Jones, 1996; Martin, 1985), where students recount and describe events that incorporate the linguistic features of written discourse. Greenberg and Walker (this volume) describe conversations that promote the use of language for literacy learning as purposeful and planned, through introducing new vocabulary, modelling complex language structures, and extending the topic beyond the here and now. This process involves creating contexts where children can, with prompting, exhibit more precise lexical choices to elaborate the context. They can use flexible variations of language, building a syntactic base to support literacy (Scull, 2013; Snow, 1991). It may, for example, include asking children to elaborate on who was involved, when and where the event took place, and how they felt about this, to build language complexity (Scull & Mackenzie, 2018). In turn, this process requires teachers to move beyond conversational exchanges, modelling syntactic complexity that supports children's increasing familiarity with written discourse patterns (Huttenlocher et al., 2004; Vasilyeva & Waterfall, 2012).

The Research Site and Study Details

The research was conducted at a non-selective, independent coeducational school situated in a three-storey heritage building in the busy central business district of a large Australian city. One of the first of its kind in Australia, the school was established in response to the growing number of families choosing to live in inner-urban areas. The school offered a personalized approach to learning and drew upon the diverse resources of the city to complement and extend the children's learning and engagement. The majority of children attending the school were Australian, while a small percentage were recently arrived from China and Korea, learning English as an additional language.

A sample of six children in their first year of formal schooling, in the teacher/researcher's class, engaged in the study. The Teacher Rating of Oral Language and Literacy (TROLL) (Dickinson et al., 2001) was conducted with all children in the class and assisted in participant selection. TROLL results provided a measure of the children's control over syntactic structures and expressive language competencies, supporting the formation of two participant groups. Three males and three females, aged between 5 years 4 months to 6 years 1 month, were selected and assigned to two mixed-gender groups, with three children in each group, balanced in terms of the children's oral language resources. Each group participated in three place-based play experiences that were filmed to capture the children's use of "language in action." Following each play episode, the teacher facilitated a discussion with the participants involved. Throughout these teacher-led discussions the children were encouraged to reflect upon their play experiences, communicating with one another in a supported yet context reduced environment. These discussions took place during the natural course of the school day. The first six minutes of these small group discussions were audio-recorded and transcribed for analysis.

The research site provided all children with access to a unique range of urban-based play learning experiences. While certain aspects of the children's learning took place within the school's flexible learning environment, much of this learning was extended through access to the array of community resources located within close proximity to the school, alongside the community partnerships that had been established in response to the children's interests in their local environment. This setting provided the impetus for the design of the three place-based play learning contexts included in this study.

Transcripts of each play episode, as *language in action* and the teacher-facilitated discussions as *language as reflection*, were coded using four aspects of language – content, syntax, vocabulary, and register – with these aspects of language recognized as foundational to and facilitative of children's future literacy learning. Descriptors for each aspect of language were based on the Oral Language and Assessment Tool, Michigan Literacy Progress Profile (Michigan Department of Education, 2000), with definitions detailed below.

> Content: Maintenance on the topic of focus, the clarity of main ideas and elaboration with supporting details.
>
> Syntax: The appropriate and regular use of words, phrases and clauses to express ideas and the developing control over the patterns and forms of language.
>
> Vocabulary: The selection of words to describe events and ideas, with increasing accuracy, precision and sophistication.
>
> Register: The degree of formality of language, or the use of language conventions appropriate to the specific context.

The discussion that follows details the play experiences and provides excerpts of the children's language. These have been selected as they illustrate the affordances for children's learning with clear reference to the aspects of language detailed above.

Urban Play Space 1: Green Grocer

The children worked collaboratively to plan, design, and construct a grocery store as a springboard for dramatic play and as an opportunity to explore other relevant concepts across various domains of learning (e.g., literacy, numeracy, humanities, and social sciences). Connections to the home and local community were evident, as the children brought to school a range of items to contribute to the store, including shopping catalogues and household recyclables (e.g., empty food boxes). The teacher supplied other resources, including dress-ups, carry baskets, a cash register, calculators, writing materials, and play money. The children were responsible for naming the grocery store, developing their own advertising campaign to market specials, creating signs, pricing and labelling stock, in addition to designing the overall physical set-up of the store. This enabled the children to make sense of some of the processes involved in food production, marketing, and consumerism, aspects of which they encountered when shopping in their local community. During imaginative play, the children assumed different roles (cashier, customer, stacking assistant, store manager). Each child's ability to negotiate, collaborate, and imagine was called upon, as they were given the agency to determine the nature of the play.

EPISODE 1 – LANGUAGE IN ACTION

The excerpt below is from the children's play in the grocery store, which highlights the importance of authentic contexts, as children maintain a focus on the content or topic discussed to build upon and elaborate ideas. The props and resources prompted the children to negotiate and assume various roles as evidenced through their language interactions and non-verbal forms of communication with one another.

> LACHLAN: Just write a list.
> ALEXANDRA: Yeah, you just write a list.
> LACHLAN: Okay ... there's no customer.
> ALEXANDRA: Maybe because she's just writing her list.
> LACHLAN: Right, that might be enough.
> GENEVIEVE: Mmm, now, this is what I need to buy.
> LACHLAN: What do you need, some cereal?
> GENEVIEVE: It looks like cat food to me.
> LACHLAN: Yeah, it's cat food.
> ALEXANDRA: Do you need some eggs, Mrs?
> GENEVIEVE: Where's the basket?
> LACHLAN: Oh, here.
> GENEVIEVE: Thank you for the basket.
> ALEXANDRA: Now here's the eggs for you.

When we consider the transcript above through the lens of language content, we see the children's ability to stay on topic as they engage in extended conservations and effectively maintain their role-play interactions. They use specific field vocabulary and show control over a variety of sentence types appropriate to the content, including statements (e.g., "It looks like cat food to me"), questions (e.g., "Where's the basket?"), and imperatives (e.g., "Just write a list") appropriate to the events. In this way, we also see the children's awareness of register, as language appropriate to the content, as they take on the roles of shopkeeper and customer.

Urban Play Space 2: Minibeast Museum

The teacher-researcher instigated a minibeast investigation in response to a number of the children demonstrating a growing interest in bugs after their recent explorations of the local parks and gardens. To further extend the children's learning, the opportunity arose for the children to visit a minibeast exhibit and participate in a related educational session at the museum. Following the children's excursion to the museum, they were asked to work collaboratively to plan and construct a minibeast museum within the class construction zone. Through their planning, the children were encouraged to consider some of the necessary features of a minibeast museum and how they might work collectively to represent their thinking using the materials they had been given. This context for play enabled the children to question, consolidate, negotiate, and extend the many concepts, language forms, and terminology specific to their minibeast research.

EPISODE 2 – LANGUAGE IN ACTION

In the play excerpt below, the children's extended responses led to more complex syntactical structures. The children were connecting their ideas, building on one another's responses, asking and answering questions, giving compliments, as well as planning, reasoning, and articulating a projected order of events. Here, the children were required to build on their prior knowledge and real-world experiences in order to engage in the dialogue.

> CHLOE: Alright then, I'll give you all of the butterflies.
> COREY: You can give me some butterflies, you don't need all of them.
> CHLOE: I'll give [make] a home for the caterpillars instead.
> CHLOE: 'Cause the caterpillars ... 'Cause when the caterpillars do turn into butterflies, I'll give them to you.
> COREY: Okay.
> CHLOE: Actually, I'll put an ant colony in there.
> COREY: Oh, good idea ... I just need one little thing.
> CHLOE: The ant colony is good going.
> COREY: That's good.
> CHLOE: This is compost.

The dialogue shows the children's ability to use word and phrase order consistent with standard usage patterns, demonstrating control over tense, pronoun reference, and regular plural nouns. Much of the discussion takes place in the present tense, which is to be expected, and there is some use of future tense to describe the children's intentions (e.g., "When the caterpillars do turn into butterflies, I'll give them to you" and "I'll put an ant colony in there"). Closely aligned to the forms and patterns of language used was the children's use of appropriate lexical choices, demonstrating their increasing knowledge of words and their meanings. We can see the children drawing upon topic-specific vocabulary (e.g., "ant colony," "compost"), to convey their knowledge of the subject area and communicative intent. They are also making appropriate lexical choices in relation to the content and accompanying action taking place (e.g., "Actually, I'll put an ant colony in there").

Episode 3 – Language as Reflection

In the excerpt below, the teacher's questions during the reflective discussion prompted the use of expository prose and the use of topic-specific vocabulary to explain and describe the features of their minibeast museum. The discussion following children's play provided an opportunity for the children to converse in a structured, scaffolded context, in contrast to the dialogue that occurs informally during play interactions.

> TEACHER: Okay, great. Can you tell me about this little room?
> COREY: Here.
> CHOLE: In the trapdoor.
> TEACHER: So why have you created a space for the trapdoor spider, so that it's not with any other minibeasts?
> COREY: Well, because the trapdoor spider is dangerous.
> TEACHER: Mmm.
> COREY: And I do not want it to kill the others.
> TEACHER: Okay.
> CHLOE: And, and the trapdoor spider is the most poisonous spider in the world.
> TEACHER: Is it really?
> …
> TEACHER: Kayden, would you like to tell me about your exhibit? Tell me about what you have created here.
> KAYDEN: I have created an ant nest and I have created different sections.
> TEACHER: You've made four different sections and each section has a different type of insect inside?
> KAYDEN: Yes.

Of particular interest in this excerpt is Kayden's command of both vocabulary and syntax during the teacher-facilitated discussion. On this occasion, the teacher introduced subject specific vocabulary, (e.g., "exhibit" and "created"), modelled appropriate use of syntax, and extended on Kayden's responses through an elaboration of his ideas. Specifically, he was able to appropriate the language model (e.g., "What have you created here?"), producing a compound sentence in his reply and using vocabulary to precisely describe his contribution to the play context. This particular example highlights the way in which children with lower-level language resources can benefit from teacher input and scaffolding to support and extend their capacity to verbally communicate with others across a range of language registers.

Urban Play Space 3: Treasure Island

Adjoining the school building was an internal courtyard, with play equipment that was interchangeable, except for a large irregularly shaped sandpit. The sandpit provided a safe haven for children to explore, imagine, and create. It was a place that provided a sense of calm or excitement as children immersed themselves in a world of fantasy, either independently or collaboratively. The third play episode was situated in this area of the school. The challenge of creating a treasure island was very much open to the children's interpretation. The children had access to a range of sandpit equipment and recycled materials, which they could use for construction purposes and to represent different aspects of the treasure island. This task required the children to articulate their thinking, listen respectfully, and compromise when working with others in order to put their ideas into action.

EPISODE 4 – LANGUAGE IN ACTION

In this excerpt, the play space affords children the opportunity to express their ideas and elaborate as necessary, building on each other's comments to collaboratively complete the task, as the register of conversation is appropriated.

>   ALEXANDRA: I think I'm digging a hole for the treasure.
>   LACHLAN: Can it be deeper?
>   LACHLAN: Oh, let's do this for gold.
>   GENEVIEVE: Why can't we dig it in the middle of the island so that it's …
>   GENEVIEVE: Lachlan, remember to join to mine.
>   LACHLAN: It's already connected [*inaudible*] actually it's going around this way.
>   LACHLAN: So, I'm going to put the treasure in here. Let's find a [*inaudible*].
>   …
>   LACHLAN: Oh, let's put a tree on top so no one knows.
>   GENEVIEVE: Yeah, they think it's not there.
>   LACHLAN: No, they'll still find it.
>   ALEXANDRA: No, they won't, so what about if we just … [*interrupted by Lachlan*]
>   LACHLAN: No, it's all mucked up, let's just muck it up so people don't know.
>   ALEXANDRA: Let's flatten it out so no one thinks we've digged in here.

In this play transcript, the children's language use was typically less formal with language use reliant on the "here and now," with this considered appropriate to the context. However, supported by accompanying action, the children's developing control over an increasing range of syntactical patterns and forms of language was evident as they used complex clause structures, signalled by the use of "if" and "so," albeit with occasional verb and adverb confusions.

Episode 5 – Language as Reflection

The post-play reflective discussion excerpt presented below placed greater demands on the children's language resources, as it was conducted in a more formal register. Register has increasingly gained the attention of researchers and educators over the past decade. Particularly upon school entry children are confronted with a multitude of communicative exchanges to support learning and engagement; these are typically formulated in the formal or academic register (Christie, 2005). The challenge of the formal register is illustrated below.

> TEACHER: Can you tell me about the treasure island you created in the sandpit?
> COREY: Um, well, we had, we were digging it up and putting it in so we could make like a nice curve shape.
> ...
> COREY: And then we put two shovels for the palm trees and we buried treasure.
> TEACHER: Great. Corey, when you said that you were digging it up, what were you digging up?
> COREY: Well, we were digging up sand.
> TEACHER: And how did you know where to put the sand?
> COREY: Well, cause Chloe made a boundary.
> TEACHER: Chloe, how did you decide how big to make the boundary or what shape to make the boundary?
> CHLOE: I decided how to make the shape of the boundary 'cause most treasure islands are like oval – round sort of.
> TEACHER: Okay.
> CHLOE: And how I knew how to make the boundary small, 'cause islands are small.
> TEACHER: And what was surrounding your island?
> CHLOE: Water.
> TEACHER: Water?
> CHLOE: Islands are usually out in the middle of nowhere.

In this excerpt, the teacher's questions were targeted towards helping the children to clarify or extend their previous response, to ensure that the response was complete from a content perspective, and the meaning was clear to all group members. The teacher's questions also act as an exemplar from which the children model the appropriate lexical and syntactical choices akin to language conventions in the more formal register. Yet with the additional demand to conform to a formal register, the syntactical complexity of children's utterances was somewhat reduced. Directing children's attention to less familiar aspects of language apparently had an impact on previously demonstrated levels of language competency. Clay (1991) described this as "the pebble in the pond" (p. 130) effect, where a focus on a new feature of text may capture the child's attention and send ripples of disturbance through responses that had previously appeared well established.

Rich Affordances of Urban Play Spaces

We suggest the play episodes described in the study provided the participants with a strong contextual frame for communicative development that built on the children's understanding of place and their familiarity with the unique urban site of the school. The orchestrated play contexts supported the language skills children brought to the classroom, drawing on the physical, social, and cultural activities of their community, and provided opportunities leading to children's language growth and development (Peterson, 2016; Sanberg & Heden, 2011). The transcripts highlight the integrated nature of language as "a complex interrelation of subsystems" (Raban, 2014, p. 1) and reinforce the idea that children do not develop individual components of oral language in isolation from one another; rather, there is a rich intermingling of each and every aspect (Clay, 1979, 2001). During each of the play episodes, the children were motivated to explore and extend their use of syntax and vocabulary, adapting their use of language content and register within the contexts for language learning that had been created.

As well as building community links and an appreciation of the local neighbourhood, the children's linguistic resources were affirmed and extended in the service of classroom learning. Through participation in play environments related to the children's community investigations and the associated experiences of "language in action," they were supported to engage in "language as reflection," using language to describe events removed from time and space. The results suggest the embedded language of play in familiar contexts of place can serve as a bridge to context-reduced language, especially for those less familiar with the discourse patterns of schooling (Scull & Bremner, 2013).

Scaffolding Context-Reduced Language

Consistent with much of the literature, our data show that children enter school as competent language users in terms of their context-embedded language use – as the language forms most commonly supported in the home and preschool environment (Green et al., 2003; Hoff, 2006) – but with limited experience in context-reduced language (Christie, 2005; Shiel et al., 2012). As literacy competence is often associated with developing control over decontextualized language, it is essential that educators are cognizant of the need to provide planned opportunities within the daily curriculum to support children in becoming competent users of this more literate discourse (Campbell & Baker, 2003; Schleppegrell, 2012).

The children's reflective discussions were illustrative of targeted, intentional opportunities for context-reduced language. The rich, familiar play contexts grounded the children's responses as the teacher-prompted language use beyond the immediate time and place. The teacher's descriptions and explanations (e.g., "Can you tell me about the treasure island you created in the sandpit?" "So why have you created a space for the trapdoor spider?") were dependent on language learned, and possibly rehearsed, during the children's play experiences. Similarly, McIntyre and colleagues (this volume) describe how the use of open-ended questions encouraged elaborated, extended responses, scaffolding children's verbal interactions and conversational skills. Intentional teaching interactions such as these are a common feature of early years pedagogies in Australia. Yet to be effective, teachers need to be closely attuned to the cultural and linguistic capital of each child (Victoria, Department of Education and Training, 2016).

The specific features of the teacher's discourse in talking with children about the play contexts also contributed to the development of the children's oral language, scaffolding a clarity of thinking and a more precise articulation of ideas. Particularly for the children with lower-level language repertoires, the teacher's prompts and modelling during the discussions provided them with the necessary support to effectively participate in the dialogue and to co-construct knowledge. Engaging in language to convey meaning removed from the immediacy of the "here and now" shifted the discourse to include opportunities for the children to adopt the more formal language registers of written texts (Snow, 1991). As discussed by Greenberg and Walker (this volume) "place and play-based learning offer many opportunities for educators to build decontextualized language as they encourage children to think creatively and use what they already know and are familiar with in a different context or to explore a new idea" (p. 222). Further, the teacher's elaboration on students' ideas extended their responses, making them comprehensible at a more sophisticated level. As a result of the techniques used to facilitate the talk interactions, the children were given the opportunity to experience a range of semiotic modalities to extend their language for learning (Wells, 1999). According to Alexander (2005), it is through this process that a cumulative effect arises, where these ideas can be linked into "coherent lines of thinking and enquiry" (p. 14).

Conclusion

We suggest that the findings from this small study afford new ways of examining the action-reflection continuum (Jones, 1996), both as discrete opportunities along the continuum but also through an exploration of notions of place that contextualizes and sequences language use and learning. The opportunities for talk that built on place through the inclusion of play environments related to the children's community provided a clear example of how teachers might support children's transition across the modes of language. Such talk supports the shift from children's use of language that accompanies action to their use of language as reflection: from most spoken-like to most written-like in form. This finding suggests that teachers might structure students' language use by connecting and building on children's experiences, as place, remembered or imagined, to effectively anchor language learning.

REFERENCES

Alexander, R. (2005). *Culture, dialogue and learning: Notes on an emerging pedagogy.* Presented at Education, Culture and Cognition: Intervening for growth. International Association for Cognitive Education and Psychology (IACEP) 10th International Conference, University of Durham, UK, 10–14 July 2005.

Bridges, A., Sinha, C., & Walkerdine, V. (1981). The development of comprehension. In G. Wells (Ed.), *Learning through interaction: The study of language development* (pp. 116–156). Cambridge University Press.

Campbell, R., & Baker, C. (2003). Children learning language. In D. Green & R. Campbell (Eds.), *Literacies and learners: Current perspectives* (pp. 33–50). Prentice Hall.

Christie, F. (2005). *Language education in the primary years.* University of New South Wales Press.

Clay, M.M. (1979). *What did I write? Beginning writing behaviour.* Heinemann.

Clay, M.M. (1991). *Becoming literate: The construction of inner control.* Heinemann.

Clay, M.M. (2001). *Change over time in children's literacy development.* Heinemann.

Comber, B., Reid, J., & Nixon, H. (2007). *Literacies in place: Teaching environmental communications.* PETA.

Dickinson, D.K., McCabe, A., & Sprague, K. (2001). *Teacher rating of oral language and literacy (TROLL): A research-based tool.* CIERA Report.

Fleer, M. (2015). Pedagogical positioning in play – Teachers being inside and outside of children's imaginary play. *Early Child Development and Care, 185*(11–12), 1801–1814. https://doi.org/10.1080/03004430.2015.1028393

Gee, J.P. (2004). *Situated language and learning: A critique of traditional schooling.* Routledge.

Green, D., Lewis, J., & Peterson, R. (2003). Language and literacy promotion in early childhood settings: A survey of centre-based practices. *Early Childhood Research and Practice 8*(1). Retrieved from http://ecrp.uiuc.edu/v8n1/green.html.

Greenberg, J., & Walker, S. (2022). The key role of the educator as a conversational partner in play and place-based learning. In S.S. Peterson & N. Friedrich (Eds.), *The role of place and play in young children's language and literacy* (pp. 211–226). University of Toronto Press.

Halliday, M.A. (1975). *Learning how to mean.* Edward Arnold.

Hill, S. (2010). Oral language play and learning. *Practically primary, 15*(2), 4–6, 12. doi: 10.3316/aeipt.182977

Hoff, E. (2006). How social contexts support and shape language development. *Developmental Review, 26,* 55–88. https://doi.org/10.1016/j.dr.2005.11.002

Huttenlocher, J., Vasilyeva, M., & Shimpi, P. (2004). Syntactic priming in young children. *Journal of Memory and Language, 50,* 182–195. https://doi.org/10.1016/j.jml.2003.09.003

Jones, P. (Ed.). (1996). Planning an oral language program. In P. Jones (Ed.), *Talking to learn* (pp. 11–26). Primary English Teaching Association.

Martin, J. (1985). Language, register and genre. In F. Christie (Ed.), *Children writing course reader* (pp. 21–30). Deakin University Press.

McIntyre, L.J., Hellsten, L.M., & Bergen, T. (2022). Place-based language and literacy learning in play: Learning from a north-central Saskatchewan Indigenous community. In S.S. Peterson & N. Friedrich (Eds.), *The role of place and play in young children's language and literacy* (pp. 227–242). University of Toronto Press.

Michigan Department of Education. (2000). *Michigan Literacy Progress Profile*. Michigan Department of Education.

Neuman, S.B., & Roskos, K. (1990). Play, print, and purpose: Enriching play environments for literacy development. *The Reading Teacher, 44*(3), 214–221.

Peterson, S.S. (2016). Research in Canada's northern rural and Indigenous communities: Supporting young children's oral language and writing. *The Reading Teacher, 70*(3), 383–387. https://doi.org/10.1002/trtr.1519

Peterson, S.S., & Greenberg, J. (2017). Teacher intervention to support oral language and literacy in dramatic play contexts. *Texas Journal of Literacy Education, 5*(1), 10–23.

Raban, B. (2014). TALK to think, learn, and teach. *Journal of Reading Recovery*, Spring, 1–11.

Sanberg, A., & Heden, R. (2011). Play's importance in school. *Education 3–13, 39*(3), 317–329, https://doi.org/10.1080/03004270903530441

Schleppegrell, M. (2012). Academic language in teaching and learning. *The Elementary School Journal, 112*(3), 409–418. https://doi.org/10.1086/663297

Scull, J. (2013). Assessing Language for Literacy: A microanalysis of children's vocabulary, syntax and narrative grammar. *International Education Studies, 6*(1). https://doi.org/10.5539/ies.v6n1p142

Scull, J., & Bremner, P. (2013). From composition to conversation. *Babel 48*(1), 20–29.

Scull, J., & Mackenzie, N.M. (2018). Developing authorial skills: Child language leading to text construction, sentence construction and vocabulary development. In N.M. Mackenzie & J. Scull (Eds.), *Understanding and supporting young writers from birth to 8* (pp. 89–115). Routledge.

Shiel, G., Cregan, A., McGough, A., & Archer, P. (2012). *Oral language in early childhood and primary education (3–8 years).* Research conducted on behalf of the National Council for Curriculum and Assessment, Research Report No. 14. Education Research Centre, Mary Immaculate College, University of Limerick.

Smith, G.A. (2002). Place-based education: Learning to be where we are. *Phi Delta Kappan, 83*(8), 584–594. https://doi.org/10.1177%2F003172170208300806

Snow, C.E. (1991). The theoretical basis for relationships between language and literacy development. *Journal of Research in Childhood Education, 6*, 5–15. https://doi.org/10.1080/02568549109594817

Stagnitti, K., Bailey, A., Stevenson, E.H., Reynolds, E., & Kidd, E. (2016). An investigation into the effect of play-based instruction on the development of play skills and oral language. *Journal of Early Childhood Research*, 1–18. https://doi.org/10.1177/1476718X15579741

Stagnitti, K., & Lewis. F. (2015). Quality of pre-school children's pretend play and subsequent development of semantic organization and narrative re-telling skills. *International Journal of Speech-Language Pathology, 17*(2), 148–158. https://doi.org/10.3109/17549507.2014.941934

Van Hoorn, J., Monighan-Nourot, P., Scales, B., & Alward, K. (1993). *Play at the centre of the curriculum*. Merrill.

Van Oers, B., & Duijkers, D. (2013). Teaching in a play-based curriculum: Theory, practice and evidence of developmental education for young children. *Journal of Curriculum Studies, 45*(4), 511–534. https://doi.org/10.1080/00220272.2011.637182

Vasilyeva, M., & Waterfall, H. (2012). Beyond syntactic priming: Evidence for activation of alternative syntactic structures. *Journal of Child Language, 39*, 258–883. http://dx.doi.org/10.1017/S0305000911000055

Victoria, Department of Education and Training. (2016). *Victorian early years learning and development framework: For all children from birth to eight years*. Department of Education and Training.

Wells, G. (1999). Language and education: Reconceptualising education and dialogue. *Annual Review of Applied Linguistics, 19*, 135–155. https://doi.org/10.1017/S026719059919007X

Woodhouse, J., & Knapp, C. (2000). *Place-based curriculum and instruction*. ERIC Document Reproduction Service No. EDO-RC-00-6.

14 The Key Role of the Educator as a Conversational Partner in Play- and Place-Based Learning

JANICE GREENBERG AND SHARON WALKER

The promotion of language development in the early years is critical to children's success in life. This is when children develop their brain's architectural foundation, on which they build the skills necessary to thrive academically and socially. During these years, the child's parent is their first teacher – encouraging first words, introducing experiences, and facilitating learning through play within their own social and cultural environment. This is place- and play-based learning at its most quintessential.

When children begin preschool, and continuing into the early school years, their educator becomes their second teacher, using specific knowledge and training to build on the parent's work and extend learning. Educators are well positioned to foster language development as children move from learning to talk to talking to learn, thus laying the foundation for future academic success (Dickinson & Porche, 2011). During this time, children also begin to transfer the language knowledge acquired through listening and speaking to the development of literacy (Dickinson & Tabors, 2001; Resnick & Snow, 2009). As oral language is strengthened, a strong foundation is established for the transfer of listening and speaking skills to reading and writing. Language learning is maximized when attentive and responsive adults talk about things that derive from the children's interests and existing knowledge (Weitzman et al., 2006). This makes place-based learning a natural catalyst for language development since it taps into children's existing funds of knowledge and draws upon local activities, values, and experiences.

This chapter will address opportunities offered through place-based learning for children growing up in a large, diverse urban setting. Place-based learning attempts to engage children with the world around them, and in a large busy city, their experiences are drawn from a wide variety of contexts, such as planting in backyard gardens, navigating busy streets, and encounters with building construction sites.

Relationship between Play and Language Development

Play-based learning also provides an ideal opportunity for language development. Play refers to any activity that children do that is child-led, joyful, and voluntary. Play does not necessarily have a specific purpose. Children's interests, not those of adults, determine how an interaction moves forward. When children lead an interaction, they do not have to switch attention from their focus of interest to an adult's interest. Since children stay engaged as they listen to and speak about what interests them, many opportunities exist for promoting language development. Moreover, the social interaction with peers and adults that is often inherent in play results in greater language use and use of more complex language.

Play and language are also connected since they both draw upon symbolic thinking. As children participate in pretend and imaginary play, they use props as symbols for real objects and events, and move beyond the here and now, as noted by Scull and O'Grady in this volume. This process of symbolic thinking is similar to that of language, in which words are used as symbols for referents, and likely contributes to language learning (Weisberg et al., 2013).

Conversations Fuel Language Development

Although place- and play-based learning provides important contexts for language learning, language does not develop from simple exposure to events or participation in activities. Children's thinking and language learning thrive when teachers subtly scaffold language in teachable moments (Weitzman & Greenberg, 2002) and support children to actively connect experiences with less familiar and abstract knowledge. By sharing the joy and working together with children towards a common goal, the stage is set for developing language in fun, meaningful contexts (Hirsh-Pasek & Golinkoff, 2011).

The everyday conversations that educators foster become important pivot points for language development. It is within these conversations that children have opportunities to think and use their language in gradually more sophisticated ways to represent ideas, provide evidence for their evolving thinking, plan, solve problems, and exchange points of view. They are also able to elaborate on their feelings and reactions towards what they have experienced (Milburn et al., 2013). Conversation gives children the chance to build empathy, understanding, and respect for different opinions (McTigue et al., 2015). Within extended conversations, children develop feelings of pride and a sense of confidence as interested adults and peers listen to what they have to say and value their local experiences, activities, and materials.

Research studies have documented the positive impact of extended conversations on vocabulary development, social communication skills, and the development of higher level "academic language" associated with school success (Gilkerson et al., 2018). More recent studies have even related children's frequency of experiences with extended conversations to greater brain development (Romeo et al., 2018). The amount and frequency of classroom conversation has been highlighted as the most important thing to evaluate in early childhood classrooms (Hart & Risley, 2003). According to Gibbons (2006), it is through participation in conversations that children become reflective, critical thinkers, and confident, competent communicators.

The Educator's Critical Role as a Conversational Partner

To capitalize on the learning within place-based play situations, educators need to consider how to best engage students in sustained conversations that draw upon their existing knowledge and promote language development (Weitzman & Greenberg, 2002). Yet, many educators say that they are unsure of how to encourage children's authentic talk in the classroom and effectively scaffold children's oral language (Peterson et al., 2016). Educators report that much of their communication with children involves directing them – giving instructions, telling children what to do, and correcting their behaviour – rather than really connecting with them in meaningful interactions (Girolametto et al., 2000).

A teaching approach that emphasizes listening, responding to, and building on child-initiated communication and conversation can be a more effective way to promote children's language acquisition, as well as their development of social skills, empathetic understanding, and the ability to pay attention. Asking for and considering children's ideas in joint dialogue can strengthen their sense of autonomy, their competence, and their critical thinking skills. Educators should aim for sustained classroom interactions that deepen children's thinking and provide ample opportunity for students' ponderings and authentic questions (Dickinson et al., 2014). This means expecting and inviting talk in the classroom and taking advantage of existing opportunities within each day to engage children in conversations with adults and peers.

As educators extend conversations, they have an opportunity to model and encourage use of the kind of language associated with language and literacy gains and academic success. This concept is noted in the targeted coaching of Layla in McIntyre et al. (this volume). This type of language is referred to as *academic language* (Van Kleeck, 2014), and is characterized by

- information density with a lot of information packed into a small number of words;
- complex syntax, i.e., multi-clause sentences, sentences with more complex verb forms;
- specific, more sophisticated vocabulary that is used less frequently and may be content-specific;
- use of language for metalinguistic purposes, e.g., talk about word meanings;
- metaphors and figurative language;
- decontextualized language characterized by abstract ideas with limited contextual support that go beyond the here and now. This includes inferencing, the reaching of conclusions through reasoning, and drawing upon background knowledge when complete information is not directly evident.

Conversations Need to Be Purposeful and Planned

Meaningful conversation and dialogue will not necessarily happen without careful forethought (Gunnewig & McGloin, 2003). Careful planning is often necessary for authentic, meaningful conversations that support language learning on a regular basis in the classroom. Although educators may spend considerable time designing and implementing learning activities, they may not necessarily focus on how they will specifically promote language development within those activities. This means planning ahead to consider

- when conversations will take place throughout the day;
- whether the conversation will be 1:1 or with a small group;
- who will be participating, with consideration of the children's varying levels of language and social skills;
- which activities/situations will be selected and how the children's background knowledge will be drawn upon;
- how the educator will support the conversation and promote language development, specifically by:
  - providing opportunities for children to reveal their existing knowledge;
  - following the children's lead by validating their knowledge and perceptions;
  - keeping the conversation going through stimulating comments and questions that encourage critical thinking and deepen the learning;

- scaffolding appropriately by making connections between the familiar and the new through adding vocabulary, modelling complex language, and extending the topic beyond the here and now with decontextualized language.

Follow the Child(ren)'s Lead

One of the key elements of a successful conversation that promotes learning is the educator's responsiveness (Girolametto et al., 2003, 2005, 2012). This means educators take the time to listen to children and then follow their lead by validating and expanding on the children's message to understand their interests, their levels of comprehension, and the background knowledge they bring to new learning. Weitzman and Greenberg (2002) describe the OWL™ strategy, which reminds educators to observe, wait, and listen to provide children with the opportunity to share their thoughts and ideas through initiating comments and questions that are not prompted by the educator. Educators can then make the most of the learning opportunities inherent to place-based learning by drawing upon the children's real-life experiences from their local environment.

When a child's lead is followed, the child comes to better understand the intentional nature of communicating, that is, talking to another recruits their interest and engagement, and their motivation to continue the conversation is increased. Allowing children to maintain rather than shift their current attentional focus to an educator-directed topic maximizes allocation of the child's cognitive resources towards the topic at hand (Justice et al., 2018). That is why play, with its inherent child-led nature, provides an ideal context for following a child's lead and supporting language development.

To consider the value of following a child's lead, consider the following example. In this busy, noisy urban setting, efforts in the classroom are devoted to reinforcing children's connection with nature in playful settings. In this example, the educator set up a pretend backyard in the dramatic centre. They provided gardening tools, pots of earth, and seeds so the children could pretend to be gardeners. In the following two exchanges, consider how well the educator follows the children's lead and the impact on the child's learning.

EXAMPLE 1 FOR GARDENER ACTIVITY

EDUCATOR: Remember when each of you planted a seed in your pot? You took care of it by watering and making sure it had sunlight. Now you can see that a small stem is growing and soon there will be a flower.

CHILD: Like at my grandma's house! She grows lots of things in her backyard.

EDUCATOR: Does she grow flowers too?
CHILD: No, carrots and potatoes.
EDUCATOR: Well, that's a bit different than what we're doing here. Who can tell me, what will happen next as the stem grows?

EXAMPLE 2 FOR GARDENER ACTIVITY

EDUCATOR: Remember when each of you planted a seed in your pot? You took care of it by watering and making sure it had sunlight. Now you can see that a small stem is growing and soon there will be a flower
CHILD: Like at my grandma's house!
EDUCATOR: Oh, you've also seen flowers growing at your grandma's house.
CHILD: No, carrots and potatoes. She grows lots of things in her backyard.
EDUCATOR: Ah, that's a bit different than growing flowers but, tell me, did she plant any seeds?
CHILD: Yes, and I helped her.
EDUCATOR: And what does she do to make sure the vegetables grow?
CHILD: Makes sure it has water!
EDUCATOR: So, vegetables and flowers are *similar*. "Similar" means that vegetables and flowers are the same since they both need water. Just like with our flowers, your grandma planted a seed and watered it! Does anything come up out of the ground like our flowers?
CHILD: Yes, but not a flower.
EDUCATOR: No, not a flower. What did come out of the ground?
CHILD: Just leaves.
EDUCATOR: So, where were the vegetables?
CHILD: We had to pull them out of the ground
EDUCATOR: So, some vegetables, like carrots and potatoes, are different from flowers since they grow under the ground. But they are similar to flowers since they still need sun and water and they have green leaves just like our flowers do.
CHILD: But not all vegetables. My grandma grows tomatoes and they aren't in the ground!
EDUCATOR: You're right. Lots of vegetables are grown above ground like flowers. Who else has vegetables at your house that grow above the ground?

In both examples, participation in the activity encouraged the child to draw upon their existing local knowledge. However, in the first example, the educator does not follow the child's lead when the child relates the activity to previous experiences at their grandmother's house and the conversation ends with a return to the educator's initial topic. In the second example, the educator does follow the child's lead by asking more about their experience and is able to extend the learning by drawing comparisons to the classroom activity. They also extend the learning for the other children by engaging them in the conversation. This example demonstrates how being responsive to children's comments can lead to new learning and connections.

Keep the Conversation Going

Engaging children in conversation by following their lead is an important place to start, but it is then important to keep the conversation going. This concept is echoed in the teacher's coaching as referenced in McIntyre et al. (this volume). This involves using comments and questions to add ideas to what children are interested in and then pausing to cue them to take another turn in the conversation (De Rivera et al., 2005; Girolametto et al., 2003, 2005, 2012; Weitzman & Greenberg, 2002).

In the previous second example for the gardener activity, as the educator follows the child's lead, they also focus on keeping the conversational turns going. They cue the child to take another turn in the conversation by

- making comments that validate what the child has said to show interest and to encourage the child to continue the conversation;
- adding interesting ideas to what the child says to stimulate the child's thinking;
- asking questions to clarify, request further information, or encourage children to think more deeply about a topic, while avoiding testing questions (e.g., What colour is that? What's that?) that tend to stop the conversation.

As a result, this conversation continues for many turns and the child is supported to flesh out the observations they made at their grandma's house and expand their knowledge of plant growth.

Here are specific ways in which this educator encourages extended turns.

> EDUCATOR: Remember when each of you planted a seed in your pot? You cared for it by watering and making sure it had sunlight. Now you can see that a small stem is growing and soon there will be a flower. [*Pauses to provide the child with an opportunity to add a comment or ask a question*]
> CHILD: Like at my grandma's house! She grows lots of things in her backyard.
> EDUCATOR: Oh, you've also seen flowers growing at your grandma's house.
> [*Makes a comment to validate what the child said and pauses to cue the child to take another turn*]

CHILD: No, she doesn't grow flowers, just carrots and potatoes.
EDUCATOR: Ah, that's a bit different than growing flowers but did she plant any seeds? [*Adds an idea to the child's comment and asks for more information to encourage the child to take another turn*]
CHILD: Yes, lots of seeds and I helped her.
EDUCATOR: And what does she do to make sure the vegetables grow? [*Asks for more information to cue the child to take another turn*]
CHILD: Makes sure it has water!
EDUCATOR: So, vegetables and flowers are *similar*. "Similar" means that vegetables and flowers are the same since they both need water. Just like with our flowers, your grandma planted a seed and watered it! Does anything come up out of the ground like our flowers? [*Adds ideas to what the child said and asks for more information to cue the child to take another turn*]
CHILD: Yes, but not flowers.
EDUCATOR: No, not flowers. What did come out of the ground? [*Makes a comment to validate what the child says and asks for more information to cue the child to take another turn*]
CHILD: Just leaves.
EDUCATOR: So, where were the vegetables? [*Asks for more information to cue another turn*]
CHILD: We had to pull them out of the ground.
EDUCATOR: So, some vegetables, like carrots and potatoes, are different from flowers since they grow under the ground. But they are similar to flowers since they still need sun and water and they have green leaves just like our flowers. [*Pauses to provide the child with an opportunity to process this new information and take another turn*]
CHILD: But not all vegetables. My grandma grows tomatoes and they aren't in the ground!
EDUCATOR: You're right. Lots of vegetables are grown above ground like flowers. Who else has vegetables at your house that grow above the ground? [*Makes a comment to validate what the child says and asks a question to draw other children into the conversation*]

At the end of this interaction, the educator also attempts to draw the other children into the conversation. As the other children become involved, interaction can develop between the peers as well as with the educator. Providing opportunities for children to engage in peer-to-peer interactions also has an important role in place-based learning. Children's language and learning is fostered when they draw upon their funds of knowledge to exchange their thoughts and ideas with their peers.

Add Vocabulary Knowledge

Through supporting back-and-forth exchanges in a sustained conversation, educators have opportunities to introduce and explain words that may be unfamiliar to the children. This is important since vocabulary knowledge is a significant predictor of literacy success as well as general academic success (Bowne et al., 2016; Ruston & Schwanenflugel, 2010).

Words that children may not know are referred to as Tier 2 and 3 words (Beck et al., 2002; Biemiller, 2009). Tier 1 words are basic and general, such as *book*, *orange*, and *sad*, and tend to already be in children's everyday vocabularies. Tier 2 words tend to be more specific or sophisticated and are generally unfamiliar to children, such as *lovely*, *grasp*, and *annoy*. Tier 3 words also occur less frequently and are generally tied to a specific topic or subject matter, such as *volcano*, *orbit*, or *addition*.

Compare these two examples that could arise in a dramatic play situation representing a grocery store in the children's community, where the child is the shopper and the educator has joined in the play as the shopkeeper.

Example A.
  CHILD: I need to buy some milk for my baby.
  EDUCATOR: Okay, two dollars please.

In this example, the conversation only continues for two turns with the child not being exposed to any new vocabulary.

Example B.
  CHILD: I need to buy some milk for my baby.
  EDUCATOR: Oh, you want to *purchase* some milk. How much milk would you like?
  CHILD: A big thing of milk.
  EDUCATOR: Oh, so you want the biggest *carton* of milk. That carton holds two *litres* of milk.
  CHILD: Yes, I want the big carton. I want two litres.
  EDUCATOR: Ok, here is your carton with two *litres* of milk. The *price* will be two dollars, please.

In the second example, the conversation continues for six turns. As the conversation is extended, the educator is able to include four words that may be less familiar to the child – *purchase, carton, litre,* and *price*. *Purchase* and *carton* could be considered Tier 2 words since these words are more specific or sophisticated compared to the Tier 1 words used by the child (*buy, thing*) and are not typically used by children in their everyday conversation. *Price* is also a word that this child may not know. *Litre* could be considered a Tier 3 word since it is associated with the specific topic of measuring liquid volumes.

In the previous second exchange in the gardener activity, the educator also added a Tier 2 word, "similar."

Extended conversations provide opportunities for educators to explain the meanings of new words and support children's conceptual learning (Barnes & Dickinson, 2017; Nanasivayam et al., 2014). Greenberg and Weitzman (2014) suggest that educators make new words sparkle by shooting for the SSTaRS. SSTaRS is an acronym that refers to how to deepen children's understanding of a new word through **S**tressing the word to highlight it in the conversation, **S**howing the meaning with gestures and other visual cues, **T**elling what the word means, **R**elating the word to children's previous knowledge or experiences, and **S**aying the words again in multiple contexts. Children's understanding of new word meanings is especially enhanced when educators make connections to children's existing funds of knowledge.

Model Complex Language

As children develop, the grammatical or syntactic complexity of their language also increases. Just as they require models and examples of Tier 2 and 3 vocabulary, children also need to hear and practise complex syntax. Acquiring knowledge and use of more complex syntax predicts language comprehension and ultimately reading comprehension (Flynn, 2016). Back-and-forth conversations provide opportunities for educators to expand on children's language with models that include diverse and complex syntactic forms. This means accepting what the child has said and providing an alternative linguistic form that adds to the child's meaning, either with a grammatically more complete form or with the addition of a new idea that results in a more complex sentence.

Knowledge of complex syntax also promotes vocabulary growth since children use cues provided by sentence structure to learn new words. For example, with the following sentence, "Martin was flabbergasted when he saw a giraffe walking towards him," a child's understanding of the grammatical structure of the sentence would reveal that *flabbergasted* is an adjective that describes how Martin felt.

Here is an example of an outdoor activity where the children are jumping into piles of leaves. As the educator follows the child's lead and keeps the conversation going, they expose the child to complex sentences with multiple clauses.

CHILD: I am making a giant pile.
EDUCATOR: Yes, and when you jump in that giant pile, the leaves are going to scatter all around you.
CHILD: Okay, here I go! [*Child jumps.*] All the leaves are flying now!
EDUCATOR: Yes, there are lots of leaves flying in the air except for the ones you are sitting on because you're very heavy! Now, I'm going to jump in the leaves! What do you predict will happen to the leaves?

During this interaction, the educator models complex sentences with main and subordinate clauses ("when you jump in the giant pile," "except for the ones you are sitting on," "because you're very heavy") as well as including the Tier 2 words, "scatter" and "predict."

The previous gardening example also includes examples of the educator modelling complex language as they keep the conversation going, such as,

Just like with our flowers, your grandma planted a seed and watered it!
So, some vegetables, like carrots and potatoes, are different from flowers *since they grow under the ground.* But they are similar to flowers *since they still need sun and water* and they have green leaves *just like our flowers do.*

Extend the Topic beyond the Here and Now

As educators build on children's interests in sustained conversations, they have opportunities to stimulate children's thinking and co-construct new knowledge that incorporates decontextualized language that goes beyond the here and now (Girolametto et al., 2003, 2005, 2012). Weitzman and Greenberg (2014) suggest eight ways to extend the topic to focus on more abstract topics beyond the immediate context. They call these options the E's and P's to refer to the initial letter of each:

1. Draw upon the children's **E**xperiences in the past.
2. Talk about **E**motions and feelings.
3. Provide **E**xplanations.
4. **E**valuate different options and form opinions.
5. **P**roblem-solve.
6. **P**redict what will happen next.
7. **P**roject and imagine what someone else is thinking or what it would be like to be in a situation you have never encountered.
8. **P**retend in an imaginary scenario.

When educators add the above elements to the conversation, they provide children with opportunities to predict, reason, plan, and hypothesize. Educators can do this with comments (e.g., "This tower fell down because there are too many blocks piled on top of each other") or questions that compel children to figure out a response (e.g., "Why do you think our tower fell down?"). Educators also show children how to think more deeply about a topic when they specifically make thinking-out-loud comments like, "I'm thinking that we better not add another block because the tower will be too high and will come tumbling down."

Place- and play-based learning offers many opportunities for educators to build decontextualized language as they encourage children to think creatively and use what they already know and are familiar with in a different context, or to explore a new idea. This means moving beyond frequently asked closed questions that typically elicit only one correct answer to more open questions that extend children's thinking and use of language. Following a child's lead with questions like "What would happen if ...?," "How would we find out?," "I wonder why ...," or "What do you think about ...?" can be a powerful way to keep the conversation going and encourage children to communicate their thinking and learning in meaningful ways. This extension of children's thinking is akin to the "language of reflection" that Scull and O'Grady describe (this volume).

Playful activities that involve imagination and pretending are especially good for building decontextualized language since they inherently represent events and objects beyond the immediate context. In the following two examples, educators have set up a pretend road, traffic intersection, and gas station in the playground for the children to navigate in toy cars. As the teacher joins in as a crossing guard, they are able to engage the children in conversation, with many opportunities to promote extended thinking and language.

Example 1

CHILD: Oh-oh. My car is stuck!
EDUCATOR: Oh dear. Has this ever happened to you before? (**Experiences**)
CHILD: Yeah, it happened with my Dad this morning. That's why I got to school late.
EDUCATOR: Why did your Dad's car get stuck? (**Explain**)
CHILD: We needed to get more gas from the gas station.
EDUCATOR: Oh, do you think that is the problem with your car?
CHILD: Yeah, I think so. I better go to the gas station. (**Problem-solve**)
EDUCATOR: Good idea!

Example 2
> JOSEPH: Jason bumped into my car!
> EDUCATOR: Oh-oh. Jason, you sound upset. (**Emotions**) What happened?
> JASON: Joseph stopped and I couldn't go!
> EDUCATOR: I think there was a reason why Joseph stopped. Joseph, can you tell Jason why you stopped? (**Explain**)
> JOSEPH: There was a red light and the red light means stop!
> EDUCATOR: Yes, it does. Jason, do you understand why Joseph is upset? (**Project**)
> JASON: Sorry, Joseph.
> EDUCATOR: Nice that you said you were sorry, Jason. So, next time you see a red light, what will you do? (**Predict**)
> JASON: Stop.
> EDUCATOR: Good to hear.

The previous gardening example also demonstrates examples of the educator extending the topic when they encourage the child to more fully describe their past *experiences* at their grandma's house and then *explained* why vegetables and flowers are the same and different.

Conclusion

Play- and place-based learning offers many opportunities for fostering children's early language learning and lay the foundation for literacy development during meaningful interactions throughout the day that draw upon children's knowledge and experiences. Through purposeful and intentional planning of sustained conversations, educators can successfully capitalize on this potential and lay the foundation for children's future academic success.

REFERENCES

Barnes, E., & Dickinson, D. (2017). The impact of teachers' commenting strategies on children's vocabulary growth. *Exceptionality, 25*(3), 186–206. https://doi.org/10.1080/09362835.2016.1196447

Beck, I., McKeown, M., & Kucan, L. (2002). *Bringing words to life: Robust vocabulary instruction.* New York: The Guilford Press.

Biemiller, A. (2009). *Words worth teaching: Closing the vocabulary gap.* Columbus, OH: McGraw-Hill, SRA.

Bowne, J., Yoshikawa, H., & Snow, C. (2016). Relationships of teachers' language and explicit vocabulary instruction to students' vocabulary growth in kindergarten. *Reading Research Quarterly, 52*(1), 7–29. https://doi.org/10.1002/rrq.151

De Rivera, C., Girolametto, L., Greenberg, J., & Weitzman, E. (2005). Children's responses to educators' questions in day care play groups. *American Journal of Speech-Language Pathology, 14,* 14–26. https://doi.org/10.1044/1058-0360(2005/004)

Dickinson, D.K., Hofer K., & Barnes, E. (2014). Examining teachers' language in Head Start classrooms from a systemic linguistics approach. *Early Childhood Research Quarterly, 29*(3), 231–244. https://doi.org/10.1016/j.ecresq.2014.02.006

Dickinson, D.K., & Porche, M.V. (2011). Relation between language experiences in preschool classrooms and children's kindergarten and fourth-grade language and reading abilities. *Child Development, 82*(3), 870–886. https://doi.org/10.1111/j.1467-8624.2011.01576.x

Dickinson, D.K., & Tabors, P.O. (2001). *Beginning literacy with language: Young children learning at home and school.* Paul H. Brookes.

Flynn, E.E. (2016). Language-rich early childhood classroom: Simple but powerful beginnings. *The Reading Teacher, 70*(2), 159–166. https://doi.org/10.1002/trtr.1487

Gibbons, P. (2006). *Bridging discourses in the ESL classroom.* Continuum.

Gilkerson, J., Richards, J.A., Warren, S.F., Kimbrough Oller, D., Russo, R., & Vohr, B. (2018). Language experience in the second year of life and language outcomes in later childhood. *Pediatrics, 142*(4). https://doi.org/10.1542/peds.2017-4276

Girolametto, L., Weitzman, E., & Greenberg, J. (2003). Training day care staff to facilitate children's language. *American Journal of Speech-Language Pathology, 12,* 299–311. https://doi.org/10.1044/1058-0360(2003/076)

Girolametto, L., Weitzman, E., & Greenberg, J. (2005). Facilitating language skills: Inservice education for early childhood educators and preschool teachers. *Infants and Young Children, 19*(1), 36–46. https://doi.org/10.1097/00001163-200601000-00005

Girolametto, L., Weitzman, E., & Greenberg, J. (2012). Facilitating emergent literacy: Efficacy of a model that partners speech-language pathologists and educators. *American Journal of Speech-Language Pathology, 21,* 47–63. https://doi.org/10.1044/1058-0360(2011/11-0002)

Girolametto, L., Weitzman, E., van Lieshout, R., & Duff, D. (2000). Directiveness in teachers' language input to toddlers and preschoolers in day care. *Journal of Speech, Language and Hearing Research, 43,* 1101–1114. https://doi.org/10.1044/jslhr.4305.1101

Greenberg, J., & Weitzman, E. (2014). *I'm ready: How to prepare your child for reading success.* A Hanen Centre Publication.

Gunnewig, S., & McGloin, D. (2003). In K. Roskos, P.O. Tabors & L.A. Lenart, *Oral language and early literacy in preschool: Talking, reading, and writing.* International Reading Association.

Hart, B., & Risley, T.R. (2003, Spring). The early catastrophe: The 30 million word gap by age 3. *American Educator,* 4–9.

Hirsh-Pasek, K., & Golinkoff, R.M. (2011). The great balancing act: Optimizing core curricula through playful pedagogy. In E. Zigler, W.S. Gilliam & W.S. Barnett (Eds.), *The pre-K debates: Current controversies and issues* (pp. 110–116). Paul H. Brookes.

Justice, L., Jiang, H., & Strasser, K. (2018). Linguistic environment of preschool classrooms: What dimensions support children's language growth? *Early Childhood Research Quarterly, 42,* 79–92. https://doi.org/10.1016/j.ecresq.2017.09.003

McIntyre, L.J., Hellsten, L.M., & Bergen, T. (2022). Place-based language and literacy learning in play: Learning from a north-central Saskatchewan Indigenous community. In S.S. Peterson & N. Friedrich (Eds.), *The role of place and play in young children's language and literacy* (pp. 227–242). University of Toronto Press.

McTigue, E., Douglass, A., Wright, K.L., Hodges, T.S., & Franks, A.D. (2015). Beyond the story map: Inferential comprehension via character perspective. *The Reading Teacher, 69*(1), 99–101. https://doi.org/10.1002/trtr.1377

Milburn, T., Girolametto, L., Weitzman, E., & Greenberg, J. (2013). Enhancing preschool educators' ability to facilitate conversations during shared book reading. *Journal of Early Childhood Literacy, 14,* 105–140. https://doi.org/10.1177%2F1468798413478261

Nanasivayam, A., Hipfner-Boucher, K., Milburn, T., Weitzman, E., Greenberg, J., Pelletier, J., & Girolametto, L. (2014). Effects of coaching on educators' vocabulary-teaching strategies during shared reading. *International Journal of Speech-Language Pathology,* Early Online: 1–11. https://doi.org/10.3109/17549507.2014.979871

Peterson, S.S., McIntyre, L., & Forsyth, D. (2016). Supporting young children's oral language and writing development: Teachers' and early childhood educators' goals and practices. *Australasian Journal of Early Childhood, 41*(3), 11–19. https://doi.org/10.1177%2F183693911604100303

Resnick, L.B., & Snow, C.E. (2009). *Speaking and listening for preschool through third grade.* International Reading Association.

Romeo, R., Leonard, J., Robinson, S., West, M., Mackey A., Rowe, M., & Gabrieli, J. (2018). Beyond the 30-million-word gap: Children's conversational exposure is associated with language-related brain function. *Psychological Science, 29*(5), 700–710. https://doi.org/10.1177%2F0956797617742725

Ruston, H.P., & Schwanenflugel, P.J. (2010). Effects of a conversation intervention on the expressive vocabulary development of prekindergarten children. *Language, Speech and Hearing Services in Schools, 41*, 303–313. https://doi.org/10.1044/0161-1461(2009/08-0100)

Scull, J., & O'Grady, K. (2022). Exploring imaginative play – as a stimulus for "language in action" and "language as reflection." In S.S. Peterson & N. Friedrich (Eds.), *The role of place and play in young children's language and literacy* (pp. 195–210). University of Toronto Press.

Van Kleeck, A. (2014). Distinguishing between casual talk and academic talk beginning in the preschool years: An important consideration for speech-language pathologists. *American Journal of Speech-Language Pathology, 23*(4), 724–741. https://doi.org/10.1044/2014_AJSLP-14-0032

Weisberg, D., Hirsh-Pasek, K., & Golinkoff, R. (2013). Guided play: Where curricular goals meet a playful pedagogy. *Mind, Brain and Education, 7*(2), 104–112. https://doi.org/10.1111/mbe.12015

Weitzman, E., Girolametto, L., & Greenberg, J. (2006). Adult responsiveness as a critical intervention mechanism for emergent literacy: Strategies for early childcare educators. In L.M. Justice (Ed.), *Clinical approaches to emergent literacy intervention* (pp. 127–178). Plural Publishing.

Weitzman, E., & Greenberg, J. (2002). *Learning language and loving it: A guide to promoting children's social, language and literacy development in early childhood settings*. A Hanen Centre Publication.

Weitzman, E., & Greenberg, J. (2014). *ABC and beyond: Building emergent literacy in early childhood settings*. A Hanen Centre Publication.

15 Language Learning in the Garden: Discoveries from a Collaboration in a North-Central Saskatchewan Indigenous Community

LAUREEN J. MCINTYRE, LAURIE-ANN M. HELLSTEN, AND TYLER BERGEN

Preschool, pre-kindergarten, and kindergarten teachers in the Canadian province of Saskatchewan are encouraged to focus on developing competent learners, promoting children's holistic development, and fostering strong positive relationships by creating a stimulating learning environment to inspire conversation and inquiry-based play (Saskatchewan Ministry of Education, 2008, 2010). By providing enriching and well-planned environments that allow children to explore and experience natural and open-ended materials, such as indoor and outdoor gardens, early childhood educators can encourage children's language development and learning (Desmond et al., 2002; Saskatchewan Ministry of Education, 2009). This chapter highlights young children's language learning in garden-based play in one pre-kindergarten classroom in a North-Central Saskatchewan Indigenous community.

In early learning environments, play-based exploration is predominantly used to support children's cognitive, linguistic, social-emotional, physical, and academic development (Jones & Reynolds, 2011; Saskatchewan Ministry of Education, 2008), and to foster creativity and stimulate children's imaginations (The Lego Foundation, 2018). In the Indigenous community highlighted in this chapter, place-based learning is central to the learning activities teachers planned and carried out as part of collaborative action research with one of the authors, Laureen. Place-based educational opportunities use "local heritage, cultures, landscapes, opportunities and experiences ... as a foundation for the study of language arts, mathematics, social studies, science and other subjects across the curriculum" (Center for Place-based Learning and Community Engagement, n.d., para. 1). Place-based and experiential learning are typically key features of

Indigenous pedagogical approaches across the various regions in Canada. As Antoine et al., (2018) outlined:

> Indigenous pedagogies are experiential because they emphasize learning by doing ... an emphasis on experiential learning means a preference for learning through observation, action, reflection, and further action ... [they] connect learning to a specific place, and thus knowledge is situated in relationship to a location, experience, and group of people. (p. 18)

Educators in Canada, particularly in Saskatchewan, are being encouraged to incorporate Indigenous pedagogical approaches in their teaching not only to better support student learners who are Indigenous but to "support systemic change through Indigenization, decolonization, and reconciliation" (Antoine et al., 2018, p. ix).

Garden-based learning (GBL) (Desmond et al., 2002) is an experiential learning approach for actively engaging and supporting students of varying ages in the learning process in their local landscapes (Lloyd & Gray, 2010). This approach is detailed in the next section.

The Garden as a Teaching Tool

Garden-based learning offers students ample opportunities to develop connections to the natural environment. They see how gardens can change over time and learn about ways in which growing their own food benefits their school and local community (Hahn, 2017). GBL supports learning in the sciences, but also in other subject areas such as language arts, math, writing, and social studies (Williams & Dixon, 2013). Additionally, GBL supports students' "sense of attachment to adults in the school setting" (Ozer, 2007, p. 854). It provides a context for promoting good health, as nutrition education and increased physical activity are a natural part of GBL (Bell & Dyment, 2008). Through GBL, children learn about "responsibility, teamwork, and respect for nature, others, and themselves" (DiClaudio et al., 2013, p. 1). They explore, move, interact with others, imagine, and play with gardening materials while planting, caring for, and harvesting the garden (Laaksoharju et al., 2012). The use of supervised agricultural experiences within classroom gardens is a novel and powerful way to teach children about the world around them, since "students thrive when they take what they have learned inside the classroom and put it into hands-on learning in real-life situations" (DiClaudio et al., 2013, p. 2). In learning environments using GBL, students can focus on building collaborative relationships with community members and studying local ecology, which has been shown to foster improved student performance on standardized tests, improved subject grades such as in science, and enhanced motivation to complete tasks and engagement in team work (Blair, 2009).

Garden-based learning programs being used in Saskatchewan are the Little Green Sprouts and Little Green Thumbs programs (Agriculture in the Classroom Saskatchewan, n.d. a). Little Green Sprouts and Little Green Thumbs are indoor gardening programs supported by the educational charity, Agriculture in the Classroom Saskatchewan (AITC SK). The aim of these programs are to use hands-on inquiry and curriculum-based resources to connect children with agriculture and help "young people value themselves, the environment and their community" (AITC SK, n.d. b, para. 1). Once a teacher applies and has been selected to be in a program, the teacher is provided with a garden kit, which includes "soil boxes, grow light, hardware, and other basic supplies … [such as] self-watering tubes and a timer for the indoor light" (AITC SK, n.d. c, para. 2). To use the kit, teachers must set aside 24 square feet of space in the classroom. AITC SK also supports students and teachers throughout the project by providing training, educational resources, and intermittent support through a coordinator. When school and classroom gardens are incorporated into early years' school curricula, educators can better support students in having more personal and direct exposure to, and experience in, nature (Blair, 2009).

In the collaborative action research project, Laureen and one of the teachers in the early years classroom focused on supporting students' language development while engaging in the Little Green Sprouts/Thumbs project. Their action research involved interprofessional collaborative practice (Abel et al., 2015; Coufal &Woods, 2018), as Laureen, a speech-language pathologist and researcher, worked with teachers to learn how to best support the diverse linguistic needs of the children in teachers' classrooms. They found coaching to be a helpful approach to support teachers' professional learning and students' language learning (Vicker, 2009). As Greenberg and Walker highlight in this volume, educators play a critical role as conversational partners. A coaching model specific to teaching language learning strategies is described in the next section.

Collaboration and Coaching to Implement Language Learning Strategies

Coaching is a helpful and facilitative method that can be used to support individuals or groups of people to learn new knowledge and skills, and to improve their current competence and performance (Ellinger et al., 2008). In Laureen's collaborative action research project with teachers, she used her expertise and experience in supporting children's speech and language by introducing, practising, and supporting teachers in implementing language stimulation strategies that they could employ during everyday classroom activities, including play activities. In the process, the coaching interactions that were part of the collaborative action research enhanced the teachers' pedagogical knowledge and skills.

Laureen based her coaching practices on the evidence-based suggestions, strategies, and materials she has used as a speech-language pathologist and those provided in the Learning Language and Loving It (LLLI; Weitzman & Greenberg, 2012) program. The goals of the program are to support teachers and parents to be able to: (1) use "natural everyday activities, routines, and play"; (2) become "attuned to children's interests so [teachers and parents] can follow their lead, which is known to foster language development"; (3) adjust "the way [teachers and parents] talk to help children develop more advanced language skills"; (4) promote "interaction among the children themselves"; (5) facilitate "language-learning in pretend play"'; and (6) foster "emergent literacy skills" (The Hanen Centre, 2016, para. 3). Greenberg and Walker in this volume also discuss various language stimulation strategies educators can use to support children's conversations and promote their language development. Their collaborative discussions started with Laureen's introduction of specific evidence-based language stimulation strategies that would meet the identified language learning needs of the students and effect change in teacher practice; these were followed by teachers practising the skills under her guidance. She and participating teachers then determined ways these evidence-based resources and approaches could be adapted to their individual classroom settings. Finally, teachers implemented and adapted these practices during interactions with students during classroom play-based activities.

In their collaborative action research project, teachers, educational/teacher assistants or parent volunteers, and Laureen worked together to facilitate children's language development and learning in language-rich play-based classrooms. In the context of this work, language can be defined as consisting of "some aspect of content or meaning that is coded or represented by linguistic form for some purpose or use in a particular context" (Bloom & Lahey, 1978, p. 11). Their action research is particularly important in participating teachers' preschool and early school years classrooms since a large portion of a child's language learning occurs during the first five years of life (e.g., Bloom & Lahey, 1978; Owens, 2012; The Hanen Centre, n.d.). The children may be developing language skills in the manner typically expected for children their age, or they may be experiencing language delays, differences (i.e., speaking dialects or a first language that differs from standard English), difficulties, and/or disorders (ASHA, 1993). We describe one pre-kindergarten teacher's action research project that involved play, garden-based learning, and coaching to support student and teacher development and learning in the following section.

Language Learning in Garden-Based Play

The authors of this chapter acknowledge that they work, and conducted this research, on Treaty 6 Territory and the Homeland of the Métis. We pay our respect to the First Nation and Métis ancestors of this place and reaffirm our relationship with them.

During the course of a seven-year action research/collaborative inquiry study Laureen, the first author of this chapter, had the opportunity to form a close collaborative relationship with the teacher of a pre-kindergarten classroom in a rural North-Central Saskatchewan Indigenous community. We will call her Layla. This classroom was located in a community school of approximately 350 pre-kindergarten to Grade 12 students in a community of approximately 600 people (Government of Saskatchewan, 2017; Statistics Canada, 2016).

The pre-kindergarten classroom had a maximum of 16 students at any one time and offered attendance to 3-year-olds for up to two half-days a week and to 4-year-olds for up to four half-days a week (Government of Saskatchewan, n.d.). As explained on the Government of Saskatchewan website (n.d.), "the prekindergarten classroom targets vulnerable three- and four-year-old children and their families" (para. 7). When school programs are selecting students for placement in these classrooms, they consider vulnerable circumstances such as: the home language of the family is a language other than English, or the child has language or communication delays (Government of Saskatchewan, n.d.). Layla observed that the majority of her students' parents felt their children's language skills were behind their same-aged peers when they started in her classroom. She also estimated that 80% to 90% of the students currently attending the community school were from an Indigenous background. English, French, and Cree are the predominant languages reported to be spoken in this community and the surrounding area (Statistics Canada, 2016). Therefore, students in this classroom may have been exposed to, and have familiarity with, more than one language in their home environments.

Layla had been teaching in this school for over five years at the time of the study. She was greatly interested in inquiry and supporting students' learning through interactions with their environment. The goals of her action research were to help students learn how to care for plants and recognize where the food that they eat comes from, and to support their language skill development. As Scull and O'Grady discuss in this volume, it is vital for educators to understand the benefit of using planned opportunities to support children in becoming competent language users.

After being accepted by AITC SK to participate in the Little Green Sprouts/Thumbs program, Layla began to create her classroom garden (see Figure 15.1). Layla knew that most of her students did not have gardens at home so she chose a variety of seeds to plant that she thought the students would enjoy eating and that were relatively easy to grow. She planned and implemented a variety of inquiry and play-based activities to support the learning goals, such as manipulating, planting, maintaining, and monitoring vegetable, flower, and herb seeds/plants in a classroom garden; and creating, maintaining, and monitoring a red wiggler worm habitat, which provided compost for the garden.

Layla talked to her students about working together to help take care of their classroom garden. She encouraged students to check the garden regularly. Students were to stick their fingers in the hole in the bottom of the gardening containers to feel the soil to determine whether the plants needed to be watered. Students were to touch the plants' leaves to determine whether the leaves were dead (if they crumbled or crunched), and thus, needed to be removed from the plants. Students and Layla removed plants that had died. They also determined whether there were vegetables ripe enough to pick and eat by looking under the leaves of each of the plants. Layla was continually striving to foster an appreciation of how plants within a garden needed to be cared for to thrive.

In the context of these activities Laureen, who is a Canadian- and American-certified SLP, a Hanen-certified SLP in the LLLI program, and a university-based researcher, coached Layla and the educational assistant assigned to her classroom to use strategies and techniques to support the language and literacy skill development of her students. The collaborative partnership between Laureen and Layla developed and deepened over the course of the seven-year project. They met in person on at least a monthly basis and co-created the language and literacy goals to target during each school year to enhance students' language and literacy and their own language modelling skills. They also reviewed classroom videos of child-child and their own child-adult interactions and had reflective discussions on the implementation of language stimulation strategies that were part of the action research.

In the following sections, we highlight ways in which coaching was used during these learning activities. The activities are introduced in terms of the language goals that they addressed, and these goals reflected what Bloom and Lahey (1978) explained are the three major components

Figure 15.1 The Pre-kindergarten Classroom Garden

of language: language form (phonology, morphology, syntax), content (semantics), and use (pragmatics).

Language Form (Phonology, Morphology, Syntax)

Language form relates to how the features of language (rules for combining speech sounds or phonology, rules for forming words or morphology, and rules for combining words to create utterances or syntax) are organized in a particular order, which is often referred to as the grammar of a language (Bloom & Lahey, 1978; Owens, 2012). Coaching teachers on the use of language stimulation techniques such as language expansion and language extension (The Hanen Centre, 2016; Stuckey, 2009), and using correct grammar and syntax (Spivey, 2009), can give teachers tools to better support students in developing their language form. Layla and Laureen found that the garden project provided many occasions for children to manipulate and explore the materials used to create, maintain, or care for the plants in the garden. While children are engaged in these activities, Layla was coached to look for opportunities to encourage individual children to understand, form, and combine words to express these experiences.

Layla observed that her students did not often use complete and complex sentences when speaking. Therefore, one of the action research project goals that Laureen and Layla co-created involved modelling language forms, with the purpose of enhancing students' understanding and use of increasingly complex and grammatically correct utterances/sentences. This involved responding to children's language initiations. Layla followed each student's conversational lead and modelled grammatically correct rephrases of each child's utterance or language expansion. She was also encouraged to add new information when rephrasing statements or extending what students had said, in order to provide models of standard language use and create a conversation with the child (Spivey, 2009; Stuckey, 2009; The Hanen Centre, 2016). We use as an example one of the videos involving Layla asking one of her students to stick her finger in the hole at the bottom of a gardening container to see if the dirt was dry or if she could feel wet soil to determine if the plants had enough water.

STUDENT: "Der's water in dere."
LAYLA: "You felt water in there."

Layla repeated what the student had said to indicate she had understood her (ASHA, n.d. a, n.d. b) and then moved on to another topic. When Laureen and Layla engaged in conversations about ways to improve on language modelling in future interactions, as part of the collaborative action research process, they noted that Layla not only could have expanded the student's utterance but also could have added information or extended her statement. This would have helped the student to increase the length of her statement. For example, Layla could have said, "You felt water in there. The plants have enough to drink today," or "You felt water in there. The soil is wet."

In this same video clip, after the class had finished checking the water levels of each gardening container and she was moving them to look at the plants in the container, Layla also modelled a grammatically correct rephrasing of a child's utterance.

STUDENT: Flowers growed.
LAYLA: There are flowers growing in there.

She then went on to direct the students to organize themselves in a line so everyone could see the gardening containers. As in the previous instance, Layla demonstrated that she understood the student's message and provided a grammatically correcte model of his utterance but missed the opportunity to extend this statement. In their reflections on this interaction while viewing the video clip, Laureen and Layla discussed how Layla could have replied, using extended statements such as, "There are flowers growing in there. I see three purple flowers growing on the plant," or "There are flowers growing in there. The flowers are hiding under the leaves."

Layla and Laureen found the place-based learning environment of the classroom garden was a context for students to use oral language to communicate meaningfully with peers and their teacher. As students expressed themselves verbally during play-based activities, Layla could extend and expand what they could do with language forms. She could follow their conversational leads and adjust the way she was speaking to provide grammatically correct extensions and expansions of their verbal utterances during classroom activities (Spivey, 2009; Stuckey, 2009; The Hanen Centre, 2016). As we show in the next section, Layla also encouraged the development of students' language content skills or use of more or varied vocabulary words in play- and place-based activities.

Language Content (Semantics)

Language content involves the meaning of language (Bloom & Lahey, 1978) or the "rules governing the meaning or content of words and word combinations" (Owens, 2012, p. 23). Students can be taught and encouraged to understand and use new and varied vocabulary words when they are immersed in language-rich environments and exposed to a variety of new learning experiences (The Hanen Centre, 2016). Layla's action research was guided by observations that her students' language could be enhanced through the introduction of opportunities to use different vocabulary. Therefore, a second goal co-created by Laureen and Layla was modelling, explaining, and encouraging the use of context-specific and increasingly more advanced vocabulary words.

As part of her action research, Layla was coached to use new and varied vocabulary words and provide age-appropriate or student-friendly explanations of the meaning of these words in the context of the classroom garden. Laureen provided coaching to support Layla's professional learning in the use of such language-stimulation strategies related to language content (ASHA, n.d. a, n.d. b; Biemiller & Boote, 2006; Spivey, 2013; The Hanen Centre, 2016). In the classroom garden context, Layla's students were exposed to new and increasingly advanced vocabulary related to both the seeds and gardening materials being used, and the actions related to planting, maintaining, and caring for the varied plants being grown. For example, in all of the gardening activities in the classroom, Layla modelled and encouraged her students to understand and use the proper names for vegetables the class had planted (e.g., "tomatoes," "peppers"), the parts of the plants (e.g., "root," "stem"), and verbs or action words related to caring for their garden (e.g., "pollinate," "prune"). In one of the video-recorded interactions in the classroom garden setting, Layla talked with her students about the jobs they needed to complete to care for their garden, leading a student to comment on what was being grown in their classroom garden:

STUDENT: And we can grow our apples too.

Layla responded that the round vegetables that were growing in their garden were not apples, and asked the students to help identify what the green and red vegetables growing on the vines were called. Students took turns offering what produce they thought were growing in the classroom garden:

STUDENT 1: Crab apples
STUDENT 2: Pumpkins
STUDENT 3: Tomatoes
LAYLA: Tomatoes, we are growing tomatoes.

In this example, Layla led the students to use the fruit's or vegetable's name and describe how it looked (i.e., its shape and colour) when they were working in their classroom garden. In collaborative action research conversations, Laureen and Layla proposed that Layla could have also discussed the variety of ways tomatoes can be prepared, processed, and eaten to further improve the students' understanding of the word "tomato." For example, Layla could have said, "Tomatoes, we are growing tomatoes. Ripe tomatoes can be mashed up to make sauce for our spaghetti," or "Tomatoes, we are growing tomatoes. I like to wash and cut up red tomatoes with a knife and put them on my sandwich."

Repeatedly saying a new word and describing what the word means, including discussing the use or function associated with the word, in the context of garden-based play activities can help a student to better understand and use new and varied vocabulary words (ASHA, n.d. a, n.d. b; Biemiller & Boote, 2006; Spivey, 2013; The Hanen Centre, 2016). As we show in the next section, teachers can also encourage the development of students' language use or pragmatic language skills in classroom garden activities.

Language Use (Pragmatics)

Pragmatics is the language component related to the reasons for communicating, or the functions of language in a communicative context

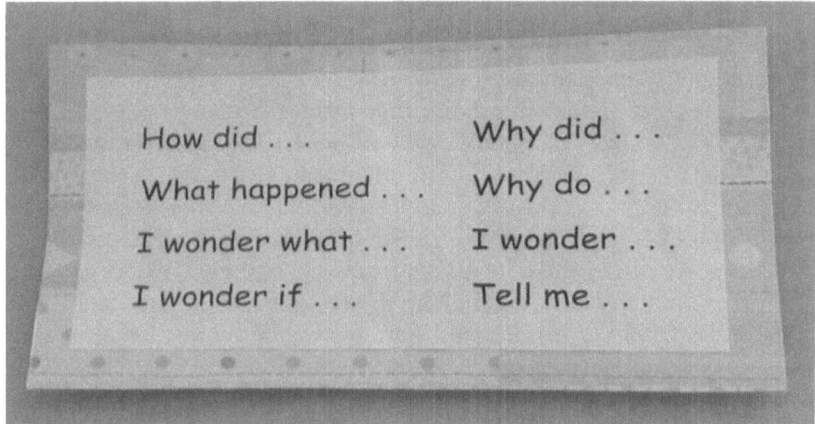

Figure 15.2 Open-Ended Statements and Process Questions Classroom Poster

(e.g., using language for different purposes such as giving or gaining information). Knowledge of pragmatics guides speakers as they vary what is said to meet the needs of different listeners in varying contexts (Bloom & Lahey, 1978; Owens, 2012). Language-stimulation strategies for supporting students' pragmatic skills include using open-ended statements and questions, which can help students develop their conversational language skills (e.g., encouraging conversational turn taking) or skills related to language use (Girolametto et al., 2003; Tofade et al., 2013; The Hanen Centre, 2016).

A starting point for Layla's action research was her observation she was continually asking her students questions that seemed to limit student responses to one or two words. Therefore, a third goal co-created by Laureen and Layla was to decrease the number of closed or yes/no questions asked in garden-based play interactions. By encouraging students' elaborated responses through open-ended questions, Laureen and Layla hoped to increase students' verbal interactions and build their conversational skills. In their collaborative action research conversations, Laureen and Layla discussed question stems that encourage students' elaborated talk. They proposed that Layla use open-ended statements (e.g., "I wonder ..." "Tell me ...") and more process-oriented questions (e.g., "How did ..." "Why did ...") to encourage students to use more words to communicate. Layla created a sign for her classroom wall listing some of the open-ended statements and process questions she could use (see Figure 15.2). This way if she was interacting with a child and was stuck on how to further stimulate conversation, she could refer to the sign for a prompt she could use.

In our assessment we used excerpts from videos taken during children's play with the red wiggler habitat, which Layla created and had the students help her maintain, as examples. These worms compost food scraps and create a fertilizer from their casings that can be used in the garden to help plants grow. One of the videos Layla collected when using this activity in her classroom showed students interacting with the worms. She had taken some of the worms and placed them on the surface of one of the low child-height classroom tables with some of the dirt and shredded newspaper from the habitat. Four students at the table were holding the worms in their hands and talking to them. One of the students had a worm crawl from her hand, across her elbow, and towards her shoulder.

LAYLA: Look, where's he going? [*Pointing to the worm*]
STUDENT: Up ... in my shirt.
LAYLA: I wonder why he'd like to go in your shirt.
STUDENT: Because it's dark in there ... That's why he wants to go in my shirt.

Layla's "I wonder why ..." probe was useful in encouraging the student to demonstrate what the class had been learning about worms – that they like dark environments. The student expressed this verbally in a conversational exchange with her teacher. If Layla had phrased this probe as a close-ended or yes/no question (e.g., "Does the worm want to go in your shirt because it's dark?") the student would have likely just responded "Yes" and the conversation would have ended in two conversational turns.

Layla found that Laureen's coaching and the reminder poster on her classroom wall supported her development of skills that fostered students' elaborated talk. Creating a classroom environment integrating elements of the natural environment, such as the classroom garden and red wiggler worm habitat, provided rich opportunities for students to engage in meaningful conversations that drew on their concrete experiences with plants and worms. Layla's observations underscore that open-ended statements and process-oriented questions support students in participating and expressing themselves in conversations with their peers and teachers (Girolametto et al., 2003; Tofade et al., 2013; The Hanen Centre, 2016).

Effecting Change in Teacher and Student Learning

Layla's and Laureen's experiences show that teacher modelling during play activities in place-based classroom environments (Sobel, 2004), such as a classroom garden and red wiggler worm habitat, can support students' language development. The garden and red wiggler worm habitat gave students a natural experiential context in which to play, explore, and learn. It also allowed Laureen and Layla to use natural learning opportunities to support the development of children's language form, content, and use. Additionally, as part of collaborative action research, coaching by a speech-language pathologist supported teacher development and learning, as Layla enhanced her own personal use of language stimulation techniques.

REFERENCES

Abel, C.D., Nerren, J.W., & Wilson, H.E. (2015). Leaping the language gap: Strategies for preschool and head start teachers. *International Journal of Child Care and Education Policy, 9*(1), 7. https://doi.org/10.1186/s40723-015-0009-8

Agriculture in the Classroom Saskatchewan Inc. (AITC SK). (n.d. a.) *Little Green Thumbs.* http://www.littlegreenthumbs.org/.

Agriculture in the Classroom Saskatchewan Inc. (AITC SK). (n.d. b.) *Programs.* https://aitc.sk.ca/programs

Agriculture in the Classroom Saskatchewan Inc. (AITC SK). (n.d. c.) *Little Green Sprouts.* https://aitc.sk.ca/programs/little-green-sprouts

American Speech-Language-Hearing Association (ASHA). (n.d. a). *Activities to encourage speech and language development.* https://www.asha.org/public/speech/development/activities-to-Encourage-speech-and-Language-Development/

American Speech-Language-Hearing Association (ASHA). (n.d. b). *How does your child hear and talk?* (Developmental Milestones). https://www.asha.org/public/speech/development/chart/

American Speech-Language-Hearing Association (ASHA). (1993). *Definitions of communication disorders and variations* (Relevant Paper). www.asha.org/policy

Antoine, A., Mason, R., Mason, R., Palahicky, S., & Rodriguez de France, C. (2018). *Pulling together: A guide for curriculum developers.* BC Campus. https://opentextbc.ca/indigenizationcurriculumdevelopers/

Bell, A.C., & Dyment, J.E. (2008). Grounds for health: The intersection of green school grounds and health promoting schools. *Environmental Education Research, 14*(1), 77–90. http://www.tandfonline.com/loi/ceer20

Biemiller, A., & Boote, C. (2006). An effective method for building meaning vocabulary in primary grades. *Journal of Educational Psychology, 98*(1), 44–62. https://doi.org/10.1037/0022-0663.98.1.44

Blair, D. (2009). The child in the garden: An evaluative review of the benefits of school gardening. *Journal of Environmental Education, 40*(2), 15–38 http://dx.doi.org/10.3200/JOEE.40.2.15-38

Bloom, L., & Lahey, M. (1978). *Language development and language disorders.* John Wiley & Son.

Center for Place-based Learning and Community Engagement. (n.d.). *What is place-based education?* https://promiseofplace.org/what-is-pbe/what-is-place-based-education

Coufal, K.L., & Woods, J.J. (2018). Interprofessional collaborative practice in early intervention. *Pediatric Clinics, 65*(1), 143–155. https://doi.org/10.1016/j.pcl.2017.08.027

Desmond, D., Grieshop, J., & Subramaniam, A. (2002). *Revisiting garden based learning in basic education: Philosophical roots, historical foundations, best practices and products, impacts, outcomes and future directions.* Food and Agriculture Organization/United Nations International Institute for Educational Planning. http://www.fao.org/fileadmin/templates/ERP/2013/link_Virtual_pub/pub_16_intro.pdf

DiClaudio, D., Hughes, L.J., & Savoca, L. (2013). *Learning through the garden.* http://njaes.rutgers.edu/pubs/fs1211/

Ellinger, A.D., Hamlin, R.G., & Beattie, R.S. (2008). *Coaching, HRD, and OD: Towards three "silo" fields of practice or a single unified profession?* Paper presented at the Academy of Human Resource Development International Research Conference in the Americas, Panama City, FL. (ERIC Document Reproduction Service No. ED501611). https://files.eric.ed.gov/fulltext/ED501611.pdf

Girolametto, L., Weitzman, E., & Greenberg, J. (2003). Training day care staff to facilitate children's language. *American Journal of Speech-Language Pathology, 12(3)*, 299–311. https://doi.org/10.1044/1058-0360(2003/076)

Government of Saskatchewan. (n.d.). *Pre-kindergarten.* https://www.saskatchewan.ca/residents/education-and-learning/prek-12-education-early-learning-and-schools/prekindergarten

Greenberg, J., & Walker, S. (2022). The key role of the educator as a conversational partner in play and place-based learning. In S.S. Peterson & N. Friedrich (Eds.), *The role of place and play in young children's language and literacy.* (pp. 211–226). University of Toronto Press.

Hahn, K. (2017, November). *School gardens are the perfect medium for place-based education.* Michigan State University. https://www.canr.msu.edu/news/school_gardens_are_the_perfect_medium_for_place_based_education

The Hanen Centre. (n.d.). *Research summary: Learning language and loving it.* Author. http://www.hanen.org/Helpful-Info/Research.aspx

The Hanen Centre. (2016). *Learning language and loving it – The Hanen Program for Early Childhood Educators.* http://www.hanen.org/Programs/For-Educators/Learning-Language-Loving-It.aspx

Jones, E., & Reynolds, G. (2011). *Play's the thing: Teachers' roles in children's play*. Teachers College Press.

Laaksoharju, T., Rappe, E., & Kaivola, T. (2012). Garden affordances for social learning, play, and for building nature–child relationship. *Urban Forestry & Urban Greening, 11*(2), 195–203. https://doi.org/10.1016/j.ufug.2012.01.003

The Lego Foundation. (2018, October). *Learning through play: Strengthening learning through play in early childhood education programmes* (Advocacy Brief). United Nations Children's Fund (UNICEF). https://www.unicef.org/sites/default/files/2018-12/UNICEF-Lego-Foundation-Learning-through-Play.pdf

Lloyd, A., & Gray, T. (2010). Place-based outdoor learning and environmental sustainability within Australian primary school. *Journal of Sustainability Education.* http://www.susted.com/wordpress/content/place-based-outdoor-learning-and-environmental-sustainability-within-australian-primary-school_2014_10/

Owens, Jr., R.E. (2012). *Language development: An introduction* (8th ed.). Allyn & Bacon.

Ozer, E.J. (2007). The effects of school gardens on students and schools: Conceptualization and considerations for maximizing healthy development. *Health Education and Behaviour, 34*(6), 846–863. http://journals.sagepub.com/home/heb

Saskatchewan Ministry of Education. (2008). *Play and exploration: Early learning program guide* (PDF document). Author. http://publications.gov.sk.ca/documents/11/82946-ELPG%20Complete%20document.pdf

Saskatchewan Ministry of Education. (2009). *Children first: A resource for kindergarten* Saskatchewan curriculum PDF document). https://www.edonline.sk.ca/bbcswebdav/library/Curriculum%20Website/Kindergarten/Resources/Core/Children%20First%20A%20Resource%20for%20Kindergarten.pdf

Saskatchewan Ministry of Education. (2010). *Kindergarten* (Saskatchewan curriculum PDF document). https://www.edonline.sk.ca/bbcswebdav/library/curricula/English/Master_K_Curr_2010_Final.pdf

Scull, J., & O'Grady, K. (2022). Exploring imaginative play – as a stimulus for "language in action" and "language as reflection." In S.S. Peterson & N. Friedrich (Eds.), *The role of place and play in young children's language and literacy* (pp. 195–210). University of Toronto Press.

Sobel, D. (2004). *Place-based education: Connecting classrooms and communities.* The Orion Society.

Spivey, B.L. (2009). *Teaching the fundamentals of grammar and syntax at home* (Super Duper Handy Handouts! No. 233). Super Duper Publications. https://www.superduperinc.com/handouts/pdf/233_TeachingFundamentals.pdf

Spivey, B.L. (2013). *Help students develop strong vocabulary skills: Instructional strategies for teachers and parents* (Super Duper Handy Handouts! No. 380). Super Duper Publications. https://www.superduperinc.com/handouts/pdf/380_Vocabulary_Skills.pdf

Statistics Canada. (2016). *Census profile, 2016 census.* Retrieved 22 May 2017 from http://www12.statcan.gc.ca/census-recensement/2016/dp-pd/prof/index.cfm?Lang=E

Stuckey, K. (2009). *Language expansion vs. language extension – What's the difference* (Super Duper Handy Handouts! No. 227). Super Duper Publications. https://www.superduperinc.com/handouts/pdf/227_langexpext.pdf

Tofade, T., Elsner, J., & Haines, S.T. (2013). Best practice strategies for effective use of questions as a teaching tool. *American Journal of Pharmaceutical Education, 77*(7), 155. https://doi.org/10.5688/ajpe777155

Vicker, B. (2009). The 21st century speech language pathologist and integrated services in classrooms. *The Reporter, 14*(2), 1–5. https://scholarworks.iu.edu/dspace/bitstream/handle/2022/9142/23.pdf?sequence=1

Vygotsky, L. (1988). *Thought and language.* (Alex Kozulin, Trans.). MIT Press.

Weitzman, E., & Greenberg, J. (2012). *Learning language and loving it – A guide to promoting children's social, language and literacy development.* Hanen Centre Publication.

Williams, D.R., & Dixon, P.S. (2013). Impact of garden-based learning on academic outcomes in schools: Synthesis of research between 1990 and 2010. *Review of Educational Research, 83*(2), 211–235. http://dx.doi.org/10.3102/0034654313475824

16 Conclusion: Questions and Implications Arising from Playce-Based Learning in Communities across Four Continents

SHELLEY STAGG PETERSON

The concept of playce-based learning, introduced in this book, comes from a recognition of the influence of social, historical, and cultural factors, not only on what counts as *play*, but also on roles of teachers, family members, and other adults in children's play, and on contributions of play to young children's language and literacy learning and development (Nuttall et al., 2019). From a playce-based learning perspective, *place* is also viewed as a cultural construct and an important part of any learning context (Gruenewald, 2003; Sobel, 2005). Place influences children's identity and language development, and their literacy learning.

Place is visible in each chapter in this book. Focal communities are identified as rural, urban, or suburban, and their social and physical environments are described. Young children's play(ful) learning experiences are viewed from a place-conscious perspective that recognizes the influence of cultural constructions of place on young children's language and literacy learning (Gruenewald, 2003), or from a place-based perspective, where place is highlighted within context-rich learning activities (Sobel, 2005). Influential to children's play and to children's language and literacy learning and development are the physical/natural features and social constructions of place, together with the identities of those who live in a particular place.

This book offers new ways to think about equity and educational opportunity in young children's language and literacy learning and development. A sense of belonging and its contrast, a sense of otherness, do not come only from relationships and identities related to ethnicity, race, language, socio-economic status, gender, and sexuality – factors that permeate the literature on educational inequalities. The place in which children live is also a significant factor, as children are constructed in different ways by their teachers and by society as a whole, depending on where they live.

In each chapter, featured examples of children's playce-based learning are located in places that are not typically acknowledged or valued in educational research. Readers are introduced to children and teachers in northern Canadian and Swedish rural and Indigenous classrooms, a family playgroup and childhood education centres in Aotearoa New Zealand and Australian cities, playgrounds in urban Brazil, and a daycare in a northern Canadian Indigenous community. When defining diversity, the contributors integrate children's and teachers' place-related constructions of identities while engaged in play(ful) teaching and learning experiences. Coming from a range of educational fields, the authors bring this expanded notion of diversity to the fields of early literacy, language learning and development (including the work of speech-language pathologists and educators of multilingual children), and Indigenous education.

Through playce-based learning, alternative meanings and possibilities for addressing social justice issues can be created as children draw on their place-based funds of knowledge and imagination in their play. New issues and questions related to diversity and equity arise when educators and researchers take up a playce-based learning perspective. The following questions are addressed, along with their implications for research, curriculum development, and practice, in this concluding chapter:

- How does playce-based learning build on the concept of funds of knowledge to offer opportunity for all children's learning?
- How does playce-based learning build on Indigenous knowledges and pedagogies to position Indigenous children as agentic, powerful language and literacy learners?
- How can playce-based learning challenge dominant pedagogies and support diverse populations of young children's language and literacy learning and development?

Playce-Based Learning, Funds of Knowledge, and Young Children's Learning

Recognition of the contributions of children's interests and experiences is described as a "cornerstone argument within early childhood education" (Nuttall et al., 2019). Teachers accept as a given the importance of drawing on children's "funds of knowledge" (Moll et al., 1992), facilitating their learning through connecting new information and ideas to what is familiar to them. There is no denying the importance of the social histories and the socio-political and economic bodies of knowledge of families and communities to young children's learning (Gonzalez et al., 2005).

It must be recognized, however, that these funds of knowledge are created within particular places. Perceptions of particular places and of the identities and relationships of children and adults who live within them are socially constructed.

When planning playce-based learning activities, teachers integrate local knowledge about the natural world, about the human activity connected to the local environment, and about the cultural perspectives of this activity. In her chapter, Nicola Friedrich describes how a northern rural teacher and her students engaged in ice-fishing play. The children assigned roles to classroom objects such as ice-fishing huts, ice-fishing holes, and fishing rods. In recreating the cultural practices of family and community members in relation to the natural world, the children's play narratives positioned them, their families, and their communities in powerful roles. Children engaged in valued community practices that had been constructed through generations of families' relationships with the nearby lake and the seasonal rhythms of their environment.

Two chapters in this book show how new immigrant children's place-related funds of knowledge came from the places where their families lived before moving to a New Zealand city. Traditional dances and music, together with interaction patterns involving meaningful and conscious silences, reflected the values and land-based cultural practices of Pasifika families in playce-based learning activities in an early childhood education centre (Maria Cooper and Helen Hedges), and in a family playgroup (Mary Jacobs). The researchers' analyses of the children's interactions in these playce-based learning contexts stemmed from their familiarity with the children's funds of knowledge gained through home visits and informal interactions with family members.

Two chapters, situated in place-based theory (Sobel, 2005), draw on Hirsh-Pasek's and Golinkoff's (2011) notion of "guided play," where teachers provide a physical environment with materials that support children's language and learning, and where teachers interact with children in ways that enhance the children's self-discovery (p. 113). Laureen McIntyre, Laurie-ann Hellsten, and Tyler Bergen show how a northern rural kindergarten teacher consciously drew on the place-based resources of her rural community by modelling language form, content, and use as she and the children planted, weeded, and harvested vegetables from a class garden. Janice Greenberg and Sharon Walker, who draw on their speech-language pathology backgrounds, discuss guided play interactions centring on the urban gardening experiences of working-class children. In both the rural and urban contexts, the teacher validated the experiences and identities of the children and their families as growers of vegetables in their backyards. Local cultural conceptions of gardening were valued (e.g., gardening is a vegetable-growing activity for the purpose of feeding the family). Teachers built on those experiences and cultural constructions of gardening to support the children's language development and to value the worldviews of their rural and working-class communities.

Implications

In conversations about funds of knowledge, place has been treated as a background to other cultural constructions that are important to children's experience and understandings. It is important for researchers, educators, and curriculum developers to recognize place, in terms of children's relationships to the immediate environment and cultural constructions of places in which they live, as integral to children's funds of knowledge and to their language and literacy learning and development.

Playce-Based Learning: Valuing of the Land Is Foundational to Indigenous Knowledges

The understandings and perspectives of Indigenous knowledges, which are foundational to research discussed in many chapters of this book, help us to understand the integral role of place in young children's language, culture, and literacy learning. Indigenous knowledges and worldviews are informed by "spiritual, emotional, intellectual, and physical relationships" with place, which is "particular, it is storied, it is experienced" (Styres, 2017, p. 46). Place is at the centre of Indigenous languages and knowledges. Teaching and learning cannot be imagined except in relationship to the land/place.

In his chapter, Jeffery Wood explains that the linguistic and cultural variations across Indigenous communities reflect the specific human interactions with the natural environment in which each Indigenous community is situated. The Indigenous teachers, with whom he collaborated, designed, and implemented Indigenous language teaching practices that involved storytelling, songs, and games carried out in their community's natural environment. As was the case with the playce-based teaching of northern Canadian Indigenous teachers highlighted in a chapter by Karen Eppley, Shelley Stagg Peterson, and Denise Heppner, relationships to the land/place of children's communities were essential to curriculum and pedagogy supporting young Indigenous children's language and literacy learning.

The concept of "all my relations" is an inclusive Indigenous meaning-making framework that can transform teaching and learning in non-Indigenous communities as well. This framework is highlighted in chapters set in northern Canadian Indigenous communities by Sharla *Mskokii* Peltier, Jeffery Wood, and by Lori Huston and Stephanie Michano-Drover, and in a chapter by Judy Parr set in New Zealand schools attended by Māori children. When taking up an "all my relations" perspective, researchers and educators recognize that relationships with family and community, with broader society, and also with the living and non-living elements of the physical environment are important and necessary sources of young children's identity construction and all learning. Pedagogy and curriculum start with sensory explorations of the children's immediate environment, particularly with natural elements. The design of learning spaces, such as the outdoor play space in Stephanie Michano-Drover's Indigenous community, reflects local cultural practices, perspectives, and understandings of a universe of relationships.

Chapters in this book make a valuable contribution to early childhood education by foregrounding Indigenous knowledges and the centrality of relationships in creating knowledge. Those who take up teaching roles within an Indigenous knowledges perspective highlight for children the interconnectedness and interdependence of all life. Making these connections is viewed as foundational to children's meaning-making. Teaching and learning based on these understandings can enhance young children's language and literacy learning in Indigenous and non-Indigenous communities.

By locating research in northern Indigenous communities that have been considered by researchers to be peripheral to the assumed urban, southern, non-Indigenous centre, contributors to this book are also "challeng[ing] the ideological circuitry of hegemonic knowledge" (Giroux, 2004, p. 74). Assumptions about places that are worthy of educational researchers' attention are upended in chapters written about northern Indigenous communities that are hundreds, and in some cases thousands, of kilometres from university cities. Researchers send powerful messages about the significant contributions of Indigenous pedagogies and knowledges and the importance of finding ways to counter the historical and ongoing marginalization of Indigenous children, their communities, and Indigenous knowledges. Kristina Belancic's chapter, set in northern Sweden, positions young Sámi children as agentic, flexible users of multiple languages. Children used the dominant Swedish language when taking up dramatic play roles that reflected mainstream culture, such as playing with toy cars. They used Sámi, the language spoken in their homes, when taking up traditional Sámi roles, such as herding reindeer. Kristina and fellow contributors who write about Indigenous children's playce-based language, cultural, and literacy learning provide alternative views of Indigenous children as learners to counter the deficit views often presented by researchers.

Implications

Conversations about pedagogy, curriculum, and research must challenge the marginalization of Indigenous children, teachers, and the knowledges of their communities. The normative models of early childhood learning and teaching, reflective of colonialist Euro-Western perspectives (Ritchie & Rau, 2010; Viruru, 2014), should be replaced with Indigenous knowledges models that reflect relationships with the land and those who live in particular places.

Offering Alternatives to Dominant Constructions of Place

Place is invisible in much of the early literacy research conducted over many decades. Occasionally, researchers conclude that children in rural communities do not have the same access to literacy resources that their urban and suburban counterparts have (e.g., Donehower & Beagle, 1998; Makin, 2003; Neuman & Celano, 2001). Apart from perpetuating a deficit perspective on rural children's literacy opportunities, place is not explicitly considered to be influential to literacy teaching and learning. Similarly, research examining sociocultural influences on play rarely considers place. A review of literature on the impact of race and culture on play (Adair & Doucet, 2014), for example, identifies the countries in which research has been conducted, but makes no mention of whether the early childhood classrooms with diverse populations are in rural, urban, or suburban settings. Descriptions of the natural and physical environment within which participating classrooms are located are absent. The influence of place on children's construction of identities as members of their classrooms and communities and on their meaning-making when engaging in play activities is overlooked and disregarded.

An assumption of a universal "every place" that can be superimposed on all places where young children live and learn appears to have filled the void created by the invisibility of place. Given that much of the extant educational research, policy, and curriculum is conducted in urban communities, the socially constructed "every place" is urban (Corbett, 2007, 2014; Donehower et al., 2007). Northern rural and Indigenous communities, and those who live in these places, are often constructed as lacking when compared to an urban norm.

A playce-based learning perspective challenges the stereotypes and deficit constructions of places that are other than non-Indigenous urban places. In her chapter, Christine Portier makes place visible in her report of rural teachers' guided play as they and their students walk through the bush close to their school. She explains how children explored place-related meanings, identities, and relationships with the natural environment as they created various types of multimodal texts. Children and their teachers were positioned as active meaning-makers and there was no sense of comparison with the standard of the "every place" urban cultural constructions of meanings and identities.

It is not only the experiences and identities of rural children that are marginalized when place is invisible to researchers, educators, and curriculum developers; the hegemonic construction of urban places misrepresents the experiences, perspectives, and identities of urban children as well. The cultural identities of children living in cities are as diverse as the political histories, geographies, climates, economies, and immigration trends of their urban communities. The contributors to this book who situate their research in urban early childhood settings provide examples of this diversity. In her chapter, Gisela Wajskop describes the Brazilian flora and the birds, amphibians, and insects that they attract in an outdoor school play space in São Paulo. She constructs this urban place as one where teachers' respectful listening and thoughtful questioning support children in their development of scientific understandings in outdoor play. The human-created features of an Australian city are highlighted in Janet Scull's and Kim O'Grady's description of young children's language learning in a grocery store and an insect museum dramatic play setting. By highlighting particular features of urban settings salient in young children's playce-based learning, Gisela, Janet, and Kim resist the normative constructions of children's identities within a perceived universal urban place.

Implications

Taking up a playce-based perspective, researchers, theorists, and educators can move conversations about the cultural appropriateness of curriculum, children's learning experiences, and teachers' pedagogy in helpful new directions. Based on an assumption that the local experiences of all within the communities in which children live are valuable resources for children's language and literacy learning, we encourage researchers and educators to seek out local experiences, world views, and practices to inform their research and teaching. By reflecting on why these meanings and perspectives are important within the local environment, and how they have been constructed by generations of children and adults living within a particular place, teachers and researchers will develop a richer understanding of the children's funds of knowledge and will expand their own understandings and views of teaching and learning. Given the importance of perspectives, understandings, and values connected to the places in which children and their families live, notions of cultural appropriateness should be broadened to include the influence of place.

REFERENCES

Adair, J.K., & Doucet, F. (2014). The impact of race and culture on play in early childhood classrooms. In L. Brooker, M. Blaise, & S. Edwards (Eds.), *The Sage handbook of play and learning in early childhood* (pp. 354–365). Sage.

Corbett, M. (2007). *Learning to leave: The irony of schooling in a coastal community.* Fernwood Publishing.

Corbett, M. (2014). Towards a geography of rural education in Canada. *Canadian Journal of Education, 37*(3), 1–22. https://doi.org/10.1080/0161956X.2014.956532

Donehower, K., Hogg, C., & Schell, E.E. (2007). Toward a sustainable citizenship pedagogy. In K. Donehower, C. Hogg, & E.E. Schell (Eds.), *Rural literacies* (pp. 155–193). Southern Illinois University Press.

Donehower, S. & Beagle, K. (1998). The print environment in kindergartens: A study of conventional and holistic teachers and their classrooms in three settings. *Reading Research and Instruction, 37*(3), 161–190. https://doi.org/10.1080/19388079809558263

Giroux, H.A. (2004). Cultural studies, and the politics of public pedagogy: Making the political more pedagogical. *Parallax, 10*(2), 73–89. https://doi.org/10.1080/1353464042000208530

Gonzalez, N., Moll, L.C., & Amanti, C. (Eds.). (2005). *Funds of knowledge: Theorizing practices in households, communities, and classrooms.* Lawrence Erlbaum.

Gruenewald, D.A. (2003). Foundations of place: A multidisciplinary framework for place-conscious education. *American Educational Research Journal, 40*(3), 619–654. https://doi.org/10.3102%2F00028312040003619

Hirsh-Pasek, K., & Golinkoff, R.M. (2011). The great balancing act: Optimizing core curricula through playful pedagogy. In E. Zigler, W.S. Gilliam, & W.S. Barnett (Eds.), *The pre-K debates: Current controversies and issues* (pp. 110–116). Paul H. Brookes Publishing.

Makin, L. (2003). Creating positive literacy learning environments in early childhood. In N. Hall, J. Larson, & J. Marsh (Eds.), *Handbook of early childhood literacy* (pp. 327–337). Sage.

Moll, L., Amanti, C., Neff, D., & Gonzalez, N. (1992). Funds of knowledge for teaching: Using a qualitative approach to connect homes and classrooms. *Theory Into Practice, 31*(2), 132–141.

Neuman, S. & Celano, D. (2001). Access to print in low-income and middle-income communities: An ecological study of four neighborhoods. *Reading Research Quarterly, 36*(1), 8–26. https://doi.org/10.1598/RRQ.36.1.1

Nuttall, J., Edwards, S., Grieshaber, S., Wood, E., Mantilla, A., Chepkwesi Katiba, T., & Jacinta Bartlett, J. (2019). The role of cultural tools and motive objects in early childhood teachers' curriculum decision-making about digital and popular culture play. *Professional Development in Education, 4*(5), 790–800. https://doi.org/10.1080/19415257.2018.1511456

Ritchie, J., & Rau, C. (2010). Kia mau kit e wairuatanga: Countercolonial narratives of early childhood education in Aotearoa. In G. Cannella & L. Diaz Soto (Eds.), *Childhoods: A handbook* (pp. 355–373). Peter Lang.

Sobel, D. (2005). *Place-based education: Connecting classrooms and communities.* The Orion Society.

Styres, S.D. (2017). *Pathways for remembering and recognizing Indigenous thought in education: Philosophies of Iethi'nihsténha Ohwentsia'kékha (Land).* University of Toronto Press.

Viruru, R. (2014). Postcolonial perspectives on childhood and literacy. In N. Hall, J. Larson, & J. Marsh (Eds.), *Handbook of early childhood literacy* (pp. 13–21). Sage.

17 Places and Players: An Afterword

MICHAEL CORBETT

What Is a Place?

Understanding terms of reference is, in most inquiries, an important starting point. I would like to begin by considering how the term place is defined in a source typically considered to be authoritative. I think definitions are interesting not because they help us understand the accuracy of a concept for describing phenomena, but rather for the way that phenomena themselves are imagined and represented in the definitions given. While I recognize that the broad context of this collection focuses on the complex and nuanced relationships between culture, language, place, and play, I want to start by bracketing this complexity to focus on a definition. One well-recognized definition machine is the Oxford English Dictionary (OED), and so I will start there to begin thinking about the question: what is a place?[1]

The first of four OED definitions of place reads: "A particular position, point, or area in space; a location." This imaginary is all too common and two dimensional; it is a point on a flat Cartesian plane. Here place appears as a particular location in infinite space; it is either intriguing or perhaps a little sad that the first definition of place in the OED is a lifeless abstraction. The second OED definition elaborates another key dimension of place in current understandings: that of ownership and property. The definition reads: "A portion of space designated or available for or being used by someone." Here we encounter the way that place is understood in contemporary English as a bounded space reserved for someone's use.

---

[1] I am using the United Kingdom OED definition provided by Lexico (https://www.lexico.com/definition/place).

The third OED definition goes a bit further, linking a propertied position on the Cartesian grid with the notion of merit. Here place is defined as "a position in a sequence or series, typically one ordered on the basis of merit." Thus, to occupy a place is to be located somewhere in a meritocratic hierarchy. How these assessments of merit are made or who sets the boundaries is set out beyond the question of place, which simply exists as what Tuan (1974) called a "stopping place" in the expanse of space. The fourth and final OED definition is even more specific, referring to "a square or short street" or a "country house with its grounds." Thus, concrete instances of rural and urban locales, and arguably social class, are neatly juxtaposed as illustrations.

I think it would be quite possible to write an entire chapter unpacking this definition, but for my purposes here, the point is to draw attention to the limited vision of place that this definition contains, and also to suggest that it is precisely this way of thinking about place that causes trouble when it thought with/in education. The boundedness of place defines what it is, and what it is not, in rather stark terms. The first of the OED definitions is followed by the quote "you can't be in two places at once." But of course, we can, as every schoolchild understands when they playfully write their address indicating a street number, a suburb, a city, a country, and then on to a continent, the earth, the solar system, the universe, etc. I am in my chair, in my office, in my house, in my village, etc., etc. In my chair are steel, plastic, fabric, paint, chemical compounds, and so forth. This is all relatively simple. In the current debate concerning racism today, many people are struggling to understand what structural or systemic means. To get it, the thinker needs to think about various systems that operate in relation to places, bodies, and things, and what is required is a rethinking or a more expansive way of considering ordinary notions like place as more than a container or a point on a line or plane. Place, like race, is systemically and relationally produced in ways that are often invisible to those who produce it, and who are produced within it.

First of all, places are relational entities. Every place contains within it multiple places, and, by the same token, every place is a subset of other places. In the wake of the global pandemic of 2020, it is abundantly clear that the novel coronavirus, which is a kind of place in itself, cannot easily be contained within places. This viral metaphor can be extended to thinking about how information moves and how markets function, for instance, illustrating how places are drawn into complex and mutable networks or what John Urry (2000) calls "scapes and flows" of bodies, things, and information. There are no places that are truly separate and isolated from the tentacles of contemporary capitalism; polluted water and air circulate everywhere on the planet.

Secondly, places are not naturally occurring phenomena, and physical and human geography are tangled together in the complex geopolitics that have been developing rapidly over the past five hundred years since the European colonial projects began. Ferdinand Braudel's magisterial studies of the development of trade and markets paints a picture of a world largely defined and created by movement, connections, contracts, and "hybridities," as Homi Bhabha (1990) writes. As such, space is no longer seen by geographers as a container, but rather as a "production" (Lefebvre, 1992) which is literally shaped by capitalist development and global movements. We are all caught up in the consequences of these processes. The long history of spatial production configures and reconfigures places often in violent and oppressive ways, and colonial/capitalist projects transform places, generating unpredictable response (Scott, 1985, 1999; Tuck & McKenzie, 2015). Indeed, as the second OED definition illustrates, we conflate the idea of place itself with ownership, and how we define place tends to be caught up in ideas of property that are often enshrined in law and that often dismiss other ways of thinking spatially. To consider place otherwise would, as Tuck and McKenzie (2015, p. 154) point out, require a consideration of genocide.

And finally, in the fourth OED definition it is not just a question of boundaries and ownership; the very image of the English country house and its grounds is invoked to reference a quintessence of place itself. To quote the example given for this fourth definition, "Foots Cray Place was the home of the one-time Chancellor of the Exchequer, Nicholas Vansittart, Lord Bexley." These definitions all generate a particular understanding of structure and stability, which in turn come to be associated with commonsense understandings of place as a point in linear space and a material backdrop/container for human agency, but also as something possessed as a birthright and/or as a form of capital acquired in the market. The right to access and use places, for instance, the right of the commons (Bowers, 2006; Theobald, 1997), or the rights to the city (Soja, 2010), or indeed questions about the very idea of land ownership raised by Indigenous thinkers (Tuck & Yang, 2012), illustrate in different ways how conceptions of place are contested and political, and indeed the source of many if not most forms of violence. Place is not innocent.

Playing in Place

Some of the limitations and possibilities of place-based education have been examined in the academic literature, adding complexity and nuance to early iterations of this idea (Bowers, 2006; Corbett, 2020; Nespor, 2008). I think it is somewhat safe to say at this point the question of place in relation to education, and indeed to literacy, is ground that has been well travelled, but perhaps in ways that have created place-understandings that may not adequately come to grips with the politics and complexity of the spatial. At the risk of getting overly abstract, connecting play and place is a bit like thinking about quantum objects which can be seen as either stable points or "particles," or as moving "waves." The trick is to think about the uncertainty, emergence, and creativity inherent in play to disrupt our tendency to see place as something fixed in space, which itself is understood as a kind of container in which action happens. Another way to say this is perhaps that many of us have not been flexible, broad, and indeed playful enough in the way we think place and education together.

But there is another figure caught in the theoretical transformations in education that are finally catching up with the last two centuries of philosophical investigation: the perceiving subject, or what we might call in this context, the "player." Through the past century, and particularly from the work of the pragmatist tradition under the influence of John Dewey and Heidegger's inflection of the phenomenological tradition incorporates a conception of place at the centre of ontology (Malpas, 2016). Subsequently, the lonely figure of the self-contained and self-referential Enlightenment humanist subject has been subject to relentless critique. To be is to be some place. The player needs a place in which to play, and that place shapes play just as it is shaped and transformed by play, which is, of course, a metaphor for agency. For Heidegger and his descendants, place is generative, foreshadowing emerging flat ontologies, and aligning in some ways at least, with spiritual, Indigenous, and other ontologies that do not so easily separate the Enlightenment subject from the material world (Haraway, 2016). As a result, place has not only moved to the centre of social science analysis, it has poetically come to life (Bachelard, 1969; Perac, 2008; Pinar & Irwin, 2004). Mary Jacobs in this volume puts it very nicely, I think, when she writes, "Play is a social practice through which children represent and communicate meanings, allowing them to participate in the communities they belong to." And, of course, the communities they belong to are nested in wider geographies. Indeed, each of the pieces in this collection illustrates the intimate connections fostered by sensitive educators between playing children and rich and generative places.

Taking spatial questions seriously removes what Foucault (1986) famously called the "pious descendants of time" (I'm imagining a lecturing teacher) from the centre stage of philosophy and social sciences, challenged, if not replaced, by the "determined inhabitants of space" (I'm imagining a child exploring beside a pond). What I take this to mean is that spatial theory in the hands of Foucault and human geographers confronts established ideas of the epoch, generation, decade, or other temporal descriptors, which in turn creates a conception of how things are or were at a given time (e.g., the notion that the 1950s was a period of conservativism while the 1960s was a time of revolutionary social change). Each epoch functionally implies a curriculum "relevant" to the technologies, occupations, hierarchies, and markets of its time. Yet, the introduction of a spatial sensibility persistently demonstrates how things can be very different in places that have passed through the same time. In a sense, there is no unitary time, only events which are subjectively and locally experienced (Rovelli, 2018). Contemporary social theory has moved on to combine the sociocultural, the spatial, and the historical to create more challenging multi-dimensional understandings of phenomena (Soja, 1996). Simultaneously, Foucault's geography, and of course, that of his Marxist geographer contemporaries Lefebvre (1992), Harvey (2006), and Massey (2005), assume struggle and contestation over what place means as well as who gets to define its character, its boundaries, what and how it values, and its future.

Through Rousseau, it is Dewey who elevates play and the child's experience onto education's centre stage (Egan, 1998). I think Dewey understood the spatial aspects of the human experience, even if his ontology is distinctly humanist, privileging the human subject over the material. His focus on experience and the importance of the management of learning spaces have formed the basis for the "progressive" schools we see today, and indeed the sorts of place-informed, rich pedagogical practices described in this volume. Laurel Tanner's (1997) lovely description of Dewey's laboratory school illustrates the depth of this tradition, but as I read it, there is a kind of seriousness in the whole business designed perhaps to show early twentieth-century teachers and others that an experiential curriculum was not unstructured play. Here the body represents a place that incorporates the material and the ideal; it is neither one nor the other as social theorists in the tradition of Pierre Bourdieu have understood. For Dewey, the body in motion was important, and his embodied pedagogy and curriculum are clearly engaged in these chapters as learners build places of living and learning. Indeed, the management of learning space itself, in the sense of intentional place-making, and learning artefact invention (from natural objects to manufactured environments, apparatuses, manipulatives, and toys), that is, creating laboratories and naturalistic affordances for learning, are part of Dewey's school as a place in which the player (the child) might show us how learning transpires. What has followed, of course, is generations of psychologically oriented child study, which has provided a behavioural, cognitive, and neurological mapping of learning processes.

While the pragmatic theoretical grounding for education initiated under Dewey's longstanding influence is more easily spotted in the work found in this collection, many of the pieces also take up at least some of the theoretical implications of phenomenological and new materialist work. Here we see a view of place and the material that does not abstract out human experience as something separate from where it happens. This move is not only radical, it is hard to do because it requires a way of thinking that takes us out of the comfortable subject-object and human/material binaries most of us have used to think with throughout our lives. And yet, it is becoming increasingly clear that earth has a voice and an agency that we feel all too keenly as the shore erodes, as species vanish, and as landscapes are rendered "dead" (Latour, 2018; Lovelock & Margulis, 1974; Sassen, 2014). This appears most clearly in work that draws upon Indigenous and new materialist ontologies and epistemologies, for example through land-based pedagogies that extend the pedagogical and curricular sensibilities found in the work of communitarian and critical place-based educational theory (Gruenewald, 2003; Greenwood & Smith, 2007; Sobel, 2006; Theobald, 1997).

In this collection, we can see the emergence of a new discourse of place that retains the flavour of established place-based educational models, but which also opens up to emerging understandings. Opening up a conversation between the North American place-based education tradition, environmental and ecological education, Indigenous scholarship, and particularly land-based education is perhaps the most important contribution of this volume. There are tensions, gaps, and considerable space for critique and thought in the cultural interface opened up in dialogue between worldviews.

Play as Place-making

What appears most powerfully in this collection for this reader is the way that children create and recreate place in their play. The geography of their play generates both known and yet-to-be-known worlds. They plant gardens and create kitchens in which they prepare real and imagined foods for one another. They negotiate activities; they gather, collect, assemble, represent, present; they build castles; they navigate between cultures, genders, social classes, and abilities. They share and learn languages, and indeed they create new languages, explore their affinities, relations, and connections, including the development of languages of affinity with the non-human world. As Jeffrey Wood and Sharla *Mskokii* Peltier point out in this collection, language, culture, land, and place are intimately interconnected in Indigenous epistemologies and ontologies.

If educators open their classrooms up and out to their broader communities and the ecologies they are a part of, place-sensitive education is not particularly difficult to enact. It requires, as the chapters in this collection illustrate, curiosity and openness, and the courage to give up a certain amount of control over space to students and human and more-than-human others beyond the school walls as a way to, as Huston and Michano-Drover put it in their chapter in this collection, "place the child's hand on the land" to touch the earth.

We also see educators and researchers working to promote the idea that play is educationally useful, a conversation that goes back at least to Rousseau. This, I think is the most powerful lesson in this book. We have known for a long time that play is essential to language learning and particularly the learning of young children. We have also known for a long time that learning "takes place" somewhere. There are debates about how close the school experience should be to the landscape of everyday life, but it is well understood that geography matters, from the micro-geography of the school classroom and the school building and its grounds to the macro-geography of the planet. This theme is developed in this collection in a number of national contexts and across rural, urban, and Indigenous geographies.

What we are also starting to recognize better in settler societies, principally through the insurgent scholarship of Indigenous scholars, disabled scholars, and scholars of colour, is the nature of place as a socio-political construction, one which has been forged in the furnace of colonialism and capitalism as well as in the institutions and "laboratories" of normalization (Foucault, 1977). Places, and the ways in which they are experienced and co-constructed, involve the ongoing negotiations relating to the constitution of settler societies and, in particular, the political and material questions of property and land that these societies have created and which generate the stable formulations found in the OED definition cited above. Land-based education, which is represented in this volume in several chapters, transcends earlier iterations of place-based education to challenge the very ways in which we understand place, and what we often call "community" is, in fact, the material traces of theft and violence (Alfred, 2009: Sassen, 2014; Tuck & Yang, 2012) but offers the promise of regeneration, productive remembering, and a different future.

I think we can help children navigate this increasingly complex and hopefully postcolonial social geography that they will inherit. This collection teaches that children can also help us understand life more flexibly, creatively, and with more openness, because in their play they often achieve a transcendence of boundaries and the fixed categories, thus creating possibilities. The central character in the award-winning graphic novel *Rusty Brown* (Ware, 2019) illustrates (literally) this childhood playful sensibility in which the central character transforms his dismal surroundings and banal relationships, including those with his parents, teachers, and classmates, into an exciting heroic imaginative adventure. *This Place* (Akiwenzie-Damm et al., 2019), another recent award-winning Canadian graphic novel, goes further, combining text, image, and heroism with a clear-eyed analysis of 150 years of Indigenous survival in the real-world apocalypse of colonialism.

But the case still has to be made to those who see abstracted "basic skills" and other forms of placeless curriculum as essential to cognitive and moral development, and, indeed, to learning one's place in fixed space. Place-based (or sensitive) education as well as play-based education are still radical propositions more than a century after Dewey's analysis of experience as the basis of education. It is immediately obvious how different the research in this collection into place, play, and literacy learning is so distinct from the technical-rational neoliberal human capital global capitalist imaginaries found in the OECD publications and in standardized testing reportage and analysis. Thinking play and place together, as the authors in this collection do, destabilizes the lingering stasis of our geographic imaginations. But so too do children as they explore and work with familiar objects to build imaginative worlds, negotiate and make space, and show us how places not only endure but also emerge.

REFERENCES

Akiwenzie-Damm, K., Assu, S., Mitchell, B., Qitsualik-Tinsley, R., Qitsualik-Tinsley, S., Robertson, D.A., Sinclair, N.J., Storm, J., Camp, R.V., Vermette, K., Vowel, C., & Elliott, A. (2019). *This place: 150 years retold.* HighWater Press.
Alfred, T. (2009). *Peace, Power, Righteousness: An Indigenous Manifesto.* Oxford University Press.
Bachelard, G. (1969). *The poetics of space.* Beacon Press.
Bhabha, H.K. (1990). *The location of culture.* Routledge.
Bowers, C.A. (2006). *Revitalizing the commons: Cultural and educational sites of resistance and affirmation.* Lexington Books.
Corbett, M. (2020). Place-based education: A critical appraisal from a rural perspective. In M. Corbett & D. Gereluk (Eds.), *Rural teacher education: Connecting land and people.* Springer.
Egan, K. (1998). *The educated mind: How cognitive tools shape our understanding.* University of Chicago Press.

Foucault, M. (1977). *Discipline and punish*. Pantheon.
Foucault, M. (1986). Of other spaces. *Diacritics, 16*(1), 22–27. https://doi.org/10.2307/464648
Greenwood, D., & Smith, G.A. (Eds.). (2007). *Place-based education in the global age: Local diversity*. Routledge.
Gruenewald, D.A. (2003). The best of both worlds: A critical pedagogy of place. *Educational Researcher, 32*(4), 3–12. https://doi.org/10.3102%2F0013189X032004003
Haraway, D.J. (2016). *Staying with the trouble: Making kin in the Chthulucene*. Duke University Press.
Harvey, D. (2006). *Spaces of global capitalism: A theory of uneven geographical development*. Verso.
Latour, B. (2018). *Down to earth: Politics in the new climatic regime*. Polity.
Lefebvre, H. (1992). *The production of space*. Wiley-Blackwell.
Lovelock, J.E., & Margulis, L. (1974). Atmospheric homeostasis by and for the biosphere: The gaia hypothesis. *Tellus, 26*(1–2), 2–10. https://doi.org/10.3402/tellusa.v26i1-2.9731
Malpas, J. (2016). Placing understanding/understanding place. *Sophia*, 1–13. https://doi.org/
Massey, D.B. (2005). *For space*. Sage.
Nespor, J. (2008). Education and place: A review essay. *Educational Theory, 58*(4), 475–489. https://doi.org/10.1111/j.1741-5446.2008.00301.x
Perac, G. (2008). *Species of spaces and other pieces*. Penguin Classic.
Pinar, W.F., & Irwin, R. (Eds.). (2004). *Curriculum in a new key: The collected works of Ted T. Aoki*. Routledge.
Rovelli, C. (2018). *The Order of Time* (Illustrated edition). Riverhead Books.
Sassen, S. (2014). *Expulsions: Brutality and complexity in the global economy*. Belknap Press.
Scott, J. C. (1985). *Weapons of the weak: Everyday forms of peasant resistance*. Yale University Press.
Scott, J.C. (1999). *Seeing like a state: How certain schemes to improve the human condition have failed* (New edition). Yale University Press.
Sobel, D. (2006). *Place-based education: Connecting classrooms and communities*. Orion Society.
Soja, E.W. (1996). *Thirdspace: Journeys to Los Angeles and other real-and-imagined places*. Blackwell.
Soja, E.W. (2010). *Seeking spatial justice*. University of Minnesota Press.
Tanner, L. (1997). *Dewey's laboratory school*. Teachers College Press.
Theobald, P. (1997). *Teaching the commons: Place, pride, and the renewal of community*. Westview Press.
Tuan, Y.-F. (1974). *Space and place: The perspective of experience*. University of Minnesota Press.

Tuck, E., & McKenzie, M. (2015). *Place in research: Theory, methodology, and methods*. Routledge.
Tuck, E., & Yang, W. (2012). Decolonization is not a metaphor. *Decolonization: Indigeneity, Education & Society*, *1*(1), 1–40.
Urry, J. (2000). *Sociology beyond societies: Mobilities for the twenty-first century*. Routledge.
Ware, C. (2019). *Rusty Brown*. Pantheon.

Contributors

Kristina Belancic is currently a postdoc in the Department of Language Studies at Umeå University and in the Department of Curriculum, Teaching and Learning at the University of Toronto. She is part of the Northern Oral Language and Writing through Play (NOW Play 2) project, focusing on Sámi-language learning through play-based learning activities.

Tyler Bergen is a PhD student at the University of Saskatchewan. His research interests include coaching and virtual coaching, with a focus on supporting teacher professional development in the areas of classroom management and behavioural support.

Maria Cooper is a senior lecturer at the University of Auckland. Her teaching and research interests include early years curriculum, educational leadership, infant and toddler pedagogies, and diversity. Her current research explores notions of leadership in early childhood education from a Pacific Indigenous perspective.

Michael Corbett is a professor of education at Acadia University in Atlantic Canada. He has studied literacies, theorizations of space and place, rural youth educational decision-making, mobilities, and education in rural contexts. His recent co-edited book (with Dianne Gereluk) is *Rural Education in Canada: Connecting Land and People*.

Karen Eppley is a former fifth grade teacher and a lifelong resident of the Bald Eagle Valley in Central Pennsylvania. Her work explores ideas around rural literacies, textual representations of rurality, rural education as a matter of social justice, and policy analysis. She edits the *Journal of Research in Rural Education*.

Nicola Friedrich, PhD, is currently participating in the NOW Play Project to assess and support young children's oral language and writing development through play in classrooms and early childhood programs in northern rural and Indigenous communities. She previously worked as a classroom teacher, reading clinic teacher, and special subject tutor.

Janice Greenberg, BSc, DSP, Reg. CASLPO, is a speech-language pathologist and director of Early Childhood Education Services at the Hanen Centre in Toronto, Canada. She develops and evaluates Hanen training programs targeted at enhancing the language and literacy facilitation skills of early childhood educators/teachers.

Helen Hedges is a professor of early childhood education at the University of Auckland, Aotearoa New Zealand. Her research centres on children's interests revealed through their play, and the decisions teachers make about whose and which interests will be developed in curricula.

Laurie-ann M. Hellsten is a professor and dean in the Faculty of Education at the University of Winnipeg. Prior to this, she was on faculty at the University of Saskatchewan for 17 years. Laurie's expertise in measurement and evaluation has led to research involving survey and mixed methodologies in education and health domains.

Dr. Denise Heppner works in the Department of Educational Psychology and Special Education at the University of Saskatchewan. Her current research focuses on professional development for educators, culturally responsive pedagogy, and play-based outdoor education. She also works as a Special Education Resource Teacher in Prairie Spirit School Division.

Lori Huston, MEd, RECE, is a Métis scholar from Red Lake, Ontario. Her cumulative experiences in research and graduate work have focused on Indigenous ECE leadership, which highlighted Indigenous pedagogies connected to reconciliation, place, and land-based teachings. Lori is a doctoral student in curriculum and pedagogy in the Faculty of Education, University of British Columbia.

Mary M. (Meg) Jacobs is a lecturer in the School of Education, Faculty of Culture and Society, Auckland University of Technology, Aotearoa New Zealand. Meg's research aims to privilege the expertise of families to understand literacies underrecognized in the valued institutional knowledge of educational settings.

Dr. Laureen J. McIntyre is an associate professor in the Department of Educational Psychology and Special Education at the University of Saskatchewan. Her research focuses on meeting the diverse needs of individuals with varied language/literacy/learning abilities (i.e., professionals' education, knowledge, and practice; early, targeted, and lifelong intervention/services; creating safe/enabling learning/work environments).

Stephanie Michano-Drover, RECE, is an Ojibway educator from Biigtigong Nishnaabeg First Nation, Ontario. She is the early childhood supervisor at the Biigtigong Nishnaabeg Children and Family Learning Centre. With many years in the early learning sector, Stephanie has experience designing and building culturally responsive child care programs and supporting educators, children, and families living in her First Nation community.

Sharla *Mskokii Kwe*, member at Mnjikaning (Rama) First Nation, Ontario, is an assistant professor in the Faculty of Education, University of Alberta. Her research and teaching experiences in community and postsecondary contexts are rich with storytelling, community land-based pedagogy, and relational teachings. *Mskokii Kwe's* scholarship centres on Indigenous teaching-learning practices.

Kim O'Grady is a PhD candidate at Monash University. Her current research seeks to explore the home and preschool influences that shape and develop young children's emergent skills and attitudes towards writing in preparation for formal literacy learning at school.

Judy M. Parr is a professor of education at the University of Auckland, Aotearoa New Zealand. Her research, much of which has been large-scale and collaborative in nature, is grounded in improvement science, focusing on enhancing professional practice and student learning in literacy, particularly writing.

Christine Portier, PhD, is an educational researcher whose activities include conducting in-house studies for school boards, reviewing literacy documents and consulting with international educators, teaching graduate courses, and providing professional development for K–12 teachers. Recently she worked with northern rural Canadian educators to support children's oral language and writing development through play.

Janet Scull is an associate professor in language and literacy at Monash University. Her research interests focus on the areas of language and literacy acquisition, literacy teaching, and assessment practices that support the continuity of children's literacy learning across early childhood settings and the early years of schooling.

Shelley Stagg Peterson is a professor in the Department of Curriculum, Teaching and Learning at the University of Toronto and a former elementary school teacher. Her current research project, Northern Oral language and Writing through Play (NOW Play), involves collaborative action research with teachers, early childhood educators, and family members in remote northern communities.

Gisela Wajskop, PhD, is currently collaborating in the NOW Play Project as an international researcher from Pontifical University of São Paulo. She is the principal at the Escola do Bairro and president of the Turma da Touca's NGO Advisory Board. She has recently participated as co-investigator in the Play and Oral Language–Based Learning Project with educators in a São Paulo suburb.

Sharon Walker, EdD, is a speech-language pathologist currently in a leadership role with Hearing and Speech Nova Scotia in Halifax, Canada. Over her 20-year career, Dr. Walker has focused on language, literacy, and speech development with early learners and their caregivers in the education, health, and non-profit sectors.

Dr. Jeffrey Wood is of Métis and settler background and is an associate professor in the Faculty of Education at Laurentian University as well as the early learning lead for the Moosonee and Moose Factory DSABs. His research interests include new/multiple literacies, critical literacies, early childhood education, and Indigenous education.

Index

Page numbers in *italics* represent tables/photos/figures.

abstract thinking, 162–3
adult-guided play, 7
agency, 135
Agriculture in the Classroom Saskatchewan (AITC SK), 229, 232
Aki/Land, 34, 35, 41–2, *47*, *48*, 246. *See also* land-based education/land literacy
Alberta, 20, 23–4, 179
Alexander, R., 6, 207
"all my relations" concept, 110, 112, 246–7
Änggård, E., 61
Anishinaabe ecological relational knowledge (AERK), 34, 36–42, *45*, 46–7
Anishinaabek, 33–4, 84
Anishinaabemowin, 35, 38–9
Antoine, A., 228
Aotearoa New Zealand, 67–70, 73, 96–7, 128–9, 131. *See also* Māori; playgroups
Asemaa/tobacco, 39
Ashton-Warner, Sylvia, 130, 131
Aspen, AB, 20, 23–4, 179
assimilation, 22, 25–6, 53, 109
Australia, 206
autonomy, 182

Baker, C., 76, 77
Barton, D, 6, 145
bears, 87
Bell, N., 22
Belonging/Mana whenua, 98
Bhabha, Homi, 255
Biigtigong Nishnaabeg Children & Family Learning Centre, 81, 84–9. *See also* play space designs
bilingualism, 76–7, 103–4. *See also* language: of Sámi people
biophilia, 35, 36
Black classrooms, 27
Bloom, L., 232–3
blue-collar workers, 24
book overview, 3–4, 9–13
Bopp, J., 36
Bowers, C.A., 19, 26
Boyd, M.P., 168
Brant, T., 22
Braudel, Ferdinand, 255
Brazil. *See* Escola do Bairro; São Paulo, Brazil
Britton, James, 127
built environments, 181

Cajete, G., 84
Caldeira, T.P. do R., 159
Calls to Action (TRC), 48, 115

capitalism, 255, 259
care-horizon, 39
Casey, E., 3
cedar, 84
Child Care and Early Years Act (CCEYA), 85, 87
children: autonomy, 182; decentring, 112–13; exploring environment freely, 86; as gifts, 34, 83; holistic view of, 112–13, *112*, 115–16; leading conversations, 215–17; leading play, 212; life-stage transitions, 46; peer teachers, 133; raising, 85. *See also individual children*
Clay, M.M., 204
coaching, 229–31, 232, 233–6
collaboration: developing ideas, 182–3; and discussions, 168; with Elders, 25; as fluid, 24; garden-based learning (GBL), 228–9; joint meaning-making, 6; on nature walks, 180; between teachers, 232; viewpoints about writing, 135. *See also* relationships
colonization, 22, 49, 259, 260
Comber, B., 96, 100
Communication/Mana reo, 97–8, 101–6
complex trauma, 48–9
conceptual knowledge, 44, *45*
constructing meaning. *See* meaning-making
conversations, 212–13. *See also* teachers as conversational partners
Cooper, M., 71, 73–6
Corbett, M., 27
Corbiere, A., 114
COVID-19 pandemic, 254
Cresswell, T., 22
critical pedagogy of place, 8, 18–19, 25–6
cultural norms, 75
culture: culturally sustaining pedagogy, 25; and expectations, 19; and identity, 110; and language, 110; and place, 8–9, 118; teachers as brokers, *118*; unlearning dominant culture, 25. *See also* assimilation; sociocultural theory
culture of silence, 75
curriculums. *See* standardized curriculums

Day, C., 189
debwewin, 44
decolonization, 18, 25–6
Deerview, Alberta, 179, 182
Developmental Reading Assessment (DRA), 121
Dewey, John, 256, 257–8
dialogic teaching, 6
Dickinson, D.K., 147, 150–1
disrupted attachments, 48
diversity, 244, 249
dominant discourses, 22, 25, 27, 49, 248
Donovan, E., 146
drawing, 169, *172–3*, 181
Durham, R.E., 143, 153
D'warte, J., 105
Dyson, A., 24

Elders: as closing generational gaps, 81; culturally sustaining pedagogy, 25–6; designing play spaces, 83; grandfather's teachings, 91; Grandmother Teaching Story, 37–40, 41; and language programs, 113–14; as nurturing guides, *111*
elevators, 167–74, *170–3*
enjoyment, 136
environmental stewardship, 19, 84
equity, 244
Ermine, W., 35
E's and P's of abstraction, 221–3
Escola do Bairro, *165–6, 168, 170–3*; overview, 161–2; classroom context, 163–4; inquiry practices, 166–74
"every place," 248–9
experience, 35, 130–1, 132, 228
Exploration/Mana aotūroa, 97, 98

family knowledges, 100–1, 106
farmer's markets, 149–50, 153
fences, 88
Festival of Trees, 182
fires, 33–4
fish ponds, 165–7, *166*
fishing, 25, 26, 41, 143, 151–2, 154
Fjørtoft, I., 57
Fleer, M., 97
flower shops, 150–1, 153
Foucault, M., 256–7
four directions/colours, 39, 40–1, *40*, 92, *112*
four Rs of Indigenous research, 19
funds of knowledge, 244–6

Gaaniniigaaniijek/Ancestors, 41, 44, *48*
Galda, L., 168
games, 60–1
garden-based learning (GBL), 228–38, *233*
gardening, 89–90, 215–16
gathering and collecting, 186, *187*
Gee, J.P., 196–7
Gibbons, P., 213
globalization, 19
goals, 7, 153
González, N., 96
Goodrich, C.G., 23
grammar, 118–19, 233, 234
grandfather's teachings, 91
Grandmother Teaching Story, 37–40, 41
green grocers, 199–200
Greenberg, J., 220, 221
Grøver, V., 63
Gruenewald, D.A., 8, 18, 25, 100, 145, 151, 154, 181–2

haka, 71–3
Halliday, M.A.K., 105
Hamilton, M., 6, 145
Hammer, M., 97
Haskell, L., 48–9
health services, 19
Hedges, H., 71, 73–6

Heidegger, Martin, 256
hip-hop, 137–8
Hoff, E., 197
holistic view of children, 112–13, *112*, 115–16
Hornberger, N., 55

ice fishing, 143, 151–2, 154
identity: and culture, 110; and language, 120–1; and learning, 117; and place, 129; and relational interactions, 76; through play in Aotearoa, 74; through play in Tipiyimisiw, 21–2; valuing, 26–7
imagination, 3–4, 183–4, 189–91
immigrants, 67, 68–9, 72–3, 95, 97, 101–5
Indigenous Knowledge: *Anishinaabe* ecological relational knowledge (AERK), 34, 36–42, *45*, 46–7; challenging dominant discourses, 22, 27, 248; as cultural capital, 22; defined, 35, 49–50; experience as knowledge, 35, 228; fishing in Poplar Lake, 25, 26; and modernity, 19; oral tradition, 40; and outdoor play space, 84; and *The School Journal* (NZ Ministry of Education), 131–2; schools teaching, 114–15; traditional stories, 21–2; valuing of land, 246
Indigenous research, 19
intergenerational trauma, 48–9
intervention specialists (IS), 146
"irate island" project, 183, 190, *190*
isolation, 5

Johnson, J.T., 23

Kinoomaadiziwin, 44
kinship, 46
knowledge: conceptual, 44, *45*; family, 100–1, 106; funds of, 244–6; hegemonic, 247. *See also* Indigenous Knowledge
kotahitanga/holistic development, 70

Lahey, M., 232–3
land-based education/land literacy: and balance, 81; Biigtigong Nishnaabeg Child Care Centre, 89–93; challenging notions of place, 259; Indigenous Knowledge as, 84–5, 246; and language, 110, 119, 122; as life-long, 44–5. See also *Aki*/Land
language: in action, 197, 198–9, 200, 201–2, 203–4, 205–6, 207; in Aotearoa playgroup, 100–1; bilingualism, 76–7, 103–4; *Communication/Mana reo*, 97–8, 101–6; content of, 199, 205, 235–6; and context, 196–7, 205–7; and conversations, 212–13; and culture, 110; decontextualization, 206, 221–3; and DRA, 121; English, 77; E's and P's of abstraction, 221–3; experimenting through play, 196, 197; extinction of, 109–10; forms of, 233–5; as important in early years, 211; and land, 110, 119, 122; language experience, 130–1; of Māori people, 69, 77, 128; and meaning-making, 105; of migrants, 67, 68–9, 72–3; morphology, 233; phonology, 233; as place-based, 114; as reflection, 197–8, 202–3, 204, 205–6, 207; register, 199, 204–5; of Sámi people, 53, 54, 56–8, 59–61; and socializing through play, 59–60; sociocultural view of, 5–6; speaking outside school, 120, 121, 122; specialist, 197; SSTaRS, 220; stimulation strategies, 230, 233, 235, 237 (*see also* teachers as conversational partners); Swedish, 57–8, 59–60, 61; syntax, 199, 205, 214, 220, 233; teaching approaches to, 110–11, 115, 116–23; use of, 236–8; vocabulary, 199, 205, 235–6
language programs, guiding principles, 113–19

language programs, measures of success, 120–3
Laureen (SK teacher), 229–31, 232–5, 237
listening, 75, 115, 163, 213, 215
literacy: defined, 6; and guided play, 146–7, 154; local and official, 24; and oral language, 6; and peer teachers, 133–4; play as maximizing skills, 174; and role-playing, 150–1, 154; scores, 143–4; sociocultural view of, 6–7, 145. *See also* land-based education/land literacy; writing
Little Green Sprouts/Little Green Thumbs, 229, 232, 233–9, *233*

Malaguzzi, L., 115
Mana whenua, 130
Māori, 67–77, 97, 128, 129–34
maps, 185–6, *190*
Mara, D., 74–5, 77
Marathon Paper Company, 84
McDonnell, S., 24
McKenzie, M., 255
meaning-making: and action, 184; Aspen sand centre, 23; cultural context choices, 61; and everyday lived experiences, 7; human-built environments, 181; joint meaning-making, 6; and language, 105; and oral tradition, 40; of places, 8; and social activities, 5–6; Story Circles, *43*
Medicine Circle cloth, 39, *40*
Medicine Circle/Wheel, 36–7, *38*, 40–1, *47–8*, 92
Michano-Drover, Stephanie, 82, 88, 89
migration, 67, 68–9, 72–3, 77, 183–4, 189–91
minibeast museum, 200–3
Mishomis/Grandfather Rock, 39, 42, *43*
Mnjikaning, 41
modernity, 19
Moore, S., 22–3
motifs, 182–3

movement, 184–5
Muchoo Wapuss, 21–2
multiculturalism, 100–1
music, 71–4

natural spaces in Brazil, 159–60, 161–2
nature walks, 90, 180, 183, 184, 185–6
Negwaadodem/family clan, 40, 46
A Nest of Singing Birds (O'Brien), 131
Neuman, S.B., 196
New Zealand, 67–70, 73, 96–7, 131; about, 128–9. *See also* Māori; playgroups
Ngāhononga/relationships, 70, 130
Nibi/water, 39, 41, *47*
Nibwaakaawin/a state of Being, 39–40, 45
Norling, M., 61
Northern Oral Language and Writing (NOW Play): overview, 143, 147–9, 178; guided play projects, 143, 149–55; human-built environments, 181; nature walks, 180, 183, 184, 185–6; play motifs, 183–91
nurturing guides, *111*

Odehwegan/drum, 39
Odenang/where the heart is, 46
official curriculum. *See* standardized curriculums
"onsters," 181
Ontario: Pic River, 84; Poplar Lake, 20–1, 24–6; Red Lake, 82; Wikwemikong Unceded First Nation, 33–4. *See also* Biigtigong Nishnaabeg Children & Family Learning Centre; Northern Oral Language and Writing
ontology, 256–7
open-ended statements, 237–8, *237*
oral language. *See* language; talking
Oral Language and Assessment Tool, 199
oral tradition, 40
Orellana, M.F., 105

"othering" of place, 8
Outakoski, H., 54, 55
OWL strategy, 215

parenting, 83, *111*
Parr, Judy, 22
pedagogies of place, 145–6
peer teachers, 133
Peltier, Sharla *Mskokii*, 109
Pic River, Ontario, 84
place: as backdrop, 3, 5; and broader ties, 161–2; and constructed meanings, 8; and culture, 8–9; and decades of literacy research, 248; defined, 69, 100, 253–5; geopolitics, 255; and identity, 129; in language and literacy theories, 7–8; as mediated, 8; and multiple places, 254; as "other," 8; as pedagogical, 3, 18, 145–6; and personal reflection, 41; sociocultural view of, 8–9; as third space, 22, 23; and traditional stories, 21–2; as universal, 248–9; and writing, 129–30. *See also* playce-based learning; reinhabitation
place-based educational theory, 8–9, 11–13, 18–19, 177–8
place-based learning: and committing to communities, 190; defined, 68, 91; environment as third teacher, 116; goals of, 153; and guided play, 149–54; and land literacy, 34; language as, 114; and meaningful communication, 235; and social context, 162. *See also* playce-based learning; urban place-based learning
place-conscious educational theory, 8–10
place-conscious learning, 55, 59
plants, 165–7, *166*
play: absence in São Paulo curriculum, 160–1; children-led, 212; cultural construction of, 5; defined, 96; as disruptive, 4; as educationally useful, 259;

guided, 7, 145, 146, 149–54, 153, 182–3; as initiation, 135, 145; interpreting, 96; and language development, 212; and language experimentation, 196, 197; learning from expertise, 98, 134; maximizing literacy, 174; motifs, 182–3; and normalization of power structures, 49; and oral language, 5–6; as place-making, 258–9; and popular culture, 26–7; and relationships, 173; replacing homogenized play, 17–18; role-playing (*see* role-playing); in Sámi curriculum, 54–5; sociocultural view of, 7; sociodramatic play, 54–5, 185; student-directed, 147–8; supporting children's learning, 17; teachers learning about children through, 17; and writing, 134–5, 137–8. *See also* Northern Oral Language and Writing; role-playing
play space designs: barriers, 82, 86, 88; and Canadian Standards Association, 87; and CCEYA, 87; and community involvement, 83; funding for, 88; and Indigenous Knowledge, 84; and land-based teachings, 89–93; and Ontario weather, 87; and wildlife, 88
play-based learning, overview, 162, 227–8
playce-based learning, 4–5, 56–61, 243–50
players, 256, 257
playgroups: overview, 96–7; Aotearoa snapshot #1, 95–6; Aotearoa snapshot #2, 101–2; Aotearoa snapshot #3, 103–5; Aotearoa study design, 99–101; as culturally negotiated place, 100
pleasure, 136–7
poetry, 137–8
Poplar Lake, Ontario, 20–1, 24–6
popular culture, 26–7
poverty, 159
pragmatics, 236–7

process questions, 237–8, *237*
protection, 33–4
pulleys, 167–74, *168*, *170–3*
puppets, 188–9, *188*

rabbits, 21–2
radical imagination, 3–4
Randall, M., 48–9
rap, 137–8
reading. *See* literacy
Red Lake, Ontario, 82
Reid, J., 22
reindeer, 55, 59
reinhabitation, 18, 25–6
Relational Way of Being, 39
Relational Wheel Teachings, 39
relationships: "all my relations" concept, 110, 112, 246–7; connecting through conversation, 213; importance in learning, 111–12, *111*, 115, 138–9; place determined by, 161; play as understanding, 173. *See also* collaboration
residential schools and Elders, 81
respect, 115
roads, 23–4
Rogoff, B., 144
role-playing: blue-collar workers, 24; farmer's markets, 150; fishing, 25, 143, 152–3; flower shops, 150–1; green grocer, 199–200; minibeast museum, 200–3; "onsters," 185; as stimulus, 145; and symbolic thinking, 196; talk shows, 185; and traditional stories, 21–2; treasure island, 203–4
Roskos, K., 196
Roth, W.M., 68
rural communities: as close-knit, 179–80; concerns of education in, 143–4, 153, 154, 248; honouring ways of, 26–8; and place-based learning, 18, 146, 153, 239; and place-conscious learning, 10; and play-based education, 178; and standardized curriculums, 8.

See also Aotearoa New Zealand; Aspen, Alberta; Northern Oral Language and Writing; Sámi; Tipiyimisiw, Saskatchewan
Rusty Brown (Ware), 260

safety, 159
Sageie, J., 57
Sámi, 53–63
Sámi National Curriculum (SNC), 54
Samoan relational ethics, 75
Sampson, K.A., 23
sand centres, 23, 203
Sandberg, A., 61
Santos, M., 161
São Paulo, Brazil, 159–60. *See also* Escola do Bairro
Saskatchewan, 19–20, 21–3, 231. *See also* Little Green Sprouts/Little Green Thumbs
scaffolding: cultural and lived experiences, 153–4; defined, 144, 145–6, 147; familiar and new language, 215, 219–20; language independent of context, 197, 206–7; props for play, 196
Schafft, K.A., 78
The School Journal (New Zealand Ministry of Education), 131–2
science, 163, 167–74, *170–3*
seasons, 116
segregation, 159
self-awareness, 36
semantics, 235–6
settler societies, 259
seven directions, 40, 46, *47*
Shefatya, L., 54
Shkagamik-kwe/Mother Earth, 41, 42
silence, 75
slam poetry, 137–8
Small Kauri Early Childhood Education Centre, 70–1
small worlds, 183–4, *184*
Smilansky, S., 54
Smith, G.A., 153, 180, 183
Smith, P.J., 153

Sobel, D., 178, 181, 183, 184, 186, 189–90
sociocultural theory, 5–7, 68, 98, 144, 145
sociodramatic play, 54–5, 185
songs, 118
spatial theory, 256–7
spirituality, 84
sports, 72–3
SSTaRS, 220
standardized curriculums: in Aotearoa New Zealand, 128–9; and local literacies, 24; and local places, 9; and rural ways of being, 8; in São Paulo, Brazil, 160–1; as undervaluing, 27
Story Circles, 37, 41–4, *43*
story-telling, 37–40, 41
Sweden, 53–63

talking, 127, 130–1, 133–4, 162–3. *See also* oral language
Tanner, Laurel, 256–7
te reo/Māori language, 69, 77
Te Tiriti o Waitangi (Treaty of Waitangi), 67
Te Whāriki (curriculum): overview, 67, 69, 129–30; and biculturalism, 97–8; challenges in, 77; and play, 134; principles of, 70, 129
Teacher Rating of Oral Language and Literacy (TROLL), 198
teachers: Ashton-Warner methods, 130; benefiting from language programs, 121; as champions of language programs, 116–17; coached, 229–30, 232, 233–6; conflicting responsibilities, 27; as cultural brokers, *118*, 145; directors vs. guides, 182–3; engagement with students (*see* relationships); listening/observing children's play, 59, 60, 164, 167; peers as, 133; training, 117. *See also individual teachers*
teachers as conversational partners: overview, 211, 229–31; academic

language, 213–14; connecting with students, 213; language form, 233–5; pragmatics, 236–8; purposeful and planned conversation, 214–23; semantics, 235–6
teu le va/relational ethics, 75
This Place (Akiwenzie-Damm et al.), 260
tikanga Māori/Māori cultural practices, 69, 77
tipis, 92, *119*
Tipiyimisiw, Saskatchewan, 19–20, 21–3
Toub, T.S., 146
Toulouse, P., 113
toys, 162–3
traditional food, 90, 103
traditional stories, 21–2
traditional ways of knowing. *See* Indigenous Knowledge
trauma, 48–9
treasure island, 203–4
tree roots, 90
treehouses, 167–74, *168*, *170–3*
trust, 49
Truth and Reconciliation Commission of Canada (TRC), 46, 48, 49
Tuafuti, P., 75
Tuan, Y.F., 254
Tuck, E., 255

Under the Wings of the Hawk game, 60–1
underneath/ancestors, 40

urban place-based learning: overview, 195, 198; play scenarios, 199–205; rich affordances of, 205–6
Urry, John, 254

Valsiner, J., 127
Vygotsky, L.S., 62, 163, 171

walking trails, 90, 180, 183, 184, 185–6
Wason-Ellam, L., 152, 153
Weh/feelings of connection, 45
Weisberg, D.S., 151, 153
Weitzman, E., 220, 221
Western discourses. *See* dominant discourses
whakamana/empowerment, 70
whānau tangata/community, 70, 97–8
whāriki, 130. See also *Te Whāriki*
Wikwemikong Unceded First Nation, 33–4
wildlife, 90, 180, 186, 188, *188*. *See also various animals*
Wilson, R., 181
Wood, E., 7
worms, 238
writing: explaining ideas, *172–3*; and language reflection, 197–8; and place, 129–34, 138–9; and place-based learning, 146; and play, 134–9; and role-playing, 150, 151; and talking, 127, 130–1, 133–4. *See also* literacy

Young, R., 136–7
Youngblood Jackson, A., 78

www.ingramcontent.com/pod-product-compliance
Lightning Source LLC
Chambersburg PA
CBHW030309080526
44584CB00012B/498